If Only They'd Told Me

For our children Jack and Sasha, Ruby, Jonah and Xavier
for teaching us well.
For John and Matt for believing in us.
And for our parents Alec and Magda
and Peter and Lynley
for showing us the way.

If Only They'd Told Me

JACQUELINE LOCKINGTON
and
NATALIE CUTLER-WELSH

About the authors

Jacqui and Nat are two mums living in New Zealand with their families.

 Jacqui is British, loves tea and is a self-confessed neat freak. She is mum to Jack (7) and Sasha (5), and is married to a very patient Kiwi, John. She has lived in New Zealand for nine years and now considers it home, although she has never forgotten her British roots and still misses her Yorkshire tea, Walkers crisps and Marks and Spencer.

 Nat, on the other hand, is organised chaos. She's a Canadian/New Zealander married to Matt, an Australian/Englishman, and has lived in New Zealand for 16 years. Mum to Ruby (7), Jonah (5) and Xavier (2). Nat is a mover and a shaker, constantly on the go. She knows all her neighbours and has friends far and wide. Nothing has affected her like parenthood.

Together Jacqui and Nat give you the 'real deal' on parenting. They're not the experts, they're the best friends you never knew you had.

Because the book is a tale of two different mums and to make it easier for you, the reader, we have decided to explain who has written what by the inclusion of two small shoe motifs.

 is Jacqui as she was pregnant in heels.

 is Nat as she's constantly on the go.

 We have put a sample of our podcast links throughout this book. This indicates a recommended podcast episode (audio recording) and related blog on that particular topic. There are over 100 additional episodes to listen to on our iTunes and stitcher radio pages.

Contents

About the authors   8

Prologue   9

CHAPTER ONE: *Life before baby*   11

What makes a mother?, Getting preggers, The missing red stain, You and your body in the preggie stage, Blooming pregnant, Signs and symptoms, Buying maternity clothes, Tips for being pregnant in heels, The big announcement, Getting ready for baby, What they say and things they never tell you, Couplehood in the pregnancy stage, Exercising while pregnant, If Only They'd Told Me (IOTTM) tips

CHAPTER TWO: *Baby on the way*   36

Get this baby outta me, Bonding with strangers at antenatal, Forty+ weeks and counting, Best intentions and unwanted advice, Maternity leave and your plan for the future, Have a plan, The birth plan, The hospital visit, The hospital bag, Labour signs and the birth, Those first few hours and days, Breastfeeding, IOTTM tips

CHAPTER THREE: *Now you're parents!*   59

Welcome to parenthood, Baby blues, Thoughts from other parents, Physical changes and challenges, Sex after childbirth, What to say and what not to say to new parents, Couplehood redefined, What other parents say, A dad's view on parenthood, Murphy's Law, Sleep deprivation and settling baby to sleep, Sleeptime sweetheart, Dorothy Waide's top tips for settling young babies, Synchronised naptimes and sleepless nights, The exhausted contest, Top tips for sweet sleep, Challenges and words of wisdom, IOTTM tips

CHAPTER FOUR: *The new you and home sweet home*   84

The new you, Get me outta here, Tips for getting out of the house with a new baby, One thing a day, The witching hours, It's 7 o'clock, now go to sleep!, Attitude is everything, Do something or get things done, The domestic grind, The domestic divide, Domestic dad, Do's and don'ts for dads, Confessions of a neat freak, Organised chaos, Top tips for domestic bliss, Supermarket dramas, IOTTM tips

CHAPTER FIVE: *Keeping the love alive*   105

Refuelling your romance, Dating again, You owe me!, Appreciation and thanks, Give the boys a break, What to do when hubby walks out, Happy blended family, Different types of families, Striving to thrive, Love language and personality types, Woo me again, Between the sheets, Words of wisdom, Sex after baby, Attraction and distraction, Honey, we need to talk, An 'I love' list, Marriage mentors, We're drifting apart, Who cares wins, Marriage maintenance, Create a mission statement for your marriage/ relationship, Relationship traditions, IOTTM tips

CHAPTER SIX: *Changing friendships*   134

Non-baby friends, Differences between Baby Friends (BFs) and Non-Baby Friends (NBFs), What NBFs *really* think, The high-school factor, But what if it is you?, Playground Mummy Mafia, Coffee groups, Nat's story: Putting yourself out there, IOTTM tips

CHAPTER SEVEN: *What about you?*   157

You time, What about you?, Do something for you!, Taking care of Number One, 'You seem overwhelmed', Post-natal depression, A post-natal depression case study, Signs of post-natal depression, Getting your body back, Finding time for fitness, Drawing the line, Helpful parenting phrases, Things we thought we'd never do, The happiest mother in the world, IOTTM tips

CHAPTER EIGHT: *The more the merrier?* 181

You want another one?, The more the merrier, Just the one, Twins, Twins plus one, The toddler years, Mealtime mayhem, A helping hand, How to help a friend and how friends can help, Tips for visiting a mum with a new baby, Power hour or 'tick the list', Meals on wheels, Where is the village?, Grandparents, Out-of-town grandparents, In-town grandparents, Hosting guests and staying sane, House rules, Putting things into perspective, IOTTM tips

CHAPTER NINE: *Whatever works* 209

Returning to work, Working mum, Stay-at-home mum, Blue sky, Whatever works, Work-life balance and earning a crust, Do what works for you, Mothers' guilt, Nat's story: Look out Super-mum, here comes Wonder-mum, Choosing childcare, 'Hot Nanny', Getting out the door, Couplehood and work, IOTTM tips

CHAPTER TEN: *Keeping kids safe* 230

Being sick while pregnant, Accidents happen, Missing child, Stranger danger, Family emergency kit, Nat's earthquake story, IOTTM tips

CHAPTER ELEVEN: *Family times* 241

Mind your manners, Lead by example, Lessons from our little ones, Catch them being good, Family traditions, Special outings, Slow down and smell the coffee, Live in the moment, Birthday parties and special occasions, Hosting a fab birthday party, Getting your child ready for school, Thriving (not just surviving) in the school holidays, IOTTM tips

Life after babies: What lies ahead? 262

Recommended reading 265

In my role, I work with a large number of parents each year and over the years have witnessed how wonderful but emotionally challenging parenthood can be.

Nat and Jacqui have done a great service to parents worldwide by being open, honest and genuinely entertaining about the tough times (as well as the great times).

I've been following 'If Only They'd Told Me' on Facebook and have had the pleasure of being interviewed a number of times for their podcast.

I think it's wonderful that they are now making their ideas and stories available in the form of this book!

Dorothy Waide, Dorothy Waide's Consultancy 'Baby Help'

The story behind If Only They'd Told Me

Even before Jacqui (a working mother of two), and Nat (at-home mother of three) met, they were each writing their own parenting book.

A devastating earthquake in Christchurch, New Zealand threw the pair together and as they got to know each other they discovered that by combining their individual books they would be able to cover a wealth of topics that every parent needed to know. Between them they had different views, different material and a whole host of stories they wanted to share with other parents. They decided while they wrote the book they could still share their material to help other mums and dads who were struggling so they started their highly successful blog-site and podcast, *If Only They'd Told Me*. Now, with over 46,000 downloads of their podcast on parenting and over 170 blogs under their belts, Nat & Jacqui are so excited to bring you *If Only They'd Told Me*, the book!

Prologue

I really had no idea. No understanding at all of the profound difference between a person's life with children compared with a person's life without.

Call it the naivety of the childless. The selfishness of the childless. Well, that's what it was for me — a naive, self-absorbed, career-climbing girl.

I was visiting my family in Yorkshire, in the north of England, for a few days, long before I had children of my own. One of my best friends had just had her first baby. I decided to swing on over to meet the new baby, drop off a gift and lend my support.

I gave her a quick call. 'Hey, Sarah, it's Jacqui.'

'Hey, Jacqui.' Sarah sounded quite strained.

'How's it all going?'

'Well, you know. It's pretty tiring. I'm shattered actually and she won't stop crying.'

'Oh. Well, anyway, do you fancy coming out for a quick drink?'

Silence followed this question, then what sounded like a sob. 'Jacqui, Ellen is five days old.'

'Right.' I didn't know quite what to say to this. Did this mean she didn't want to come out for a drink? I would have thought that a drink — a stiff one — was just what she needed.

'Why don't you come here instead?' she asked.

'OK. What time suits?'

'Well, I try to get Ellen to bed around seven.'

'OK, I'll come around seven-thirty then.'

'I meant to come earlier, so you can meet her,' Sarah said, clearly exasperated.

'Right, right, yes, of course. I'll be there around six-thirty,' I announced.

When I turned up with a bottle of nice red wine it was chaos in the new baby house. The place was a tip, clothes strewn everywhere, the bed unmade, dirty dishes piled up, dirty laundry stuffed into a corner of the living room, the heating so hot the room was almost stifling... not to mention a strange, sweet, mustardy smell that I couldn't quite place.

Sarah, my normally glamorous friend, was a sight. She looked as though she hadn't slept in days. Her hair was greasy, she wore not a scrap of make-up and she was wearing a pair of old, baggy pyjama bottoms with an old baggy T-shirt and (it seemed) no bra.

I was taken aback. 'Erm, hi. You look, erm, nice,' I said, thrusting the bottle of wine into her hand.

She sighed and gave me back the bottle. 'I can't drink,' she stated. 'Breastfeeding. Help yourself to a glass in the kitchen.' She turned away and walked into the lounge.

I scooted into the kitchen to collect a glass before following her into the lounge, which looked as though it had been camped in for the last few days.

'Not even one glass?' I asked. She shot me a withering look. It was then I noticed the tiny bundle in the corner of the sofa. I almost sat on it. It seemed to be asleep. 'Aaah, you must be Ellen,' I said, picking her up abruptly and clearly startling her. She made a little coughing noise before screwing up her face into a tiny, tight red ball and crying. The crying was horrible. A very loud, high-pitched cry that pierced your soul.

Sarah looked like she too was about to burst into tears. She pulled her hand through her hair. Her nerves seemed on edge. 'Erm, she's crying,' I said, holding the baby towards Sarah. I had absolutely no idea what to do with a crying baby and no desire to learn.

'You don't say,' Sarah shot back before putting her face into her hands and crying herself. Faced with a crying infant and a crying Sarah, I was lost. This wasn't quite the night out with my best friend I had planned.

'She just won't stop,' Sarah sobbed. 'She doesn't stop crying *all night long*. I can't do this.'

I didn't know what to say, apart from 'Are you sure you don't want a glass of wine?'

CHAPTER ONE

Life before baby

What makes a mother?

What qualifies a typical woman to become a mother? Is it an amazing ability to single-handedly hold down a writhing six-month-old on a change table while the other hand manages to whip, wipe and wrap (whip the culprit nappy off, wipe off the evidence and wrap up the baby in a clean nappy)? Or is it the way we manage to simultaneously manoeuvre a buggy with one hand, drag a screaming, kicking toddler with the other, while holding a conversation with a shopkeeper? Or perhaps it's our knack of putting an arch-backed, non-compliant passenger into a baby car seat? Is it our ability to tell the same story night after night with enthusiastic character voices? Or is it the pleading and bribery we resort to when taking them . . . wait for it . . . supermarket shopping!

Answer:

All of the above, plus the ability to be the washing fairy, bedroom partner, cleaner, friend, shoulder to cry on, incredible hostess, great conversationalist, contortionist, diplomat *and* to continue to be the witty, gorgeous girl you were pre-baby.

Getting preggers

'If only they'd told me it's harder to get pregnant than you think ...'

Following countless years of being vigilant with birth control and a few false alarms, we find ourselves at the stage of life where we are 'ready' (if such a moment actually exists). For some, getting pregnant is not as easy as they expect. The Murphy's Law aspect of parenthood starts way back at conception. Some people hear that it can take a year or so to become pregnant so start 'trying', only to find they become pregnant straight away. Other people decide that they want a baby now, but it takes ages and doesn't happen for years!

When you get married, you often assume that kids will come along a couple of years later. And so, you come off the pill, quite nervously at first as you really don't want children straight away. I mean, you've only been married a year, you're doing really well at work, you're saving to go to Fiji next year and you've just bought a new Karen Walker dress which cost one month's salary and it will be a real shame if you get pregnant straight away and can't wear it ...

So, it's with relief when your period arrives on the twentieth of the month like clockwork, and then again the following month. By month three you begin to relax ... and start to wonder what is taking so long. I mean, you don't necessarily want it *right now* but *soon* would be good. A couple more months go by, then a few more again. By which point you have transferred from polite indifference as to whether you are going to get pregnant to a deep worry that *something might be wrong*!

Before long, a year has gone by and you have read up on everything about getting pregnant. Spontaneous sex has become a thing of the past as you're constantly timing sex to ensure that you are doing it at the optimal time. You start trying different positions because someone you know knows someone who knows someone who got pregnant doing it in a handstand position. You cross your legs after sex very firmly to ensure as little as possible escapes. Still nothing happens.

Then you start to really worry. You contact fertility specialists, start peeing in pots, have blood tests, more peeing in pots, start talking about *other options*, get acupuncture, visit a homeopath and spend a fortune on Chinese herbal remedies, pee in a few more pots. You cut out anything bad for you in case it's ruining your chances of getting pregnant, such as alcohol, fat and sugar. You talk to your specialist about low sperm count, low egg production, pee in a few more pots, start seriously talking to specialists about those *other options*, and your husband gets to spend an afternoon with a few magazines, a video and his own 'special pot'.

 After being told that we needed to start an IVF process, my husband and I poured ourselves a strong gin and tonic (being healthy was, at that time, giving us no advantage) and decided to forget about the whole children thing for a while. We would, we decided, have a holiday, and give ourselves a few months' break from trying, worrying and visiting specialists.

So, things settled down. We planned a holiday for a few months later. We both started training for a half marathon and sex went back to being the pleasurable thing it had been before. A couple of months later, after a particularly big night on the town, I realised that I hadn't actually had my period for a while. The old me would have known every day I was overdue but the new me had completely lost track of the time. I counted my way back to my last period, and realised I was indeed two weeks overdue!

I'm not the only woman to share a story like that. We know a couple who tried for years to get pregnant. They had six goes at IVF before they finally gave up and adopted a child. Two months after the adopted child joined their family, the wife fell pregnant.

And, we know another couple who had IVF three times after failing to conceive naturally. After the third time they were told the likelihood of them conceiving was virtually nil. They stopped trying and eight months later fell pregnant naturally.

We each have our own stories: some of us can breed like rabbits, while others struggle. Don't assume that you will get pregnant straight away. Many women put everything into their careers, working long hours and not even thinking about children until their late thirties. This may be one of the reasons women are finding it more and more difficult to conceive naturally. There are more 'assisted' pregnancies than ever before; more older mothers and, ironically, more sets of twins as when we get older our eggs 'split' more frequently causing a higher risk of multiple births.

 For some it really is about fertility challenges and for others it's just bad math. The 'window' of opportunity (fertile time) of the month is 14 days *before* your period, not necessarily day 14 of your menstrual cycle. We made this mistake when trying for our first baby and I've talked to so many other people who have been confused and doing it (literally) at the wrong time of the month.

So, brace yourselves, girls … it just means bonking like rabbits until it happens!

'It took so long to figure out if we were ready, then we found out we had fertility problems. We were warned it would take a long time to get pregnant. My husband handled it well.'

Lucy, Christchurch, 39 weeks pregnant with first baby

'Approximately two years trying first time around, now approaching three years the second time. I am finding the second time harder, I think because my expectations are higher. Lately I've been frustrated about being the one on medication, doing tests etc. and wishing some of the pressure was on him. We set a time limit on actively trying, just to get some control back and impose our own certainty. But the limit is approaching and I don't know if we will actually be able to let it go.'

Anne, Christchurch, daughter aged 4 years

'It was very difficult for us to get pregnant. I could write an entire book about it! It forced my husband and me to really talk about our hopes/ dreams/vision of our lives in the future. It made us stronger as a couple (but I wouldn't wish it on anyone). We had assumed that we'd have kids, and then when we thought that we couldn't, we eventually got to a point where we were OK with that. As a last-ditch attempt we were shocked and thrilled to be successful with our first round of IVF. Not a day goes by when I don't think how lucky we are to have our two little miracles in our lives (even when they wake us up screaming in the middle of the night). Our twins are double blessings.'

Ann, Toronto, twins aged 20 months

The missing red stain

 When at last your period fails to arrive, it's amazing how your first reaction is disbelief.

I remember quite clearly clutching at the little stick, staring with growing nervousness at the clear blue line. Then, of course, you spend your first trimester pretending that you aren't pregnant (ironic really), and trying to carry on life as normally as possible without alerting work colleagues to the fact that you have something inside that has nothing to do with lunch.

You can't drink, you suddenly become ultra-aware of every pregnant woman around you and there's baby stuff everywhere. You Google everything about pregnancy and babies. You pin cute 'kid's room' ideas on Pinterest. You sneakily buy pregnancy magazines and books that tell you the weekly size of your baby in relation to fruit.

Weirdly, you are actually classed as pregnant before you are pregnant. For example, you are classed as five weeks pregnant when you are only actually three weeks pregnant, as pregnancy timing starts from the end of your last period although you don't actually conceive until halfway through the month.

You and your body in the preggie stage

> *'If only they'd told me that being pregnant wouldn't just be feet up, eating chocolates ...'*
>
> **Jo, Auckland, two daughters aged 2 and 3 years**

 Being pregnant brings to mind images ranging from women with a 'healthy glow' to women who are exhausted and vomit throughout the day. The reality of being pregnant is ever-present, but for men reality seems to kick in when they first hear the heartbeat or see the baby at the first scan.

Now, I don't know about you, but I had the idea that pregnancy was supposed to be fun. Isn't it about being looked after and pampered, putting your feet up while your husband massages them; having dinner cooked for you and basically swanning around looking, well, blooming?

I know that idea came from somewhere, quite possibly from the many

American movies that I have watched over the years. The women always seemed to be eating chocolates!

Well, if you are pregnant and reading this I dare you to go ahead and eat a box of chocolates right now. You'll probably soon be farting like crazy and suffering from serious heartburn.

Yes, you might look totally gorgeous when you are pregnant, but you will also be unable to keep tabs on your bodily functions. Those hormones racing around your body will be making you cry at just about everything. Even if you are a mean, hard-nosed cow at work, if someone so much as says *boo* to you now you'll just blub like a baby. And don't mention the farting! You can try all you like to blame everyone else for the smells but, let's face it, everyone knows that it's the preggie ones who are letting off the mingers.

And, don't forget the heartburn which haunts you after every meal. Even though they say it's caused by curries, it's actually caused by pretty much everything — sugars, dairy, bread, pasta, tomatoes, strawberries; the food acid burns your insides and all the Mylanta in the world doesn't seem to help.

Have they told you about the leg cramps? They seem pretty harmless, except when they jolt you awake at 4 a.m. with spasms like electric shocks.

Standing up for too long causes leg pain as most of your blood supply is being given to the baby to grow and there isn't enough left for you to stand around all day. Sitting down isn't much better as your lower back aches constantly. Lying down is even worse, if it's possible. You can't lie on your stomach for obvious reasons and you're advised not to lie on your back — although it's not comfortable to lie on your back anyway!

The only slightly comfortable position is on your side and even then, the bigger you get, the harder it is to keep your legs together. You end up putting pillows in between your legs to try to get more comfortable.

You're hot, you're bothered, you're uncomfortable, you have acid burning your insides, cramps killing your legs, pains in your lower back, blood pumping around furiously, nausea, someone inside your stomach kicking you ... no wonder you can't sleep.

Everyone tells you to 'catch up on your sleep, dearie, you'll need it when bubba comes along'. Fat chance! By the time baby comes along you'll be a walking zombie.

As for baby brain, you can now breathe a sigh of relief every time you forget something because it really does exist. The *Sydney Morning Herald* reported that an analysis of 14 research studies around the world since 1990 concluded that pregnancy impairs memory for up to 80 per cent of pregnant women and new mothers. Phew...

I am lucky that I can blame so many of my blunders on baby brain. For starters, I crashed the car. The weird thing was, I'm sure that car just appeared out of nowhere. Oh well, who knows, but at least my bump and I were OK. The car wasn't though. It was at the panelbeaters for quite some time. Thank goodness I was pregnant so hubby couldn't be too cross with me.

I constantly forgot people's names. I sent an email to a client twice, rewriting the whole email and sending it through just 10 minutes after I had sent the first one. I also forwarded an email to a client from someone else who had slagged off that same client in their email to me — I had to spend quite a bit of time digging myself out of that particular hole.

The scary thing is that your memory never fully recovers. Apparently when you have a baby it destroys so many brain cells that you never get back the same level of memory that you had before you were pregnant.

 I really liked being pregnant. I'm not sure if I was 'glowing' as such, but I certainly liked having a bit more shape and big boobs. I didn't suffer from morning sickness or food aversion. No pregnancy horror stories here! In saying that, each pregnancy is progressively harder on the body (my back and legs mainly).

Blooming pregnant: signs and symptoms

Most pregnant women will at some point be able to tick off many of the following:

- nausea
- tiredness
- increase in need to urinate
- heartburn
- vomiting
- leg cramps
- sore or tingling breasts
- swollen or enlarged hands and/or feet
- swollen or enlarged breasts
- mood swings
- visible veins
- metallic taste in mouth
- heightened sense of smell
- spotty or dry skin

- greasy hair
- swollen belly
- increased saliva and vaginal secretions
- backache
- period-like pains
- indigestion
- spotting
- bleeding nose or gums
- sensitive teeth
- increase in weight.

Sounds like fun, huh?

Buying maternity clothes

 Talk to anyone who has ever been pregnant and they will tell you how they couldn't wait to burn or throw out their maternity clothes once they had completed their family. We end up wearing our maternity clothes so often that, no matter how exciting we found them at the beginning, we just end up hating them. Despite this, you'll have to buy maternity clothes. There is a period of time when you may think you can get away without buying any, but you're just kidding yourself. If you want to save money, buy pre-loved (second-hand) maternity clothes rather than new.

You see, you don't just 'bloom' overnight. Your body takes time to adjust from your normal pre-pregnancy weight to carrying a baby and it's that second semester when you're neither one thing nor the other — size-wise, I mean. You may well have been svelte before and you may well go on to carry a compact little bump and be 'all baby' (which is what non-pregnant women should say to you anyway to make you feel fabulous when you're looking like a turkey is stuck up your jumper). But, the fact of the matter is, there are a few weeks of just looking like a big heifer. Your body starts producing extra blood, extra skin and a large tyre around your middle, in preparation for protecting the baby as it grows. Before the baby bump shows, you go through a really uncomfortable few weeks where you just look like you've put on a heap of weight. None of your clothes fit and you are still in denial that you have to buy maternity clothes so you start wearing your trousers with your zipper down and really long floaty tops and dresses. Your boobs are falling out of your bra and you start to wear XL T-shirts.

You tell everyone who even slightly looks at you that you are pregnant, to ensure they don't think you're actually fat. I would look in the mirror daily to see if there was any change in my body and even started walking with my stomach stuck out to make it more obvious until my hubby told me it looked weird.

I asked all my pregnant friends when they started looking pregnant, but everyone had different memories so it didn't really help.

Then just a couple of weeks later it happens. You go to put on your jeans and *wham*! You can't do them up. That's when you realise it's finally time to bite the bullet and buy yourself the dreaded maternity clothes. There is no point denying it any longer. To just buy bigger sizes of favourite garments is a complete waste of money; they'll only last a few weeks and you may well never be able to wear them again.

However, why should being pregnant mean you can't be stylish? These days you can flick through any trashy magazine and find photos of celebrities strutting their pregnant designer bellies around the hip hangouts. In fact, it can seem that being pregnant is the equivalent of wearing the latest handbag on your arm.

The rise of the 'yummy mummy' has increased the pressure on mums to dress well during pregnancy, instead of pulling on any old baggy T-shirt and jogging bottoms. Who can forget how beautiful Demi Moore looked when she was pregnant? Who wasn't envious of that beautiful pregnant body?

Personally I *was* pregnant in heels, spending my entire nine months strutting around the streets of Auckland in my Marc Jacobs wedges. Of course, my legs and back ached the entire time but I couldn't let pregnancy get in the way of vanity.

Don't forget that you'll have a cleavage to die for. Those boobs are going to be ruined soon enough so get them out and flaunt them in plunging necklines while you can.

Tips for being pregnant in heels

Now, you could spend a fortune on the very best maternity clothes. Or you could save your money and buy a couple of pairs of cheap maternity trousers and skirts, and borrow a heap of large T-shirts and shirts from your partner.

Buying maternity clothes online is a great option — some celebrities have their own designer collections that they promote on their websites. Some of the more popular online chain stores have maternity sections, such as UK sites Top Shop, Next, Sara, Dorothy Perkins and H&M. There are independent maternity boutique stores popping up all over the place, lots of the big department stores stock maternity clothes and don't forget the maternity sections in children's shops such as Pumpkin Patch, Mothercare and JK Kids*. You can also buy second-hand online at eBay or TradeMe.

* At the time of publication JK Kids has gone into receivership.

If you want to look stylish while pregnant, here are a few tips to follow:

Jeans

First of all, invest in a decent pair of maternity jeans. It's worth it. Your jeans are going to be worn practically every day for the duration of your pregnancy, and possibly your second, third and fourth pregnancies, so it's worth spending some money on a decent pair. It doesn't have to be a pair of designer preggie jeans — yes, they do make designer preggie Sevens (and they are pretty nice) — but they just need to look good. Look for something smart and flattering, in the style of jeans you normally wear (you can even get skinny preggie jeans, flared bottoms, boot-cut and three-quarter-length cut-off denim). They need to be comfortable, so make sure you try them on — some jeans sit below your bump (this is my preference), some have the adjustable buttons on the sides, some have elastic middles to 'support' the bump. Buy what suits you.

Leggings

Maternity leggings are another staple, especially for those days where you are not planning to see anyone and just need to be comfortable. Leggings can be worn under maternity skirts or with big shirts, tunics or maternity tops. They're also great for pregnancy yoga. They are comfortable, pretty much go with anything and will last you the entire way through your pregnancy.

Trousers

If you're at work then a smart pair of maternity trousers are recommended. I bought just one pair of smart black trousers from a chain store. They went with pretty much everything and saw me through any client meetings I needed to attend as well as a few nights out.

If there's a special occasion to attend you could get away with a smart pair of black maternity trousers and a nice top, or you could splash out on a stylish maternity dress. I had quite a few functions to attend during my two pregnancies — weddings, races, Christmas, birthdays and awards ceremonies — so it was important to me to have a nice dress to wear out and about.

Tops

A few nice tops are essential — floaty, dressy ones that don't interfere with your bump or casual stretchy ones. You can get away with buying larger-sized tops at the standard chain stores. A few large, stretchy boob tubes in different colours are fantastic — you can wear them under your normal tops as they can cover from your boobs to down over your bump so there's no preggie skin on show. A belly band is another good buy as it can be worn with skirts, shorts or trousers, ensuring your expanding tummy doesn't play peek-a-boo.

One nice top or dress

You won't be able to go though your entire pregnancy and avoid all social activity so it is worth buying one or two nice maternity tops to wear with your smart black trousers or investing in a maternity dress.

Shoes

Many women's feet swell while pregnant, and some women suffer from leg cramps and varicose veins. Even if you don't, you'll probably want to invest in some comfortable flat shoes. They don't have to be shoes your grandma would wear. I bought a stylish pair of knee-high chocolate brown boots when I was pregnant with my second child and still carrying around my first one. I also invested in a pair of plain black ballet flats for everyday wear for both pregnancies and a pair of smarter black ballet flats with gems on them for nights out.

Second-hand

Here's another tip: borrow from friends whenever you can. I had a very generous friend who lent her entire maternity wardrobe to me for both my pregnancies.

The big announcement

 It's ironic that the first trimester of your pregnancy is spent trying to hide the fact that you are pregnant while bursting to share the news with family and friends. You'll be reading anything you can get your hands on during those first few weeks of pregnancy, trying to soak up as much as possible about the baby being created in your belly.

You are usually advised to wait until the first trimester is complete (12 weeks) before telling people, but by the time you actually do get to tell them your excitement is starting to wane. Also, it's typically your first trimester when you are the most tired and nauseous. If you don't share your pregnancy news then, how will you gain the support you need during that time? And by the time you get through your first trimester, the questions you had wanted to ask your mummy friends are no longer as pertinent.

In my first trimester, the company I was working for at the time was in the midst of a huge renovation project, painting and bulldozing offices. The two second-trimester pregnant women were moved to a quieter, paint-fume-free office at the other end of the building. I was at the more crucial first trimester stage (but hadn't announced the pregnancy) and struggled among dust and paint fumes the entire time. In retrospect I wish I had said something and requested a change of location as well. Imagine if I had lost the baby.

Once we told our families, I actually started to feel justified reading all those pregnancy magazines and books. I also started to get excited about the pregnancy for the first time — it started to feel 'real'. John's parents were as pleased as punch, but the real surprise was telling my own mum and dad in the UK.

They were delighted but very shocked. 'I thought you always said you didn't want children,' Mum demanded, as though the whole thing wasn't real. 'I did,' I explained patiently, 'but I changed my mind.'

I could tell by the tone of her voice that she was genuinely caught off guard. So was Dad — he had already gone to get himself a whisky, despite the fact that it was 9 a.m. their time when we called to tell them.

Once we'd told our parents, John and I went back to normal life. I continued working, albeit at a slower pace, and we continued our social lives, although I was always thinking of ever more elaborate excuses as to why I couldn't join the girls for a few glasses. Over that first trimester I was 'detoxing', 'seriously training', 'not feeling that sharp tonight', 'driving', 'had a big night the night before', 'had an early start the next morning', and was 'saving myself for a big night out the following night'.

It all came to a head one weekend. We were visiting John's brother and sister-in-law in Sydney; it was the weekend before the half-marathon so I was using that as my excuse not to drink. That same excuse didn't work for the oysters or the swordfish they served up for dinner that night though. 'Jacqui doesn't really like oysters,' John improvised wildly, seeing my distress as a plate of beautiful oysters, which I love, was put down in front of me.

'What?' said Paul. 'I've seen her eat them before.'

'I've gone off them,' I mumbled, pushing the plate away. 'I had a bad experience,' I added, thinking quickly.

While Paul was happy to help himself to my oysters not thinking anything of it, Monique looked at me sharply.

The next course was swordfish, a fish pregnant women should try to avoid because of the high mercury content. How was I going to get out of this one? I picked at my swordfish and pretended to sip at my wine, feeling uncomfortable. Monique stared at me knowingly.

The same thing happened the week after the half-marathon. It seems no one ever believes that I would choose not to have a drink! I had already used the 'detox', 'hard night out the night before' and 'got a big day tomorrow' excuses with these friends. So, this particular night, when we out for dinner and the waiter came around to pour the glasses of wine and I said 'No, I'm driving,' my friend Jenny clapped her hands in delight.

'I knew it, I knew it!' she cried. 'You're pregnant, aren't you?'

I burst into tears. I'm not sure whether it was the relief of finally being able to tell someone, frustration that she had guessed or the beginnings of the pregnancy hormones which plagued me right until the end of my pregnancy.

I nodded, hanging my head. 'How did you know?'

'Jacqui, it's pretty obvious when *you* of all people don't even have one glass of wine,' she cried, hugging me in delight.

'Well, I'm only eleven weeks — I haven't even had my twelve-week scan yet,' I said. 'Please don't tell anyone.'

'Of course not, and I am absolutely thrilled!' she grinned.

I didn't have to wait much longer to tell my other friends and the rest of our families. The 12-week scan proved beyond doubt that yes, I was definitely pregnant, and all was well. It wasn't some weird dream. John and I looked at the scan of the Martian-like figure in my belly.

The doctor had tried to point out the baby's nose, eyes, mouth, hands and feet but we couldn't make out anything at all. Strangely, rather than feeling really excited, we both felt pretty let down — the baby didn't look like a baby at all. Nevertheless, we only had one week to go before our trip to the UK.

The plan had been to tell our New Zealand friends about the pregnancy when we got back from the UK but Jenny had foiled that plan. We felt we should come clean with our other mates before we disappeared for our five-week trip.

We frantically phoned around friends that week and got lots of excited squeals and 'welcome to parenthood' from friends who had already been there, done that.

'I'm not going to tell work until we are back from the UK,' I told John. Work had been pretty tough lately. My client had put the business up for pitch and we had been pitching for months against my former boss, who had gone to work for a competing agency.

That week — my final week at work before my holiday — we were due to find out which agency had won the business.

I was determined that whatever the outcome, I would keep quiet about being pregnant until I came back from the UK. Perhaps by then I would have a better idea of what I was doing with my life — God knows, until that point I hadn't even considered when or whether I would go back to work.

Unfortunately circumstances gathered pace that week and carried me along with them. The day after my scan we discovered that we had been unsuccessful in the pitch, losing out to my former boss's company after having the business for over 22 years. I burst into tears when I found out — whether it was hormones or genuine dismay, I have no idea.

The clients came in to tell us in person. I tried to remain professional in the meeting but it was difficult as tears rolled down my cheeks and I sniffed into my hanky. One of the clients obviously felt dreadful and gave me a big hug as she left. It had been a hard few months for me, what with hiding the pregnancy, training for a half-marathon and long, long hours at work — late nights, early mornings and weekends of working on this pitch — and now we had lost it.

That evening I received a telephone call from my former boss. 'I want you to come and work for me and run the account,' he stated. 'I want you and they have asked for you.'

I burst into tears again — it was becoming quite a habit. 'I can't,' I stammered. 'Why not?' he demanded. 'I would make it worth your while.'

'I'm pregnant,' I sobbed. That stumped him. I do believe he was genuinely thrilled for me, but worried too. 'What's going to happen for you at work?' he asked, concerned.

'I don't know,' I replied. For the first time I started to feel worried. What if I didn't have a job due to losing the account?

I didn't have to wait too long to find out. The next day was my final day before my holiday. I was pulled in to see my boss. 'Now, I want you to know,' he started, 'that we think an awful lot of you. I want you to go on holiday and not to worry about not having a job here when you get back. We will be restructuring the agency, but we'll look after you.'

I hesitated. What exactly was he saying? Restructuring the agency? 'What do you mean?' I asked.

'Well,' he replied, 'obviously, losing that piece of business is a big revenue loss and people will have to be made redundant. But don't worry, we'll look after you.'

I knew what he said was true. They would look after me. I had been loyal and worked hard for them and they would repay that. That's what he was saying. What I was concerned about was my growing belly and the fact that other people could be out of a job yet I was going to have to leave in a matter of months to have a baby.

I took a deep breath. So much for not telling them before my holiday, I thought.

'Roger, I've got something to tell you...'

Getting on the plane to the UK, I felt a mixture of relief and excitement. Roger had been amazing, telling me how thrilled he was for me and reassuring me that despite my pregnancy, they would have something wonderful for me on my return. I didn't know what I was coming back to, but I knew that no matter what happened with work, my life was quickly changing and it was totally out of my control.

Getting ready for baby

> 'If only they'd told me I wouldn't need to spend **thousands** on items that the baby doesn't need.'
>
> **Vicky, London, one son aged 2 years, and pregnant with number two**

 Getting Ready for Baby: ifonlytheytoldme.com/22

 Not long after I announced to my friends that I was pregnant, I received an email. It was sent to me by a friend with two children, and had been sent to her by someone else with children and so on. The email was a list of what to buy and what not to buy for the new baby. It had been edited, formatted and notes had been added. It was one of the most helpful lists I received throughout my whole pregnancy. Here's my version of 'The List':

Furniture/big items

- cot
- mattress
- mobile
- buggy/pram
- sun and rain cover for pram
- sheepskin (not only a comfort for the baby in the pram but also really useful to prevent 'spillages' getting onto the pram material which is harder to clean. With a sheepskin you can throw it into the wash every day if you need to.)
- car seat
- change table

- change mat
- nappy disposer and wrap (nice to have, especially if you are in an apartment or have stairs)
- baby bath
- sunshade (car window)
- travel cot

Accessories

- mattress protector
- sheet set
- blankets (wool and cellular)
- activity mat
- bouncinette (bouncing chair)
- Baby Mozart DVD (like the Symphony in Motion mobile, it allowed me time to vacuum the house, have a phone conversation or sit down with a cuppa)
- baby towels
- face cloths
- cloth nappies (great for spillages, changing baby, drying baby, putting over your shoulder if baby vomits, wrapping baby for sleep)
- dummies (our baby didn't use one but lots of people swear by them)
- muslin wrap (softer than a cloth nappy for wiping baby, washing them, wrapping them for sleeps)
- Huggies newborn nappies (the only nappies that kept all the poo in. All the others leaked.)
- aqueous cream (useful for nappy rash, inflamed baby skin or just general baby rashes)
- Sudacrem (good for baby's sore bottom)
- nappy bags (to dispose of all those yucky nappies)
- baby wipes (with a newborn you will use a muslin with tepid water but as baby grows and from the age of around 6 weeks you will be able to move to the more convenient baby wipes)
- Calpol/Pamol (for sick babies. Never give a baby medicine without checking with a doctor first.)
- cotton wool (initially for wiping newborn bottoms but generally useful for dabbing on aqueous cream, for example).

Feeding

- steriliser (I used a microwave one and found it quick, easy and very convenient. However, there are many types of sterilising equipment available.)
- bottles (starter pack such as Avent)
- bottle and teat brush
- feeding pillow (Some people don't need anything. Others will grab any old cushion. Personally I had terrible problems breastfeeding and I wouldn't go anywhere without my cushion.)
- nursing bras (unless you want to strip every time you need to feed, you need to invest in some decent nursing bras. I bought three and washed them constantly. You only use them for the duration of the time you are breastfeeding — in my case six months each time, so I figured I could just thrash the living daylights out of them.)
- breast shields (not everyone uses them but some people who have inverted nipples or just find it hard to breastfeed rave about breast shields. I didn't use them but if you do, then it is not something you are meant to use long-term.)
- breast pump (you may think that you don't want to feel like a cow but, believe me, if you want to supply predominantly breast milk to your child and have some semblance of a normal life and go out sometimes, then a breast pump is definitely recommended. I bought an electric one which you could put over your breast, press a button and let the machine do the work, extracting milk from your breast into a little bottle. You can get manual ones too and I have heard people recommend them too, so it's just down to personal preference.)
- nursing bra pads (If you have a lot of milk then you'll need these unless you want puddles lining your T-shirt for the world to see. I went to the movies one night when my first child was just 3 months old. The movie featured a baby, and unless you have had children you will not realise the significance of this — I experienced a 'let-down'. I left the movie theatre sporting two wet patches on my T-shirt.)
- plastic bags for breast milk (not just any plastic bags but specific ones which you can use to freeze any milk you may have expressed and save it for when you are going out and your husband or babysitter will need to be able to feed your baby with a bottle in your absence).
- cabbage leaves and tea strainers (for putting over your breasts when needing to give your breasts some 'recovery time').

Baby's clothing

- vests/body suits (cotton and wool)
- nighties (envelope neck)
- stretch 'n' grows
- T-shirts
- trousers
- cardigan/jersey
- jackets
- socks
- booties
- hat
- mittens
- bibs

Things for mum

- nappy bag
- vaginal icepack/soothies

I wanted to splurge on the very best pram available. At that time the bugaboo had just hit New Zealand streets. My friends in the UK all had them and raved about them and celebrity mothers were often seen parading their beautiful children in them. I wanted one. Whether it was to keep a bit of my UK friends near me while I went through my pregnancy in New Zealand or whether it was to be a 'yummy mummy', I can't tell you.

In retrospect it was a complete waste of money. NZ$1500 on a pram is excessive considering it will have baby vomit, milk, food, poo and mud splattered on it. Yes, it looks good, when it's new at least; yes, it's light and easily collapsible; but is it a whole $800 better than the next pram?

Now I know to ask the question: will it hold its value? Once you've had your baby you realise everything has a time limit. As you and your baby outgrow all the paraphernalia you can sell it on TradeMe or eBay or to friends. Some things hold their value more than others.

No one is going to pay $1000 for a pram that cost you $1500 three years after you bought it. Someone might, however, pay $500 for a three-year-old pram that cost $800 new. So, unless you have more money than you know what to do with, don't blow it on something that is going to take a serious pounding every day for the next few years.

The other tip is to buy second-hand wherever possible. There are certain things that you don't want to buy second-hand — cot mattresses for example, and car seats in case they have previously been involved in accidents — but prams, change tables, cots, baby baths, books, toys and ride-ons can all be bought for a fraction of their retail price.

Do you need a change table? I have heard many people say they would prefer to save money and not buy a change table, but I loved having one. You will spend an extraordinary amount of time changing nappies. Unless you want to be constantly bending over your baby on the floor, I would recommend a change table. Not only does it make your life easier, as your child will be confined at your level while you change his nappy, with everything at your fingertips (most change tables have shelves in which to store nappies, wipes, bags to put soiled nappies, creams etc.), it will also save your back.

The other worthwhile investment is decent storage. You will gain so much *stuff* it is not funny. Not only will you get given a whole heap of stuffed animals when your child is born, you'll buy parenting books, you'll have books and toys coming out of your ears, nappies, creams and potions, vests, tops, jackets, jumpsuits, little shoes and socks and so on.

You can buy really cheap 'box' shelving units to store things in, either in little baskets or colourful plastic boxes straight on the shelves. It makes life so much easier if things are put away and easy to find. I've talked about a change table to store nappies, wipes etc. but it's also worth investing in a chest of drawers for baby clothes. Drawers can be picked up cheaply new or online second-hand and painted or spruced up with fun new handles.

You'll need a cot and mattress, of course. There is nothing wrong with buying a second-hand cot, giving it a quick sand and paint and just buying a new mattress and fun, colourful linen.

You don't necessarily need a bassinet although it is recommended to make baby feel as secure as possible when born, which is why you wrap them up well for the first few months. You can buy a second-hand bassinet or Moses basket, which is easy to carry around with you.

Portacots, although not a necessity, are very useful if you are moving around a lot, going on holiday or just want to keep your social life going through those early years of parenthood. It's nice to know that you don't need a babysitter every time you go out but that you can simply cart your baby and her portacot with you and pop her up at a friend's or grandparents', allowing them to sleep while you relax over a nice meal and a glass of wine.

Decorating baby's room also doesn't need to cost a fortune. We simply framed some fun, colourful alphabet-themed wrapping paper and used it as a picture in our baby's room. You can buy fun friezes, or do your own stencilling if you feel creative. Framed postcards or black and white cartoons are another way to decorate the room in a cost-effective fashion. Look for illustrations in children's books that appeal, which you can have enlarged and framed or mounted. As your child gets older you can always use their own artwork for decoration, or use blackboard paint on one wall or door that can be drawn or written on at any time with colourful chalk.

A baby bath isn't a necessity. Use a washbasin if you have one or you can buy little cloth seats to put baby in the big bath, enabling you to use your hands to wash baby and lift them in and out of the bath more easily.

'Baby-wearing' and 'natural parenting' are really making a comeback. Front-packs and slings are important to some people but not to everyone. I started using a front-pack with my first baby, and it really came into its own with my second child. It enabled me to push my eldest child in the pram while carrying my newborn in the front-pack. It also enabled me to walk around the park or garden playing with my eldest child while my new baby slept contentedly in the front-pack, and didn't need to be left in a pram parked in the corner of a park.

In terms of toys and books — don't buy any, at least until you see what gifts you receive. Do invest in a decent bouncer chair though. A bouncer chair is a soft-backed curved chair ideal for babies under 6 months. The baby bounces contentedly away, lulled to lala land by the bouncing, giving you a few moments to do other things.

A portable play mat is also useful. Buy one that you can fold up and pop in your nappy bag so when you are visiting friends, you are able to whip it out and pop baby down on the floor, safe in the knowledge that no matter how dirty the floor is, your baby is safely on their own mat.

Play gyms can be useful although they're not absolutely necessary. They are cloth mats with colourful (and sometimes musical) items hanging down so baby looks at the items and not just at the ceiling. Basically the difference between a play mat and a play gym is that the play gym has things hanging down for the child to grab, focus on, gum and explore whereas a mat is just that — a mat for you to put the baby on so they can lie and kick.

The only toy you really need to buy is a teething ring. Babies under the age of one don't need toys. They are exploring the world. Your face is fascinating to them, as is the ceiling, the rug, and other visitors' faces. You can bounce them on your knee, play peek-a-boo, show them their reflection in the mirror, and print out or draw cards with black and white shapes.

You'll get given soft toys for the baby to gum or chew but a colourful bucket of pegs, a wooden spoon and a tin or saucepan, or a home-made rattle made with rice in a plastic sealed jar will be enough to entertain an older baby.

Excersaucers are nice to have, but they're not a necessity. They enable babies to almost stand up in a safe play circle, touching items around them and not able to get into any trouble. They also enable mums to get dinner ready without having to hold baby in their arms. Bouncers do much the same.

A mobile hangs above the bed or change table. Your baby will spend most of their first six months on their back, looking at the ceiling, so this gives them something to look at. Some pretty mobiles hang from the ceiling or attach to the cot, or even play music and 'entertain' baby. They are definitely a nice-to-have. I invested in a top-of-the-range Symphony in Motion mobile, which plays several Beethoven melodies and circles around above the baby's head for 10 minutes — the perfect amount of time for a mother to have a shower. (Yes, you are allowed to leave your baby safely in their cot for 10 minutes by themselves while you have a shower.)

What they say and things they never tell you

'If only they'd told me that my boobs would grow bigger than they had ever been before, only to shrivel up and shrink to even smaller after the baby.'

Jo, Auckland, two daughters aged 2 and 3 years

As a couple you've become accustomed to living life at your own pace, whether that means working most evenings, leisurely dinners, bike riding or whatever your thing is. Let's be frank — having a baby is mind-blowing. Not only do you experience a range of emotions, from anxiety to exhilaration, but suddenly all those things people told you start becoming true. 'You'll love your baby more than words can explain.'

Life before baby feels like an entirely different universe to life with a baby. You hear the 'impending doom' comments made by friends and strangers offering advice like 'enjoy your freedom while you've got it'. People smile knowingly and make comments like 'You won't know what's hit you' and 'You know you won't be able to go out for dinner or to the movies like you used to.' It's easy to get annoyed at all the remarks but just grit your teeth and don't let them bother you. You'll probably make a pact with yourself that you will not change. I was determined that my lifestyle wouldn't change and that I would show all those know-it-alls that I could do it with flair. I was determined to maintain my lifestyle, freedom, career, friendships, relationship and heels and I swore that the baby would fit around me and my life.

There will be other friends — those with no children nor any interest in children — who will just smile vaguely, feel sorry for you and promptly stop inviting you to parties. I know when I was pregnant I found I had to gate-crash a few parties for my friends to understand that I wasn't going to change and they could still count on their good old buddy to have a good time. In fact, later on during my pregnancy, I was so determined to prove that you could be glamorous and pregnant that — aside from the designer maternity wear and the tottering heels that I wore right the way to the hospital — I partied (almost) as hard as the rest of them, just without the wine!

People will comment on how big or small or high or low your baby belly is. Strangers will smile at you and think it's OK to pat your belly. They will ask you if you know if it's a boy or a girl and whether you've chosen a name yet. But they might not tell you that pregnancy is 10 months long (not nine), you might bleed for three to six weeks after having your baby, and once you finish breastfeeding your boobs will shrink!

Couplehood in the pregnancy stage

 One of the main things people somehow neglect to mention when a baby is on the horizon is the impact on your relationship. So much focus is on 'the birth' and 'sleep deprivation', people almost forget to warn you that your relationship will be rocked! Couples receive little advice about how their relationship will change. Having a baby is a huge change to your life, and the change on your relationship is different but equally as significant. It can be quite a shock.

What makes a marriage/relationship thrive? It's little things like looking your husband (lovingly) in the eyes when he walks through the door, rather than glaring and handing him the baby!

Exercising while pregnant

While researching for this book and writing our blog, Nat and I spoke with several personal trainers to get their advice about exercising while pregnant. Here is what personal trainer Inga Fillary had to say:

Although this is an embarrassing admission to make as a personal trainer, I have to fess up — I did virtually no exercise during my first two pregnancies. After my second baby I was hugely out of shape and overweight. I got inspired, lost 20 kg and in the process became fascinated with exercise, nutrition and health and retrained as a personal trainer. I have now been a PT for five years. I'm now eight months into my third pregnancy and have exercised pretty consistently throughout.

The difference between pregnancies is amazing! Here are a few benefits that I've noticed so far:

⊙ keeping that awful morning sickness in check
⊙ better posture (and fewer discomforts associated with muscle imbalances)
⊙ better cardio; I can walk (even run!) without having to stop for a breather.

The aim of the game is to keep you fit and healthy. Obviously this is not the time to be losing weight or radically changing exercise habits. Remember you'll have the rest of your life after the baby comes to lose the weight you gain and be the shape you want to be so *safety first*! Be conservative, listen to your body and get the go-ahead from your LMC before embarking on an exercise regime.

Remember to warm up and cool down for an extended period. This means doing light cardio (walking, biking, swimming etc.) for at least seven minutes at the start of your workout and five or more minutes at the end. Otherwise blood can pool in your extremities, and with all the extra blood you are pumping this is not a good thing! Make sure you keep well hydrated.

Avoid lying flat on your back after the first trimester (I actually found crunches just felt 'wrong' quite early in the piece so dropped them from my workout). Also avoid holding your breath and performing exercises with your limbs higher than your heart as this can push up your blood pressure.

Weight-bearing exercise

Many of the discomforts of pregnancy arise from muscle imbalances, which lead to postural problems. Most commonly we tend to get a curve in the lower back, and our shoulders tend to slump forward. Some of these problems are caused by the weight increase, and others by the hormone relaxin that makes all your muscles stretchy in preparation for the birth.

Obviously you need to take it fairly easy and not lift any heavy weights. Stretchy bands, body weight and light weights are ideal. It's also really important to train in 'neutral spine'. Our spines are designed to have curves for shock absorption. However in pregnancy it's very common for these curves to get over-accentuated, so whenever you are performing weight-bearing exercises aim for a 'neutral spine'.

Cardiovascular exercise

Ligaments stretching and the weight of the baby can make high-impact exercise such as running or jumping quite uncomfortable, particularly in the latter stages of pregnancy.

The current cardio recommendation while pregnant is 30 minutes a day. Listen to your body — if you feel exhausted and very out of breath, tone it down. Likewise, if you have maintained a high level of fitness throughout your pregnancy you can push a little harder.

Walking, swimming, elliptical trainer and reclined bike are all good cardio-vascular activities.

You should not *start* a cardio programme in the last half of your pregnancy.

IOTTM tips for life before baby

- ☉ Don't just assume that babies will come along straight away. There is only a very small period of time when you can actually get pregnant. In a typical 28-day menstrual cycle, your most fertile time is day 12 to day16 (assuming a typical 4-day ovulation).
- ☉ Typical pregnancy signs can include nausea, tiredness, increased need to urinate, queasiness or even vomiting, greasy hair, swollen or tingling breasts and a metallic taste in your mouth.
- ☉ Your body will change hugely while pregnant — learn to accept it and love it.
- ☉ Invest in comfortable maternity clothes that are also stylish. You will wear the same things again and again throughout the duration of this and other pregnancies and so you need to feel good in any maternity clothes you buy. Better to spend more on a few items of maternity clothes you love than a whole wardrobe of cheap maternity clothes you want to burn.
- ☉ Don't leave the planning and buying of what you need for baby to the last minute. If you plan and research earlier then you are more likely to get good

quality second-hand items for a better price or find items on sale or special discounts.

⊙ Exercising when pregnant is fine if you have always exercised. However, talk with a specialist to get an exercise programme designed for your stage in your pregnancy. Avoid any exercise that involves lying on your back, such as lifting weights or crunches.

CHAPTER TWO

Baby on the way

> 'I think we were as prepared as you can be. You will never be fully prepared for the fatigue and demands of a child. Another mother told us at the hospital after the birth of our first child, 'My baby is so needy!' Yeah, that is a baby! You do not realise what 'needy' means until you have a child! There really is no break from this need.'
>
> **Lawrence, Brooklyn, two sons aged 3 and 6 years**

Get this baby outta me

By the end of any pregnancy, nearly all pregnant women declare that they have finally had enough. 'Get this baby outta me!' I have to admit that I wasn't much different. Surprisingly, the worst thing was my legs. My legs throbbed constantly and I felt so tired. Those last few weeks of child number one saw me develop a heavy cold, and I had to make do with rubbing Vicks VapoRub all over my neck, throat and chest and around my nose, which caused my eyes to sting. For someone who was determined to work right up to the day I went into labour, I really did start to fade.

But, the worse thing was my legs. In those final few weeks I often woke in the middle of the night with the most awful leg cramp. I would clutch at my leg, rubbing it furiously. Often I had to get out of bed and walk around to stretch it out. It took about 10 minutes before the cramp finally abated and I was able to climb back into bed and go to sleep.

And the constant peeing! I was up and down like a yo-yo, day and night. I would no sooner sit down in a work meeting when I was up again, excusing myself to visit the ladies room. I had to ensure I didn't have to travel too far in the car without a toilet break. And what was with the little leaks? Was it just me? God, it was embarrassing. When I sneezed or coughed there was a little bit of seepage — rather worrying considering I was constantly coughing and sneezing.

I asked my specialist about it the next time I visited him.

'Are you doing your pelvic floors?' he asked.

'My what?' I wondered aloud.

'Your pelvic floor exercises? Are you practising them?' Seeing the blank look on my face, he opened a drawer. 'Here you go, try reading this. Do them every day without fail — at least twice a day otherwise you'll be caught out for the rest of your life.'

'How unglamorous,' I thought to myself as I read the pamphlet later that afternoon when I was back at my desk. 'None of my friends who had babies told me about this bit.' I tried squeezing in my pelvic muscles like the leaflet said.

'Are you all right?' asked Gemma, who sat opposite me. 'You look a bit red in the face.'

'No, no, perfectly fine,' I said rapidly, putting the leaflet away in my bag and deciding that the privacy of the car was probably the best place to practise them.

But seriously, those pelvic floors are super important. If there is one thing you decide to invest in once you have had your baby, I would recommend a top physiotherapist who can give you one-on-one Pilates and pelvic floor instructions. Otherwise your life will be filled with uncomfortable wet moments from here on in.

Pelvic floor exercises don't have to take up that much time. I usually do mine sitting at traffic lights, or doing the washing up. Just suck your buttocks up and together as though you are stopping yourself peeing. Hold for 10 seconds, relax and then do it again. Just keep doing it throughout the day and you'll find you'll be able to run for buses once again. There is even a Circle of Moms blog dedicated to this very subject! (circleofmoms.com)

Back to the legs. The last few weeks of pregnancy saw the most awful changes. I've always been unlucky enough to suffer from varicose veins but in those last few weeks they just popped out all over the place and were almost bulging out of my legs. I almost cried when I caught sight of them in the mirror.

'Look at my legs!' I pointed out to hubby, hoping for some sympathy.

'Oh my *God*, they're awful! What have you done?' he said in shock, which made me feel even worse.

He was right though. I phoned my specialist straight away. 'My veins have come up and they are really ugly. What can I do?' I demanded.

'It sometimes happens with pregnancy,' the doctor replied soothingly. 'They'll go back to normal afterwards. Just put your feet up as regularly as you can and avoid wearing high heels. If they are still bad afterwards there are people you can go to who can make them better. Oh, you can wear support stockings.'

'No high heels!' I screeched in horror. 'But I always wear heels.'

It was true. I had an impressive collection of shoes of every colour, all of them heels. In fact, I don't think I owned one pair of flat shoes. The thought of putting away my gorgeous array of beautifully coloured shoes was very depressing.

The next day, however, I came around. 'I need to buy some more shoes,' I announced to hubby.

'But you've got hundreds of shoes,' he protested.

'Not flats,' I said firmly. 'The doctor said I needed to wear flat shoes for the rest of my pregnancy. I'll need at least two pairs to see me through for the next few weeks.' Feeling slightly better I trounced off for a shopping expedition.

I also checked out the support stockings that the doctor had mentioned, but put them firmly back on the shelf again in disgust. They were thick, white and looked like bandages — there would be no way I would be wearing those, no matter how ugly my legs. I would rather swelter in trousers through the whole of summer than wear a pair of those disgusting things.

In retrospect that was probably a mistake as my legs have never quite recovered from the stress of my two pregnancies and I now have to undergo surgery to fix them. Moral of the story, forget about vanity and go for comfort and support!

The other thing that sneaks up at you when you are coming to the end of your pregnancy is the 'waddling'. You swear that you won't be one of those waddlers, but you will! 'God, you've popped out,' everyone remarks as you waddle along.

In the last few weeks, your belly and boobs become so swollen that even maternity clothes stop hiding your bump. I remember one day when I had a huge presentation at work, I grabbed my smart work maternity shirt and waddled out the door. It was only when I sat down at the board table that I realised my blouse was gaping so much that not only could my clients see my bra but also my lovely belly too. I spent the whole presentation clutching my file in front of me so no one could see, and I was so paranoid that I totally mucked things up. To top it all off, I had back-to-back meetings followed by a dinner that evening. I spent the whole dinner fat and uncomfortable trying to cover my gaping buttons.

Bonding with strangers at antenatal

 The antenatal class is a huge turning point in your pregnancy. It's when the impending birth suddenly starts to become real. However, the strangest thing about it is that you are thrust into a relationship with absolute strangers and expected to 'bond' just because you are all pregnant. Now sometimes this can be great and you can strike gold with your antenatal class, making friends for life. Others aren't quite so lucky.

Personally I was part of a lovely group of girls who were wholly supportive of each other. Coincidentally many of us were from the UK, all living in NZ without our families nearby. All of us encountered problems at some point and the others would rally around supporting those in need.

I struggled with the birth and the feeding and the girls, unbeknown to me, all spoke to each other, realised I needed help and took it in turns to pop by and see if I was OK. Likewise another member of our class suffered from serious post-natal depression with both children. She was literally bed-bound after both births and we would each take it in turns to drop meals over and pick up the older child for playdates or kindy.

Years later, when I had to have an operation, the same group of girls were amazingly supportive, looking after my youngest for me while I recuperated.

Other antenatal groups, however, aren't quite so lucky. There are those who simply don't gel and never really get it together after the birth. Then there are others who have even worse experiences. One woman I know had to put caller ID on her phone due to a woman from her antenatal class, who she thought seemed really nice initially, continually phoning and harassing her. The other woman probably wasn't coping that well but the friend in question hardly knew her and was trying to get her own head around her new life as a mum and wanted space to find her way by herself. Her new 'antenatal friend' didn't let up and would ring sometimes up to five times a day or, worse still, just turn up on her doorstep unannounced.

'I would often still be in my pyjamas,' she explained, 'unshowered and certainly not in the mood for visitors. One day she even woke me up while I was trying to sleep during my baby's nap. She just didn't seem to get I needed space. I hardly knew her yet she seemed to have automatically claimed me as her new best friend, just because we lived a few streets apart. I couldn't cope with it and would just let the phone ring through to answerphone to avoid speaking with her. The worse thing was, whenever I did speak to her, she didn't even have any reason for ringing. The conversation would be awkward and full of long pauses and I could never work out why she was ringing me in the first place.'

Back to the antenatal class itself. The antenatal class covers all the stuff leading up to the birth: Braxton Hicks contractions, recognising labour, the birth itself. But it doesn't ever prepare you for the aftermath: the shock, the emotional rollercoaster, the painful breastfeeding, the relationship turmoil and the changes to your life as an individual. That, I suppose, is where the coffee groups come in. If you are lucky enough to have a good antenatal class then you will start to meet up regularly. Of course, you won't really bond until after you have all had your babies and then suddenly you are in the same boat. You can laugh and cry with people going through the same as you, and you can hopefully help each other by being honest and sharing your experiences.

And who could forget the most well-talked about part of the antenatal class — the birth video? Nowadays you can watch *One Born Every Minute* with your cup of tea each week. But when we were at antenatal classes, it was still a big deal. In our class we were given the option to miss it. Our teacher let us know the week before the screening saying, 'If any of you are particularly squeamish and would rather not watch it, then just come fifteen minutes late next week.' My husband is squeamish. He really didn't want to see it. He thought the whole antenatal class thing was a complete waste of time and I had to bribe him to come at all. So, the following week he was determined to miss the video. He purposely made us late so that when we walked into the class, the showing would be over. The problem was that it wasn't. There had been a technical hitch with the video and they were only just starting it. Not only that but, because we were late, there were only two chairs left, right in front of the TV!

Forty+ weeks and counting ...

 If you are still pregnant by the time 40 weeks rolls around, you'll be so over it that if one more person asks you if you've had your baby yet, you'll scream. I mean, do you look like you've had your baby? And you'll suddenly become inundated by well-meaning friends who phone constantly to ask 'Any news?' I mean, do they honestly think you wouldn't have bothered sending word?

If you are unlucky enough to suffer from Braxton Hicks contractions then you know how uncomfortable they are. Every day is a near-labour day. The first time I had them I thought I was in labour. I even got the towel ready and had a momentary panic attack as I realised that I hadn't ironed any of the clothes I wanted to pack in my hospital bag. I made poor hubby iron my clothes for me and spent the whole night not sleeping and being on tenterhooks as I waited for my waters to break and my contractions to intensify, only to wake up again the next morning with bump and waters still intact.

The one good thing about being 'late' in labour is the fact that finally people actually expect you to be tired and over it and to need to put your feet up. They don't complain when you say, 'I would rather stay home tonight with the telly or a good book.'

The other good thing about being late is the fact that you get to spend even more quality time with your husband, and get dinner cooked for you and people to do your cleaning and ironing because, let's face it, even bending down to unplug the iron is a struggle when you're that big.

Of course the bad thing about being overdue, apart from the constant phone calls and getting more and more uncomfortable, is the fact that the baby inside you is getting bigger and bigger, and has to come out somehow. Quite a scary thought when you are planning a vaginal delivery.

Best intentions and unwanted advice

 What is it about being pregnant or having children that suddenly opens you up to advice from any Tom, Dick or Harry? It's like the arrival of a baby in your belly makes you the unwelcome focus of every well-meaning friend and stranger. People don't mean to overstep the mark, I know. But sometimes they do.

People are speaking with absolutely the best intentions, but it does wear thin. When you're pregnant there's always a comment about what you must or mustn't eat, whether you should be wearing heels or not, whether you're too big or too small, how you're 'carrying' and what it means (big girl, small boy), what pram you need to buy, what car seat you need to buy, how much maternity leave you should take . . . the list goes on.

Strangers smile knowingly and make comments like, 'Enjoy your freedom while you've got it', 'You won't know what's hit you' and 'You won't be able to go out for dinner or to the movies like you used to.' It's easy to get annoyed at all the remarks, but just grit your teeth and don't let them bother you.

When you have your baby the advice steps up a notch: whether or not you should breastfeed and how long for; whether your baby should or shouldn't sleep in the same room as you; whether your baby should be in a routine or you should let them sleep, cry and eat when they want; how old they should be when they eat solids; when you should toilet-train them; whether they should be allowed to watch TV and at what age and for how long; should they go to daycare?

Even when they are older the advice continues. Should you teach them their ABCs before they start school? How should you discipline them? How many times should your child be allowed to eat sweets? What age should you introduce them to the computer? It's a never-ending round of questions for every parent, in every generation around the world. Advice is all well and good and yes, sometimes it is definitely useful and helpful. But sometimes people just don't know where to draw the line.

Parenting is private and personal. Any criticism dressed up as 'advice' can be frustrating and upsetting. Personally I didn't mind the advice so much when I was pregnant — the main thing that bugged me was strangers patting my belly in the supermarket. However, once I became a parent, it was a whole different story. When people told me I was doing too much with my children, or that they were unruly and too loud, that's when I took it personally. It is true that if someone criticises your children, then they criticise you. When I received an email recently from my daughter's kindergarten teacher complaining that my child had hit another child and telling me how I should be practising 'positive parenting' at home to ensure it didn't happen again, I was so upset. I am sure the person who sent it thought she was being helpful. I took it the other way. Not only was I upset to hear that my child had been hitting other children, but to be told I wasn't practising positive parenting at home was upsetting.

Here are some pieces of advice readers of our blog site, If Only They'd Told Me, received when they were pregnant or had children and have kindly shared with us.

'I struggled with the way total strangers would come up and put their hand on my stomach as if I was suddenly public property. It was very warmly intended, but it felt way too intrusive for comfort.'

Hillary

'I got frustrated with people always trying to tell me what I could and couldn't eat, and what they thought I 'should' eat! Maybe it was just my hormones but I found it really irritating.'

Melissa

'After a while, I wanted to give a little kick to people who said "giving birth is a completely natural process, women have been doing it for thousands of years, your body will just know what to do!"'

Casey

'"Get your sleep now..." drove me nuts!'

Kelly

'Lots of people telling me complete horror stories of how they gave birth. It was very depressing.'

Kay

'The horror stories really bothered me. I had two very wonderful, med-free labours (one at home), and I always tell mums-to-be how amazing labour can be. I felt amazing after both births, like I could do anything!'

Sarah K

'I got sick of people telling me I should not have found out the sex of the baby! I think that's a personal choice.'

Helen

'I bet most of you haven't heard this one: sunbathe topless because it will toughen your nipples ready for breastfeeding! Because that's what this person's doctor told her to do in the 1970s!'

Sarah P

'My male boss — gay and childless — told me how women had given birth up trees in Africa, and how infirm I'd be in the months leading up to and after the birth. Another woman at work told me how she smoked and ate sushi while pregnant and how silly I was for being so 'careful'. I wasn't uptight — I had one low-alcohol beer a month with a full meal, made my own poached eggs and walked 5 km a day until my waters broke! I had my healthy baby girl in hospital (strangely, the tree in the back garden wasn't tempting) and checked myself out 24 hours later. I've been a single mum since day one of my pregnancy and wiped the smirk off my boss's face when I returned to work a year later, glowing with health, baby weight exercised off and — oh my gosh — coping! (However the attitude did make me quit, choose to take another year off with my poppet and now I work for a family-friendly company.)'

Sarah B

Try not to take unwanted advice to heart. In most cases, people are genuinely trying to help!

On this note, we were lucky enough to meet with and interview actor and comedian Jaquie Brown about her book *I'm Not Fat, I'm Pregnant*. When she started writing the book she didn't know what a full-on time she had ahead of her. It wasn't just a vomit-plagued pregnancy but also a high-stress labour. No shortage of material for Jaquie to write about; and she does write well! Here's one of her great 'tips for new mums':

'Resist the temptation to say anything to pregnant friends about enjoying their social life, sleep-ins, sleep in general, sex life, waistline, perky boobs and sanity "while they can". It's mean-spirited, inaccurate and not every foray into motherhood will be the same.'

Jaquie Brown

 Jaquie Brown: ifonlytheytoldme.com/21

Maternity leave and your plan for the future

When you're pregnant, one big decision you have to make is deciding how much maternity leave to take.

Of course, often it depends on which country you live in and what your entitlements are in that country. In New Zealand you currently get 14 weeks fully paid government maternity leave. Companies are required to leave your job open for you for 12 months but they do not have to pay you a sausage. In the UK you are currently entitled to 52 weeks maternity leave, with 39 weeks of that leave paid. Some larger companies such as banks and law firms even pay their employees a year's wage at full pay with the proviso that they return to work for at least one full year after their maternity leave. Employees in the UK have the added bonus of having their annual leave accrue while they are on maternity leave.

Central Europe generally tends to have the longest maternity leave regulations in the world. It is fairly standard for a mother to take three years off work after having a baby. For the whole period, the mother is supported by the state.

In Australia, the government used to pay parents to have children with a baby 'bonus'. Mothers get 52 weeks off, 18 of them paid.

In the US and Canada the maternity leave is quite different again. In Canada, for example, maternity leave has recently been increased from 10 weeks to 35 weeks, paid for by the Employment Insurance system. In the US, maternity leave is surprisingly only three weeks, which means a lot of American mothers end up returning to work much earlier than in other countries.

Have a plan

 Have a serious think about how much maternity leave you want to take and how much of that will be before the baby comes along. Most people take between one and four weeks off prior to the birth. Four weeks might sound a long time but actually near the end you do need to put your feet up. At the same time, you will go into overdrive trying to organise everything in time for the baby. I didn't even start shopping for baby until I went on maternity leave.

It is unlikely your baby will arrive on your actual due date, unless you have an organised C-section. In many cases, especially in the case of high-pressure jobs, a pregnant woman will finish work only to go into labour the next day. Four of my good friends have all had babies the evening they finished work. In one case, my friend hadn't even bought a car seat or baby clothes to take to the hospital with her, let alone a bassinet or cot!

To tell the truth, I wasn't going to take *any* time off work beforehand, preferring to work right up to D-day (I was in denial that a baby was on the way). It was only because so many friends who already had a baby persuaded me not to be so stupid that I finally took note and realised, they couldn't all be telling me the same thing for no particular reason.

In the end I took four weeks off prior to the baby coming and loved it. Not only did I get to leisurely shop for baby items but I went swimming and walking daily, visited friends and generally put my feet up.

You should also take into consideration your work environment when deciding how much maternity leave to take after having the baby. If you work at a young, fast-paced company with most of the employees working late hours, then you probably are best not to rush back while you are still breastfeeding and going through sleep-deprived nights. If, however, it is a family-friendly company then you may wish to go back earlier. It also depends on your own monetary situation, of course, and how much maternity leave you can afford to take. It will also depend on *you* and your personality. You may love being at home with your baby or you may crave to be back in the centre of activity at work.

My advice is to take a longer maternity leave and then, if it isn't working out for you at home and you want to return to work earlier, just let work know. If you take a shorter maternity leave then any extra time you want to add will need to be renegotiated with your work and they are within their rights to deny it.

 When I first contemplated my maternity leave, I thought 'I'll take a few months off and then ease back into doing some work from home.' Three months sounded like *ages* and the thought of taking a whole year off sounded ridiculous! Wow, how things change! You never truly know how you will feel in your new role as a 'mother', so the best plan is to be flexible and keep your options open. In hindsight I would encourage all mothers to take a year's maternity leave if they can afford to do so. Alternatively, take seven or eight months off then return to part-time work only.

The birth plan

One of the pieces of advice they will give you at antenatal class is to make a birth plan covering the big decisions such as drugs or no drugs, what happens if you get into difficulty, and so on.

Jacqui's birth plan

I knew from the beginning that any drugs offered during my birthing experience would be readily accepted. I had no strong desire to have a 'natural birth'.

In fact, early on I had decided to have a water birth. I had a romantic notion of candles fluttering, classical music playing, me beautiful and naked in the bath with my husband, and my baby just 'gliding' out. Everyone was smiling and the nurses and obstetrician were very much in the background. Then I found out that:

1. There are no drugs allowed in a water birth.
2. Most people poo in the bath and therefore you are in a bath with your own poo floating past you.
3. My husband was refusing to be even remotely involved in a water birth due to point number 2.

I started to rethink.

So, I assured my obstetrician that I was incredibly weak and squeamish and therefore would be willing to accept any drugs or other form of pain relief offered. Other than that, I think I played it pretty straight with my birthing plan:

- No, I do not want to keep the placenta.
- No, hubby is not allowed 'down south'.
- Yes, hubby must remain with me throughout the birth but must be firmly to the north and holding my hand and under my instruction at all times.
- No, I do not want the birth videoed.
- Yes, I am willing to take all pain relief offered.
- Yes, I would be willing to undergo surgery, whether it be forceps, ventouse or a caesarean if necessary.

I know that other women are determined to give birth *au natural* and I don't belittle that at all. Nor do I see it as a major accomplishment. Giving birth is the accomplishment, no matter how you do it.

One good friend was adamant she wasn't going to have any pain relief whatsoever. We were just six weeks apart in our due dates and would talk often on the phone. I remember her asking me whether I was planning to take pain relief and after I had assured her that I definitely was, she proudly announced that she wouldn't be taking any at all. Not a jot. As it turned out, she had a terrible labour and yelled at her midwife, who tried to talk her out of gas when she screamed for it, insisting, 'You told me not to let you have it no matter what you called me.' The same friend later apologised about lecturing me for putting pain relief in my plan, admitting she hadn't realised just how hard birth would be.

Nat's birth plan

My plan for all three labours was the same: keep it as natural as possible but have medical assistance ready in case it is needed. While some friends expected me to have a home birth because of my eco values, this was not my preference. I was all about no drugs if possible but I would do what needed to be done for a healthy and safe delivery. My first birth was a water birth (no poo situation, Jacqui!) and the next two were on my 'hands and knees' on the hospital floor. All were 'no drugs', which is more a fact than a bragging point. Unlike Jacqui, I did want my husband 'down south' — he was crucial in pressing on my back when the contractions came, and he 'caught' the baby. I had the birth videoed and photographed, and had a friend along as well for support for baby number one, my mum for baby number two, and just my husband for baby number three.

All labours are different and the guilt and judgements that plague motherhood need not start in the delivery room.

One friend desperately wanted a home birth but when things went wrong, she had to contend with being rushed to hospital in an ambulance. Another good friend who wanted a straightforward hospital birth actually ended up giving birth on her bathroom floor.

The point is to plan, but to be prepared for things to change during labour. You're allowed to change your mind!

The hospital visit

Please make sure you visit your hospital before you go into labour so you know your way around. The last thing you want is to give birth in the car while your husband drives round the block looking for a car park. When we did the hospital tour the only problem was that the nurse talked so fast that I couldn't remember anything she said. She whistled us all over the hospital showing us really important places and telling us where to go and where to park and what button to press on the lift and where to go after that and if you get it wrong that you could possibly have your baby on the carpet in the main corridor like one poor woman did last month. By the time the tour was over, far from feeling reassured I actually felt quite sick. Luckily hubby was taking it all in and when the time came he went into 'auto pilot' and navigated us to the delivery suite without incident or hallway births.

The hospital bag

And then, of course, there's the hospital bag. You're told to pack for a long labour. In fact, it almost sounds like you're going on holiday. Buy yourself a nice new nightie and pack yourself some smellies to make yourself feel better is completely *useless* advice. Now here's my advice: do *not* go to the bother of buying yourself a new nightie. You will *not* be wearing it. Nor would you want to as you will bleed afterwards and who wants to ruin their new nightie? Just stick to the blue hospital gowns — yes, the backless ones where everyone sees your bum. Believe me, when you are in labour you really will not care what you look like. And afterwards, you will want to burn whatever you were wearing at the time.

As for the smellies, you will not be taking long, lingering showers. Apart from the fact that you will be exhausted, weak, sore and bleeding, you just won't feel like it.

My hospital bag consisted of the following:

- snacks for me for during labour (never even opened)
- snack for my husband for during labour (never even opened)
- a pack of cards (seriously, what was I thinking?)
- romantic music (see comment above)
- candles (don't laugh)
- massage oil (see comment above)
- magazines for me (are you serious?)
- a book for my husband (not a chance he was going to be reading)
- nice new undies (remained new until the baby was 3 months old — no way I was ruining those)
- nice new nightie and dressing gown (I stuck with the blue 'Property of this Hospital' gown)
- baby clothes, nappies, muslins etc. (finally, something useful)
- my wash things (toothbrush, hairbrush etc. . . . made me feel human)
- my leaving hospital outfit, maternity bras etc. (Note: pre-preggie jeans are not a good idea).

The only slightly useful items packed in the hospital bag were for the baby and my wash things.

You'll see that I was under the illusion that hubby and I would be spending most of the labour eating gourmet delights, listening to romantic music by candlelight and playing cards. Not even close.

Do make sure you pack some soft baggy pants/maternity leggings and a large floaty top for leaving the hospital. I thought that once the baby was out I would fit straight into my pre-pregnancy jeans. Not only was I not even close to being able to fit into them, I really didn't want to wear anything tight. Jeans were the *last* thing I wanted to wear. So, pack yourself a floaty skirt or generous trousers. Don't forget the maternity bras to make feeding easier.

You'll also be shocked about how much blood your body will expel over the six-week recovery process after having a baby. You bleed a *lot* so make sure you have your thick maternity pads packed. Put it this way, there is no point packing your sexy G-strings. Mummy knickers are what you need.

Labour signs and the birth

'It all felt very dreamlike, a bit of a blur. I didn't have a clue what I was doing. There was a sense that I had somehow changed and entered a different world. I also felt very emotional and blessed to have Charlie. I was physically extremely sore down below. I was walking like John Wayne and felt like I'd been beaten up.'

Vicky, London, one son aged 1 year

No matter what anyone tells you, giving birth is not easy. It is bloomin' painful, probably one of the most painful things you will ever have to go through in your life. The screams and puffs and countless swear words you utter while going through it are genuine. I cannot comprehend women who shrug their shoulders and talk about how they just 'popped out' a baby recently. How can anyone 'pop out' a baby, for goodness' sake?

Yes, afterwards they may look tiny. And you will probably join in with the cooing of 'Look how small their little hands and feet are' once you have recovered from the trauma of the new arrival arriving from your nether regions. But, when you are trying to squeeze them out of an area that really isn't that big, they don't feel so tiny then, let me tell you.

I had one friend who told me that giving birth was 'easy'. Imagine how annoyed I was the first time I had a baby and realised that she was talking out of a hole in her arse. Imagine the names I called her. I won't repeat them.

I'd like to reassure all you new mums-to-be that any nerves you might have about how your language and bodily functions might degenerate while giving birth are to be put aside. You may be the most prudish, sensible, quiet lady in everyday life, but when you are in labour you will turn into a monster! You will use words you didn't even know you knew. You will hate your partner and demonstrate it by gripping his arm so tightly that it will leave nail marks scarred on his arm for ever, lest he ever tries anything like that again.

During the birthing process, and indeed the days and weeks afterwards, you will get to know and embrace your body like never before. A woman's body is capable of the most incredible things. Giving life to someone else, giving food to someone else, opening up and closing up again. Amazing. In the days that follow, breasts will leak, vaginas will bleed, and everything will hurt. During the birthing process, you will probably lose control of your bodily functions. You may vomit. You may poo. You may pee. If you go into fast labour, your body will go into shock and shake. Believe me, at the time, you won't care. And, let's face it, the medical team have seen the same thing once or twice before so do *not* worry. You are no different from anyone else.

As I mentioned before, I had grand illusions of soft music and candlelight while I had a perfectly calm water birth. In reality I screamed for drugs, and shouted at the obstetrician and anyone else nearby. There was no music, no candles and the only water leaking was from me.

As for recognising when you are in labour, everyone is different. With my first it followed the antenatal hand-outs to a T. Waters broke 11 p.m. at night while in bed watching comedy TV. Hubby wasn't pleased, and accused me of wetting myself while laughing. It didn't occur to him I was 41 weeks pregnant so it might be something else. Once we had established that it was my waters breaking, he panicked, jumping up and down nervously, not knowing what to do. There were no contractions, however, and I felt fine so we went to bed, agreeing to call the obstetrician in the morning. Two hours later it was a different story. The most incredible deep backache I have ever felt, to the point it was uncomfortable to lie down, sit up, stand up ... an hour on and I was vomiting and trying desperately to time my contractions. All while hubby slept on peacefully beside me. When I did eventually manage to wake him he had the nerve to turn on the TV to watch the footie (it was the World Cup at the time, I suppose). At 4 a.m. I managed to tear him away from England vs Romania to call the specialist, while I unpacked and repacked my hospital bag five times. Then, off to the hospital we went, he insisting I sit on towels so as not to ruin his car.

I was worried about being turned away — you hear about women who go to the hospital only to be told they are only a couple of centimetres dilated and being sent home to wait. I was bracing myself for that, so was very relieved (and proud!)

when the midwife told me, 'You're eight centimetres dilated. Why didn't you come in earlier? You've done the hard bit yourself now.' My self-congratulations didn't last too long, however, when I realised:

1. She was lying. If I had done the hard bit at home then what the **** was I doing now then?
2. Because I was so far gone, they refused to give me an epidural, despite my begging, yelling and offer of marriage to the anaesthetist.

Despite that, hubby and I were under the illusion that once you were in the hospital, you had lots of time to kill. I was in stirrups on the bed in my blue hospital gown when hubby kissed me on the head and said, 'Be back in a jiff. Just going to make some calls.' The midwife looked at us both in disbelief as I nodded and said, 'I think I'll try to get a bit of shut-eye now before the baby comes.'

'You're not going anywhere,' she announced to hubby in her Irish twang. 'And as for you, missy, I don't know how you think you will be getting any sleep. Your baby is coming *now*.' She was right. Once she had said it out loud, there he was, in all his glory (although with much more drama than that, of course!).

Every birthing story is different. You might have a lovely water birth with everything serene around you. You might, like Nat, be unlucky enough to give birth in an earthquake. You may have elected to have a C-section for health or other reasons. Or you may be really unlucky and go through hours of labour only to have to be rushed into an emergency C-section after all.

Chances are your birth will be different from what you planned, in some way. Don't beat yourself up about it. Keep your eye on the goal. It's better to have a healthy baby after all, no matter how they arrived in the world.

Those first few hours and days

 Those first few hours and days can be a bit of a breeze — you might even ask what all the fuss was about. My second child shot out a straight two hours after first going into labour. She fed like a dream, slept like a dream and did everything by the book. Even to the point that two days after giving birth I sat up on the bed in my glamorous hospital gown across the tray from my beautiful husband, eating a gourmet dinner and drinking a glass of wine, to celebrate Valentine's Day together whilst my new baby slept contentedly beside me.

In contrast my first birth was pretty painful and the following days and hours were incredibly hard. My body was recovering from shock, my lower regions were in a great amount of pain. I was bleeding and sore, my breasts were huge and leaking. Other people have recovered quickly but my own experience wasn't quite plain sailing.

So, with that in mind, it is hugely important to give yourself recovery time in the hours and days that follow. Forty years ago, women stayed in hospital for 10 days or so after giving birth. Giving birth was considered a big deal. People died in childbirth, after all. Mothers were treated well, looked after and encouraged to recuperate and recover.

Nowadays new mothers are considered a dime a dozen. Sometimes you can be dismissed from hospital 24 hours or less after completing labour. You will be groggy from drugs, delirious from lack of sleep and have legs like jelly.

If you are lucky enough to stay in either a hospital or a birthing centre after your birth, then make good use of it. These places are full of trained professionals who see new mums every day. They recognise the shock and bewilderment that we all go through. They deal with babies every day so they can teach you how to put a nappy on the baby and how to get the baby to latch on to the breast for breastfeeding. They are paid to be there to help you recover so *use* them. Get them to show you again and again how to wrap your baby in muslin so they sleep more soundly. Ask their advice about how much clothing should be on the baby. Get them to sit with you while you practise latching on. Ask them to show you different techniques again and again. Soak up their knowledge. You need as much help as you can get.

If your baby isn't settling, ask them (or any dads or visitors you might have) to take the baby for a walk around the hospital corridors. It may be too painful for you to do this at this stage. Accept help. If you haven't had any sleep, there is nothing wrong with asking one of the nurses to look after the baby for a couple of hours while you rest. Rest is *crucial*. Without sleep you may not be able to produce the milk needed to feed your baby. Your rest and state of mind is so important, and these first few days will set the scene as to how you recover later on. When you sleep, your body produces milk to feed your baby. If you have milk to feed your baby then the baby will be happy with a nice full tummy and will sleep too. If baby is still hungry because there is no milk (or you have an incorrect latch) then baby will not be happy and will not sleep and will cry.

In summary:

You rest = milk = happy baby = baby sleeps = more sleep for you = you can cope.

You don't rest = weak milk = unhappy baby = baby doesn't sleep = no sleep for you = you cannot cope and everything turns to custard.

Breastfeeding

It is your decision whether to breastfeed or not. Do not let anyone bully you into anything. Not everyone is lucky enough to be able to breastfeed so persevere but please don't beat yourself up if you can't breastfeed, or decide not to. It doesn't make you any less of a mum.

Having said that, breastfeeding is pretty cool because you have baby food on tap, which is free and extremely nutritious. Breastfeeding also helps to improve the bonding between mother and baby. If you do decide to breastfeed, then it is important to get it right at the very beginning when you are at hospital. If you are lucky enough to have a baby who knows what to do and they latch on to your breasts straight away, then that's great. If not, spend the time — as much time as it takes — with the midwives showing you different techniques. Do not leave the hospital until you can latch your baby on to your breasts correctly.

If you leave the hospital without having achieved this then you may be in for a rocky ride. Not only will it affect the baby's sleeping, happiness and growth (and therefore your sanity), but you can say hello to cracked and bleeding nipples, possible thrush and mastitis and a whole lot of pain.

Nat's breastfeeding story

With all three of my kids I had a pretty easy time breastfeeding. They all took to it naturally. Apart from the painful engorgement stage on days 3–5 and a bit of nipple chaffing at the start, all was well. Please don't roll your eyes but the toughest thing for me was eating enough food to keep up milk production. Here's something I wrote in my baby journal: 'I probably shouldn't make such comments as "he's sucking the life out of me" and should think positively "I am enriching my baby's body" or something similar. I often feel like I eat (translation: shovel food into my mouth without an iota of manners as quickly as possible when I can find a spare moment) primarily to produce milk.'

Breastfeeding is lovely and wonderful for bonding and rather handy being 'on tap'. But it's still hard work. Hard on the posture, the nipples, the feeling of independence. Inde-what? And when you have other children to care for it can make things tricky, especially as the dinner hour approaches! I breastfed my first two babies exclusively for 12 months, and my third baby started 'taking the bottle' at 6 months — and I *loved* giving him one bottle of formula a day. I intentionally timed this for around 5 p.m. so he could drink while I made dinner.

Jacqui's breastfeeding story

 Unfortunately I was not one of the lucky ones. Still in shock after the birth of my son, I didn't take full advantage of the nursing staff in my birthing hospital. Hospital was a blur of crying baby, pain everywhere, sleeplessness, and breastfeeding hell.

I tried all the latches they showed me but never managed it successfully. By the time I left hospital my milk still hadn't come in (due to the fact baby wasn't latching on properly, and therefore wasn't sucking properly); baby was fast losing weight and therefore crying *all* of the time. We weren't sleeping and I had turned into a walking zombie.

It only got worse. By the time baby was 2 weeks old, I had to top him up with formula as he wasn't putting on any weight. I was advised to feed every two hours and pump my breasts with an electric breast pump in between feeding times. As baby was taking an hour to feed on each side (at the time I didn't realise this wasn't right or necessary) and I was pumping afterwards for an hour, it meant no rest or recovery. It also shredded my breasts. It hurt constantly. I would dread putting him on my breasts at feeding time. The pain would shoot through me and my nipples would bleed.

Eventually, despite the visiting midwife telling me what I was going through was normal, I woke up one morning shivering and unable to get out of bed. I had read enough by that stage to know what it was and I hauled myself off to the doctor. He confirmed mastitis and thrush in both breasts, put me on antibiotics and ordered me to continue feeding as the only way of releasing the infection.

More painful weeks went by with me feeling desperate and tearful. It still hurt constantly and the state of my breasts wasn't getting any better. I even had a hole in one nipple. It hurt to have anything touch them so I took to walking around the house with hubby's boxer shorts on and nothing on top — his boxers were loose and airy for the recovering downstairs region, and the air circulating around my breasts (and as it was winter, it was *cold*) was the only thing that gave me some relief.

I went downhill fast. Hubby would come home from work to find that I was in the same boxers and nothing else that I had been wearing for days. I stopped showering as it hurt when the water hit my breasts. I hadn't washed my hair since before the birth. I was a mess.

One day it came to a head. Baby was 8 weeks old and I had suffered enough. I picked up the phone to call La Leche League, a breastfeeding support group. I tried three of its members listed on the back of the leaflet. All went to answerphone. I collapsed in tears. Big hearty sobs. I looked on the back of the help book I had been given at Birthcare and saw the Plunket Helpline. I lifted the phone and dialled.

Plunket is 'New Zealand's largest provider of support services for the development, health and wellbeing of children under 5.' It was amazing. The woman on the other end recognised desperation straight away. She took a note of my number and my address and said she would call me back. Two minutes later she called back to tell me she had made an appointment for me at the local Plunket Family Centre at 8 a.m. the next morning.

Before I even had the chance to voice my panic about being able to leave the house by 8 a.m. — at that stage I don't think I'd actually left the house unless it was to go to the doctor — she had reassured me.

'Don't worry about showering. Don't worry about having breakfast before you go,' she told me. 'Just throw on clothes for you and baby and get there.'

I did as she advised and arrived the next morning without shower or breakfast. The women welcomed me with open arms. Showering me with tea, toast, cosy sitting chairs and magazines, they whipped baby off me, dealt with cries and nappies effortlessly while making me feel like I was home with Mum.

After watching me carefully unwrap my breasts and attempt to feed my baby, they tutted loudly, reassured me they had seen worse and proceeded to talk me through and physically show me the correct way to feed. 'You're too gentle with him,' one woman remarked. 'Let him cry, let him wait, let him not get fed until he learns how to latch on correctly.' Gripping my breast with one hand, another woman told me, 'Hold your breast with your hand like it's a hamburger between two buns' (a strange description but one that resonated with me), 'shove it in his mouth and if he doesn't take it properly then take it out and make him try again.' Suddenly I realised that this wasn't necessarily my fault. There were two of us struggling here.

They made me do it again. And again, and again, until I had it right and Jack finally got it too. Then they sent me off upstairs to bed while they babysat. I slept for two hours — the best sleep I had had since baby had arrived, safe in the knowledge that I totally and utterly trusted these women.

When I emerged from my rest, they plied me with tea and toasted sandwiches and magazines. Jack could smell me and was crying but they insisted he wait. 'You being well fed and well rested is very important. If mum is rested and fed and happy, then baby will be too.'

It was the best piece of advice anyone had given me. Suddenly a huge weight lifted. I knew I could do this now. And it was time to get started with my new life.

My biggest bit of advice is get professional help early, *before* you get to the stage of breast infection. La Leche, Plunket or a professional 'baby whisperer' like Dorothy Waide can help baby to latch properly and get you on the right track.

'When I had my first child it used to take me an age to leave the house. When he was two months old I realised I had the same amount of petrol in the car as before I had gone into hospital to have him.'

Louise, Auckland, three children

IOTTM tips for baby on the way

- When it comes to veins, forget about vanity and go for comfort and support. Wear flat shoes and invest in some support stockings and keep your feet elevated as much as possible.
- Have a birth plan but be flexible. Recognise that things might not necessarily go the way you planned and be prepared to cope with a change in how your baby may arrive in the world.
- Have a plan for maternity leave and returning to work but be flexible and open to change.
- Try to take at least a couple of weeks off work before your baby is due. It is important for the health of both you and your baby for you to have at least a little quiet time before the onslaught begins.
- Visit the hospital prior to your due date. Work out where the parking is and where to go when you are in labour. The last thing you want is to be giving birth in the hospital foyer.
- Make sure you pack plenty of comfortable clothes for after the birth. Baggy pants and tops with plenty of airing space, comfy dressing gowns and slippers and a good maternity feeding bra to make things easier and more discreet for you.
- Take maternity pads and 'mummy knickers' into the hospital with you. Forget about being sexy. It's off the agenda for a while!
- Take as much time as you need in the hospital or birthing unit to recover. Don't let yourself be pushed out before you are ready.
- Get as much advice as you possibly can from all the experts in the hospital.

Ask lots of questions and get them to demonstrate feeding, putting on nappies and wrapping baby again and again until you are quite sure you have learned it.

- Limit visitors to the hospital and sleep as much as you possibly can while there are other people there to help you with baby.
- Appreciate your man. We know you're pregnant and uncomfortable, or have just given birth, but remember, it is all new for him too, so give him the love and kindness he deserves.

CHAPTER THREE

Now you're parents!

Welcome to parenthood

So, here you are. You have a baby now and you don't have a clue what to do with it. Don't worry, you're not alone. All mothers have been there and we are the ones who will help you through it. It's true that once you have a child you suddenly become part of a club. It's a club where only its members understand what you are going through. Other mothers and fathers will look at you and understand your red-rimmed eyes. Other friends, without children, no matter how well-intentioned and helpful, will just not get what you're going through.

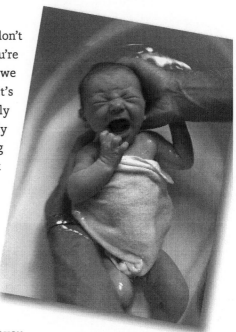

Suddenly you develop an amazing respect for all parents. You think of your own and realise how much they have given you. You look at pregnant ladies in the supermarket, knowing what they are about to participate in, or you look at other parents carting their kids around, and smile a little secret 'mummy smile', which means 'we're all in this together, gal.'

Jacqui's story: The emotional upheaval

 'I remember being in hospital with my first baby and the realisation hitting me of everything my parents had given me and sacrificed over the years. It was like someone had thrown a bucket of cold water over me to wake me up and I suddenly understood. I wanted to throw my arms around my mother right then and there and apologise for all the angst I had given her and thank her for raising me and loving me as she had. It took having a child and the opening of those emotions and feelings deep inside for me to realise how much she had sacrificed for me and my sister. It gave me a whole new-found respect for every friend and stranger who was a mother. I wanted to hug them all and shout from the rooftops, 'I get it now. I understand!'

So, you're in hospital and you've just had a baby and, even if you are normally the most confident, self-assured person, suddenly you are flummoxed. How do you go to the bathroom? Are you allowed to just leave your baby and go? What about when you need to take a shower? Who will keep an eye on the baby while you shower? What if the baby cries and you can't hear it because of the noise of the water running? And then, when the baby cries, why are they crying? He's just been fed so how come he's crying again? You struggle with wrapping up your baby in muslins and cloth nappies, and struggle some more putting nappies on them. It's a whole new world.

I was lucky enough to spend the first few days with Jack in a maternity hospital. However, because my head was in cotton wool and I was severely sleep-deprived, I didn't take advantage of it at all. What I should have done was to have asked the maternity nurses for lots of advice. I should have made them show me again and again how to wrap the baby and how to change his nappy. I should have quizzed them on how much and how often I should feed him and how often and how much he should sleep. I should have soaked up as much information and advice as I could from those experienced nurses.

But I was on a different planet in those first few days and I just couldn't see beyond a crying baby and the four walls that surrounded us. Jack cried all the time and I didn't dare leave him for one moment, even to have a shower. I hated to think that the nurses and the other mothers in the rooms around could hear my baby crying, sometimes all night. Their babies didn't cry that much, so how come mine did?

I used to wait for my husband to visit me before taking a shower and, even then, it was a quick shower. I didn't wash my hair for four weeks as I didn't think I had the time. I felt lost and confused and unsettled. My confidence vanished. I shrivelled away and let other people take over and hold him as I had neither the energy nor the confidence to take charge myself.

When I was finally discharged from hospital it was with mixed emotions. I had been dreadfully unhappy as I was so conscious that Jack cried constantly, I couldn't master breastfeeding and I was an annoyance to the nurses by my own constant tears and confusion. At the same time, I was dreading going home and having to be alone with this baby when I honestly had no clue what to do with 'it'.

I didn't use Jack's name for the first 16 weeks of his life. I just called him 'it' or 'the baby'. I didn't want to hold him and didn't feel the bond that many people talk about. I felt like a feeding machine. I would feed him then pass him on to his nana or dad or any visiting friend to hold. I just wasn't interested. I later realised that I was very close to PND (post-natal depression).

Of course, this feeling of isolation and rawness is not necessarily shared by all new mothers. Some mothers find the bond with their baby straight away. Nat, for instance, had a totally different experience.

Nat's story: The baby bond

 In contrast to Jacqui calling her baby 'it' for 16 weeks, I called mine 'sweet darling' and 'honey bear'. I felt the bond straight away. In fact with her three-hour naps (a few times each day) I initially wondered what all the fuss was about. 'This baby thing is easy,' I thought, at least for the first few weeks until all the broken sleeps caught up with me. My biggest struggle was getting the baby back to sleep after waking for a night feed. Her 'turn-around time', as I used to call it, was 2–3 hours! Oh what I would have given to have someone stand beside me and show me how to resettle a newborn.

It's easy to look back and laugh now but at the time it was very stressful. I would faff around changing her nappy and feeding and possibly over-feeding her. Then when she wouldn't settle I would get her back out of her hanging Nature Sway bassinet and change her nappy again. I would move her around so much that she would spill milk on her outfit and I would have to change her sleepsuit then I would try to read her a book (no joke — she was only 1 week old and I'm reading her stories at 3 a.m.). I just didn't know what I was doing! I also struggled with 'relaxing' (which has never been my forte) and not being productive and getting things done. You really have to shift your mindset of what you'll achieve in a day when you have a baby.

Everyone struggles in different ways in those early days. For some it's just a case of the baby blues, for others it's something deeper.

Baby blues

'Women come back from child-bearing like Arctic explorers. You see them in the foyer of the theatre, perhaps they have lost weight or dyed their hair. Their faces glow. They expect people to notice them and the amazing fact that they have come through ... Men, on the other hand, try to hold on to the thread of their lives more often and fumble it through a maze of sleepless nights, thwarted socialising, and oddly soured ambition. They end up tired out and happy enough, or they end up exhausted and bitter ...'

Anne Enright, *Making Babies: Stumbling into Motherhood*, 2005

OK, the above quote may seem a bit dramatic but there is some truth in it! For the mums, from the birth of your first child you will forevermore think of someone else before yourself (until they all grow up and leave the house). This is an overpowering change in the mother's life especially in the first five years, depending on one's work or childcare situation.

Three days after you have your baby, the adrenalin you may have experienced gives way to tiredness, and with it comes a flood of emotion. This is called the baby blues. Suddenly you become hypersensitive, crying about everything or losing your temper. There is actually a medical reason for this — you are not going mad.

While you are pregnant, your body is full of high levels of oestrogen, progesterone and endorphins. As soon as the placenta is removed, these hormones go back to their pre-pregnancy levels. The fluctuation in hormone levels as well as lack of sleep and being faced with a new, crying baby all contribute to the baby blues.

Some symptoms of the baby blues are:
- weepiness and bursting into tears
- sudden mood swings
- anxious and hypersensitive to criticism
- low spirits and irritability
- poor concentration and indecisiveness
- feeling 'unbonded' with baby
- restless insomnia.

Dad may also suffer from the baby blues as he is the one you will take everything out on! The baby blues are not the same as post-natal depression, covered in a later chapter. The baby blues will pass as your hormones return to normal.

Thoughts from other parents

When researching this book, we asked a range of people how they were finding parenthood compared to what they expected. The overall theme was 'harder'!

What have you found most challenging and most surprising so far about parenthood?

'Since having children I have made so many sacrifices in my life so that I can be all I can be to my children ... that has meant less time for me and more time for them. I don't run as often, I don't have much of a social life. Especially since I only have my one child about half the time, I make sure I schedule social outings when I don't have him. I don't feel like I have to do it, I want to. I have had my time, and I will have my time again when they are older and less 'needy' of me. I like making the sacrifice. I also believe it is my duty to do so. I feel I have a good balance of personal life and my children, and one day I can spend more time on myself again.'

Nadine, Ontario, one son aged 1 year, one stepson

'I am more hopeful about the world and see things more positively. I have never felt so important! I learn about myself each day. I am seeing the world again through the eyes of my children.'

Ava, Dunedin, two daughters aged 3 months and 2 years

'My time is spent now with focus on the baby, not so much myself. I feel very happy with this new baby, I feel more complete. Life makes sense to me more.'

Jane, Dunedin, one daughter aged 3 months

'It's made me more compassionate, but short-tempered. It's made me proud and more ashamed of myself than I've ever been before.'

Rachel, Christchurch, one son aged 5 years, one daughter aged 2 years

'I think my expectations were realistic which meant the sleep deprivation, absence of spare time and the myriad of challenges were easier to deal with. I never expected it to be easy.'

Elton, Oamaru, two daughters aged 2 and 7 years

'Most challenging is the change in lifestyle compared to having no children, and being constantly tired at the same time as trying to deal with the adjustment. Being awake so often in the night sucks. I am traditionally such a wonderful sleeper.'

Nick, Auckland, two children aged 1½ and 3½ years, and a baby on the way

'For me, the most challenging was the first three to six months with the baby. The change between the person I was and me as a mother. How to integrate being a mother; the uncertainty and lack of confidence; wanting baby to sleep then worrying and wanting him to wake up; always on edge and couldn't enjoy the moment.'

Kelly, Auckland, one son aged 4 years and a baby on the way

Physical changes and challenges

 Raging hormones and emotions are just one part of an almighty challenge ahead of you. The physical repair your body is going through is another.

Boobs

If you are lucky enough to breastfeed then you will know about the look-don't-touch *humongous* breasts and the problems they cause, not only for you but for your dying-to-touch-them partner. Let's face it, they have never been so appealing and so *big* to him. But make sure he knows that if he even tries a little squeeze, not only will he literally get milk in his face, but he will probably be kneed so hard that he will lose the ability to make another mini-version of himself.

Leaking breasts are a nightmare, and we all have embarrassing stories of squirting boobs in the gym showers, or going to the movies wearing a white T-shirt and by the end of the movie looking as though you've been in a wet T-shirt competition.

A mum to two young kids gave me some great advice: tea strainers. Yes, that's right. Insert a tea strainer into each cup of your bra to enable air to circulate and heal sore, cracked or bleeding breasts. It really does work! Make sure, however, that you just wear the tea strainers at home. Do not go out for coffee wearing them as you will look very odd indeed. (Note to all new mums: buy breast pads as a priority and *never* leave the house without them.)

Anyway, enough of breasts. Other experiences you may have to endure may be a little, ahem, more delicate than that. Now, ladies, the following is what they don't tell you at antenatal or in any of those other fluffy pregnancy books you may have read. And goodness me, I very much doubt your friends who have been there will have told you this. This is really 'not to be discussed' territory. And for that reason, I need to tell you.

Bottoms

Having a baby stretches and puts a huge amount of pressure (and sometimes tearing) on your body. Recovery time is roughly six weeks (whether you have a C-section or not). There are certain times when you will feel it more than ever. Let me give you an example — that first dump (*poop!*). *There*! I've said it. Yes. The first time you have to pass a motion, without the aid of laxatives, is a very interesting experience. Not everyone will go through this but if you do, better to be forewarned.

Firstly, advice: keep taking laxatives for at least the first week and make sure you have plenty of roughage and fruit to help you pass softer motions until you are feeling much better. I didn't. Two weeks after the birth I had to pass my first un-laxative-aided motion. Suffice to say, I spent roughly one hour in the bathroom. There is no delicate way of putting it — it got stuck. I tried pushing and the pain was so intense I cried. Luckily my parents were visiting from the UK and I had them run me a warm bath and pass me glasses of water and cups of tea and fruit and, at last, I finally managed to complete my motion.

Anything after that was a piece of cake. I had learnt my lesson and made sure I drank plenty of water and ate lots of fruit and roughage and I was OK from then on. It certainly wasn't a pleasant experience.

At least my own experience didn't have me end up in hospital, which is what happened to a friend who got caught in a similar situation. Yes, her husband had to call her an ambulance to take her to hospital to help remove her poo which was half in, half out. Honest to God. Now, *nobody* wants that to happen to them, do they? So heed the advice, girls, and avoid the ambulance run of shame.

Sex after childbirth

Now, let's talk about sex after childbirth. Yep, lovely gooshy, tender sex.

You probably won't exactly feel like participating in sex with your partner straight after you have a baby. Funny that. You actually probably shouldn't for the first six weeks of recovery time anyway, to make sure that everything has a chance to heal. And, although it is a long time for your husband to wait, quite frankly, he's going to have to. Not only is everything rather tender — you, have just squeezed something like a watermelon out, for goodness' sake — but, quite honestly, you are wearing nappies as big as your baby's to soak up the bleeding, your breasts are leaking and aching, you are operating on zero sleep and you probably haven't washed your hair for weeks. So, let's face it, he probably doesn't even want to have sex with you looking like that anyway.

I don't think I have ever been as unattractive as during those first few weeks after having my first child. As I said earlier, I walked around the house all day with my husband's old baggy boxer shorts on as they were lovely and loose around my nether regions, and completely naked on top. Yep. Stark naked. I didn't want anything touching my sore, cracked nipples so I didn't wear anything. I actually sat at the dinner table like that one night. Honestly. My husband had made an effort to cook something nice and suggested we sat at the table together for dinner that night in order to talk like we had before baby. (It was only three weeks since 'the baby' was born but a lifetime had passed between now and then.) I sat gingerly down at the table and he looked at me in horror. To his absolute credit, he didn't say a word. Now I realise what the horror was all about. I was unshowered and had been for roughly two weeks; my hair was limp and greasy, I was wearing old baggy boxer shorts and my huge dripping breasts were on display. Just lovely. If that doesn't kill the romance between you as a couple then nothing will.

The first time I got up the nerve to attempt to have sex again after having baby was eight weeks after the birth. I tentatively touched my husband in bed and told him it was time. He was very careful and tender and, yes, it did hurt. But, the more you do it, the less it hurts and you start to recover very quickly.

What to say and what not to say to new mothers

There are some things that mothers (not just first-time mothers) just love to hear.

The best thing you can say to a mother is 'What can I do to help?' This is not just music but a complete symphony to the ears.

Try some of these magic words with your new-mum friends:

- What can I do to help?
- I've made you dinner for tonight.
- I'll do that (regarding whatever task the mum is currently doing, e.g. unloading washing, unloading dishwasher, folding washing, making tea and so on).
- Don't worry about writing a thank-you card.
- I'll look after your baby. Why don't you go for a lie-down/a walk/some fresh air?
- You look fabulous!

What not to say to a new mother

- When are you going back to work?
- What did you do all day?
- Wow, you look really tired. (Translation: You look like crap.)
- When is your baby due? (Answer: I had it five weeks ago.)
- Did you get my baby card/present? I haven't heard from you.
- Have you fallen off the planet or something?

What dads *love* to hear:

- ☺ Honey, you handled that situation with (Jack) really well.
- ☺ I really appreciate how hard you are working (at work and at home) for the family.
- ☺ Thank you.
- ☺ You're doing a great job — you're a fabulous dad.
- ☺ I love you.
- ☺ Let's shag!

Couplehood redefined

> 'The most surprising thing for me was my almost total disinterest in my intimate relationship with my partner. It felt really forced. All my energy, focus and physical being was being taken up by this little person I had just birthed.'
>
> **Anna, Dunedin, one son, pregnant with number 2**

When your partner becomes a parent, things change! It's wonderful to see them in that new role as 'mum' or 'dad' but your own expectations of them shift as well. Gone are the evenings of lingering over a wine after dinner or curling up on the couch to watch a movie or *The X Factor*. Instead you'll be tagging in and out with sleep and baby-holding. Peaceful moments won't be so peaceful...

The shift from lovers to parents can rock your marriage down to its roots. Suddenly you find yourselves taking on traditional, stereotyped roles that may clash with your thoroughly modern expectations. A working mum trades the office, wisecracking colleagues and the gym for breastfeeding, bottle-washing and mountains of laundry. A husband faithfully attends childbirth classes, spends long hours in the delivery room, and cuts the baby's umbilical cord, yet all too often feels shut out during the early years of childrearing. Instead, he works longer and harder in his career in order to provide for his growing family, and feels more and more distant. You're both doing more, communicating less, and feeling vastly underappreciated.

How did your life change when your baby came along?

'More tired, more laughter, more frustration, less money.'

Peter, Tauranga, three children

'I value my me-time more, as it is a rare commodity which probably puts a strain on the relationship.'

Stu, Christchurch, one daughter aged 4 years, one son aged 2 years

'No downtime for me as a person. No couple time.'

Sarah, Melbourne, one daughter aged 5 years, one boy aged 3 years

And here's a nice, positive take on parenting:

'My relationship with my husband was changed for the better when we decided to have a child. We both enjoyed watching the other take on a new role and felt more connected as a couple. We took great pains from the very beginning to "protect" our time together and seemed to instinctively know that we needed to continue to relate to each other as "husband and wife", not to let that go and become only "mummy and daddy". We felt strongly that our children should see us as a couple that was connected, not just as their mum and dad.'

Ruth, Christchurch

In William Doherty's book, *Take Back Your Marriage*, he addresses the problem of 'solitary marriage', which he defines as when couples don't realise how common their problems are and feel like they are alone.

The roles that we fall into as 'mum' and 'dad' are a bit ironic. Mums often want the dads to 'do more'. Dads probably want the mums to 'do less' but to trust in them more and ease off on the self-pressure and take some time out. As mums, we're struggling to get our heads around our new role, let alone how dads fit into it. We need to remember that we are a team. We are in it together. We need to help each other through it and that will keep 'us' solid.

What other parents say

How have you found parenthood compared to what you expected?

'Harder. The tiredness and grumpiness is something I didn't expect. I expect so much more from my hubby, expect him to do more around the house, with the kids and allowing me to have my time out which is usually in the form of some exercise. I thought I would be so happy to be a mum that staying at home with the kids and doing all the things mums do would be enough for me.'

Cath, Nelson, one daughter aged 2½ years, one son aged 15 months

'Harder, much harder than I ever expected, and more physically demanding than anticipated. I had to quit my job and have given up most of my hobbies and interests. Taking care of the baby is all-consuming. The first four years of having kids had us basically ignoring each other completely. The children were very close together (13 months) and basically put us on a sleep-deprivation programme for two years.'

Gordon, Montreal, two boys aged 2 and 3 years

'Your baby won't remember the times you take off to spend with your partner. Don't ever feel guilty for wanting to recapture a few hours of before-kid time.'

Amy, Vancouver, two daughters aged 7 and 12 years, one son aged 8 months

If you could turn back time, what advice would you give yourself about making a healthy happy partnership and family life during the early years of parenthood?

'Realise that it's going to be hard. Look after each other, give each other breaks and help each other out. Communicate — keep talking about things like expectations so each other knows what to expect.'

Kate, Christchurch, one daughter aged 3½ years, one son aged 1 year

How has becoming parents impacted your relationship with your partner?

'Strained. Both sleep deprived, everything is harder. But we both dig deeper to a place we didn't know we would have to (or could get to) to try to make it all work.'

Erin, Ottawa

'It's not really the parenting that has affected our relationship — we both love being parents and enjoy our baby girl. I think what has had the biggest impact on our relationship is the change in roles and lack of alone time together. I feel like my husband, along with others, has forgotten who I was before I was a mother. My input regarding financial decisions isn't as important now. Being financially dependent on someone is a strange feeling. I had to ask for some personal spending money which was hard for me. It hadn't occurred to my husband that I needed my own money and that really annoyed me — I'm so stubborn and independent that I found it really hard to ask. So I think from my point of view I have felt undervalued and forgotten which has made me feel a little resentful.'

Lauren, Wellington, one daughter

Looking back, what 'skill' or 'gift' would you give yourself now that you're through the baby years?

'The gift of patience. Patience for myself to grow into the role of motherhood. Patience for my marriage to persevere through such a crazy time. Patience (to know) that all will be well and we will come out the other side of having young babies.'

SLC, Richmond Hill, two sons aged 2 and 5 years

A dad's view on parenthood

Vaughan Poutawera: *Father of three*

Acceptance: One thing that helped me was simply accepting the changes that having a baby or young family brings. Embrace and develop the 'new' you. There's no point trying to pretend that you're the same carefree, wild, party-loving animal you once were, when all you want to do is go home, see the kids and get an early night. Nine out of 10 mates will happily accept the 'new' you and you shouldn't have to make any excuses.

Friends: You may drift apart from one or two old friends, whose lives continue along their own path as yours diverges. So be it, accept it as part of life. You're still friends, right? Friends can accept their friends having young families.

Young kids can also open lots of doors to new friendships and fellowships. Accept that your motivations may change and where you once were happy to stay hours late at work, you now want to get home before the kids have gone to bed, just so that you can read them a story before lights out. It is inevitable that your new responsibilities as a parent will at times compete with your old work responsibilities. Juggling these pressures is all part of the 'big adult world'. Relax, take a big breath, you'll figure out a way to make it work best for you.

Sacrifices: Accept that sacrifices will need to be made. It is unlikely that you can continue to work 100+ hours every week, train for the Ironman, go to the gym five times a week, drink with your buddies on Fridays and Saturdays, have a happy marriage and still be the best dad in the world. Something has to give. This is part of the big adult world and its big adult choices. Don't just drop things willy-nilly. Dedicate some time to figuring out what there is time for and what there is not. Maybe you catch up with your buddies less often but still regularly, exercise of course, and it's vitally important you continue to work hard, just have a think about balance a bit more. Life is about choices. You just made one of the biggest, to be a dad, so make the most of it. Make the kids proud, and lead by example.

Acceptance: Accept that your kids are no better or worse than anyone else's. Your kids have good and bad skills, traits, behaviours and talents. So do parents. Your child is no more gifted than the neighbours'. Let your kids explore their talents in their own way, with your guidance and comforting presence, but not your forceful heavy hand or voice.

Murphy's Law

What better way to welcome you to parenthood than to list the first rule of parenting, good old Murphy's Law. This law comes in all shapes and sizes, it can't be avoided so it's best to accept it and move on!

Scenario 1: Your 5-month-old baby *finally* sleeps through the night. Your 3-year-old who usually sleeps through gets up twice.

Scenario 2: You have no social plans for two weeks and suddenly three things come up — on the same night!

Scenario 3: Your husband has a three-day business trip and an hour after his plane departs, your baby gets chickenpox.

All of these things can lead to frustration. I'm almost at the point where I just say 'of course…'.

Sleep deprivation and settling baby to sleep

Sleep deprivation is a killer. It has been used as a form of torture for many years. The importance of getting your sleep cannot be over-emphasised. During the day, when your baby sleeps, sleep. Turn the answerphone on and sleep. Do not agree to lots of visitors in the early days. Put them off until you and your baby are more settled. Make yourself a sign saying 'Mother and baby sleeping', and put it on your door so people who arrive unannounced know to leave unannounced. Use hubby, mum, mother-in-law, whoever your support is to field visitors, acting as a barrier between you and the outside world. *Rest* and do not put this off.

Let the washing pile up, or encourage visitors to do it for you. Forget the dishes, leave them to the washing-up fairy. Do *not* make the mistake of saying to yourself, 'I'll just put on one load of washing, hang up the other load, make some calls, write some thank-you letters and then I'll go to bed.' It won't happen, and even if it does, you'll be too tired to sleep. As soon as baby is in bed, then you go to bed. No excuses.

Unless you sleep, you will not be able to cope with the emotional and physical recovery process you are going through. Nor will you be able to cope with the crying, middle-of-the-night feeds. Take it from someone who knows.

Now, it's all very well advising you to get as much sleep as possible but it probably doesn't help you if you have a baby that doesn't sleep. There are many reasons this could be the case. It could be quite simply that your baby isn't getting enough milk. Often this is down to having the incorrect latch, as opposed to not spending enough time on the actual breastfeeding. Or it could be that your milk supply simply isn't full or thick enough to satisfy baby's tummy. In my opinion there is nothing wrong with topping up your baby with formula to help him sleep if it means that you get to sleep too. Remember:

A well-rested mum = a good supply of milk = a contented sleeping baby.

I personally used to find that by the time 6 p.m. rolled around, I was so exhausted that I wasn't able to satisfy my baby's hunger with breastfeeding alone. My Plunket nurse advised me to start topping him up with a bottle (either pre-pumped breast milk or formula) at 6 p.m. after breastfeeding, to see if he would take it. The fact that he guzzled it down made me realise that I wasn't supplying a good quality and quantity of milk at that time. Once I got into the habit of topping him up with formula each night, life became so much more pleasurable for everyone in the family.

Sleeptime sweetheart

 One of the things that surprised me the most about parenthood was the extent of the whole 'sleep' thing. Antenatal classes, mothers and strangers will all tell you how exhausted you will be and how hard sleep deprivation is … but that's really only one part of the sleep story.

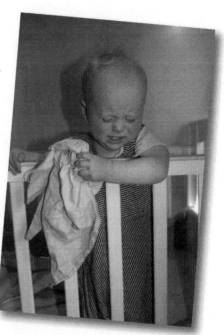

I didn't realise how tough actually 'getting the baby to sleep' (naps and at night) would be, and how much time and effort would go into getting them to sleep as they progress from baby to toddler to cheeky child.

The pursuit of sleep can become somewhat of an obsession when one enters the realm of parenthood, particularly with the mum. And this is a good thing for the dad to realise. It's not personal, but we'd often prefer sleep over sex. And during the day, once baby is down for that nap, we go into crazy mode trying to either GTD (get things done) or get some sleep ourselves.

In the first year, with naps and bedtime depending on the age, stage and nature of baby, it can take between five and 50 minutes to settle a baby to sleep. Then as toddlers with one nap a day (if you're lucky) and the bedtime routine, it can become a drawn-out affair with endless requests for books, water, cereal and so on. When my eldest, Ruby, was a baby, getting her to nap was a matter of one down, two to go! It was agonising. The sleep-stress, as I like to call it, was probably self-inflicted as I had stupidly agreed to do some work from home for my old boss, believing my baby would sleep much of the day. It was almost as if she sensed my anxiety for her to sleep, as she seemed to rebel against it.

My second baby, Jonah, was a completely different story. He was super predictable with his naptimes and often would 'melt' into the cot when you laid him down. He was what I like to refer to as a pop and walk. Pop him in bed and walk away!

My third baby was a very dozy baby when he was a newborn, so much so that I had to wake him to feed him. But when he turned 5 months old he totally changed his game! We struggled to get him to nap in his cot as well as at night. I eventually threw in the towel and stopped trying. When naptime rolled around (twice a day

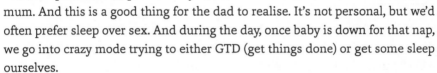

at that stage) I would put him in his stroller and rock him. Right there in the living room. I didn't even need to go out. At other times I would intentionally plan an outing in the car around naptime as I knew the movement would lull him to sleep. Even though I knew I was teaching him bad habits, this was far less stressful than listening to him cry in his own bed and still not fall asleep.

It can be extremely stressful trying to settle your baby to sleep, especially when you're exhausted yourself. It's amazing how it can make you doubt yourself and make you feel incompetent. Even though people tell you that you're 'doing a great job' as a mum, you can still feel like a failure. I definitely wish I had known about baby whisperers like Dorothy Waide who actually come to your house and helps you learn to settle your baby to sleep!

Dorothy Waide's top tips for settling young babies

Nurturing

Nurturing is the common thread that runs through every aspect of caring for your baby. It begins from day one and continues to evolve as your baby grows, bonds deepen and emotional needs change. It is not only about 'doing'; sometimes it is simply about 'being'. Feeding, burping, changing and settling your baby and helping your baby find sleep are all part of nurturing.

You cannot spoil your baby — nurturing your baby creates an environment in which your baby feels safe and learns to trust.

Sleep

Babies need to be taught (guided/encouraged/supported) to sleep; it is a learned behaviour. It is not about leaving them to cry alone or cry it out — it is about allowing them their space to find their sleep and intervening when necessary. In the first 12 weeks it is 'doing' this in arms so they are nurtured rather than rocked or put in a cot and left alone. What they want at this age is the warmth and familiarity and nurturing to soothe them.

Dark is for sleeping, light is for playing — the same as the sitting room is for playing and bedrooms are for sleeping.

Allowing your baby to sleep in your arms is not a cop-out. On the contrary, it instils a sense of security that makes them feel nurtured and ready for sleep.

Sleeping patterns determine how often you feed.

Feeding

Ensure you have a good deep latch-on technique. This can solve many of the issues mothers have in the early days.

Ensure you are feeding for hunger and not comfort. Give the baby's digestive system time to process their food and empty out before starting to feed again. Imagine if you had digestive pains and someone kept feeding you. Babies are more interested in food than a nappy change; it is the adults who worry about the nappy.

Nutrients

Babies who feed well, sleep well; those who sleep well, feed well. Both are nutrients — we talk about food as a nutrient but sleep is not often referred to as a nutrient.

Awake time

Ideally newborns should not be up longer than 45 minutes to an hour at a time; this includes feeding, burping and changing and returning to sleep. Longer waking intervals will make your baby overtired and interfere with establishing healthy eating and sleeping rhythms.

Tired signs

Trying to read tired signs can be confusing and put added stress on parents. It is easy to be fooled into believing that an alert and active baby simply requires less sleep than others. This is rarely true. It is more likely that such hyperactivity is a sign of an overtired baby.

 Dorothy Waide: ifonlytheytoldme.com/27

Synchronised naptimes and sleepless nights

 What is the best gift your spouse can give you? More sleep. With our second baby I became very preoccupied (OK, a bit obsessive) about the number of hours of sleep I was getting each night. Each time I was woken up I would check the clock and mathematically work out the number of hours, being sure to subtract time for the time it takes to fall back asleep. In the first 14 months of Jonah's life I averaged six hours of broken sleep each night (due almost equally to baby and the toddler). Thankfully hubby would give me sleep-ins to top up usually twice a week.

When Jonah was 9 months old he slept through the night for the fifth time *ever.* Fret not, there are also heaps of 'good news stories' about baby and toddler's sleep habits. I remember crawling back into bed one night (or more accurately one morning) and saying 'I'm going to a hotel'. I was so *over* being woken up in the night.

I don't think that I was actually exhausted but I always felt that I soon would be if I didn't actively try to get more sleep. There are two bits of sleep catch-up advice that I know in theory but find difficult to implement:

1. Nap when you can. My cousin gave me this advice with our first baby. She said there will always be more laundry and dishes to do. Getting as much sleep as possible is more important.

I agree with this, but it's easier said than done. When the baby (or toddler) is napping, it becomes a pressure-infused decision to clean or sleep, clean or sleep. In theory I totally agree with the logic of napping when the baby naps and I've managed to do it on a fair few occasions.

I have my little rituals:
- Put a sign on the gate (Come back later, mum and baby sleeping)
- Turn off phone (Murphy's Law says the phone will be silent all day then ring the minute I drift off into dreamland)
- Put dog inside (so she doesn't bark at people, the wind etc.)
- Ready, set, sleep.

2. Go to bed early. When the little darlings are in bed (about 7 p.m.) and the laundry and dishes are done (about 8 p.m.) I find myself wanting to get things done on the computer, relax in front of the TV or take my time with a leisurely shower, so that by the time I get into bed it's usually around 10 p.m. I know that in theory I could (or should) pop into bed at 8 p.m. and leave the house less than tidy (huge understatement). I've only done this on a handful of occasions.

During the baby years it's easy to stay home and feel house-bound by naptimes. Usually NBFs (non-baby friends) and sometimes dads don't fully grasp how precious this time is to either 'get things done' or have a bit of time out.

When baby's down for a nap I immediately shift gears into 'must-be-productive mode'. After the initial deer-in-headlights 'where do I start?' phase, I become anxious and have a 'don't-slow-me-down-don't-get-in-my-way' mindset. I rush to start (and occasionally complete) a project around the house. I love the idea of relaxing with a cuppa or having a nap in the sun when the kids are both napping but more often than not, I find myself going from busy happy mother to

Tasmanian devil. I'll start doing dishes then remember I need to make a phone call (uninterrupted) so I'll do both at the same time while also putting on another load of laundry.

Friends with kids totally get it. If they ring while your kids are napping they'll quickly hurry off the phone to let you make the most of your free time. Heaven help a neighbour or random door-knocker that arrives during my 'golden hour'!

The exhausted contest

Here's the scene: you're both sleeping peacefully and then you hear that sound of baby crying. Your heart sinks; you hope it's a dream but it's real. You both lie there nice and still, waiting for the other to make the first move. She's thinking 'I went last time', he's thinking 'I've got work in the morning' and you're both playing the 'I'm more exhausted than you are' game. In our house, now that both kids are (in theory) sleeping through the night, hubby and I have an unspoken arrangement whereby I get up to any kid in the night (usually six out of seven nights someone calls out) and hubby gets up in the morning to do the breakfast shift.

> *'There will always be dishes and laundry to do. Naps are more important.'*
>
> **Emily, Christchurch, three children**

Top tips for sweet sleep

1. Nap when baby naps. Great advice, but easier said than done when you are surrounded by piles of washing and stacks of dishes. Remember *you* are a priority and the laundry can wait! Make yourself a 'baby sleeping, please visit later' sign, turn off the phone and try to catch some zzzs.
2. Expectation management. As with many aspects of parenting, you'll need to adjust your own expectations around how much sleep you will get and how much you will get done. Some babies sleep through the night from 3 months while others take a full 12 months to get the hang of it. Just go with it as much as you can and ask friends and relatives to help you where possible.
3. Have a plan with your man. Instead of a battle of wills about whose turn it is to get up to the kids, have a plan. For example, you might agree that Mum tends to night wake-ups and Dad gets up first with the kids in the morning.

4. Tired signs and settling techniques. There are so many books and techniques around settling baby to sleep, it can be confusing. Bottom line, go with your gut and go back to basics. Look for 'tired signs'. Be aware of the pattern of feed, change, play, sleep, repeat, and learn what is realistic for babies at different ages and stages.

Babies do have different types of cries, but it's easy to over-analyse them. Don't do what Jacqui did and spend hours referring to a book to see what type of cry your baby is making each time they cry out. If it isn't obvious, just try each of the key things to see which one works: feeding, burping, change nappy. If baby is still not settling then it is probably over-tiredness. Just try whatever works for your baby to get them to finally drop off, e.g. rocking, ssshing, stroking forehead and eyes, calm soothing voice... whatever works!

Challenges and words of wisdom

Lower your daily expectations. Keep in mind that you could spend between five and six hours each day just feeding baby and if you're breastfeeding the calorie consumption is equivalent to running 10 km per day! So set your expectations accordingly. Having a shower or hanging out the laundry can be a real achievement. And dads — when you come home to a messy house, don't say anything! Better yet, start folding laundry or picking toys off the floor.

Forget doing trivial things you used to do before baby. Sending thank-you cards is an example. Of course it's polite to thank people for their gifts and messages but sometimes, the thought of sitting down for an hour to write 10 thank-you cards is just too much.

People who have been there get it. They will understand. Others may not, so why not just send a one-page email out en masse or Facebook message to every-one who has supported you. Send a photo of baby and say a heartfelt thank you to everyone, explaining that you are getting yourself sorted and into a routine and trying to cope with the trials and tribulations of having a new baby. Trust they understand and say you hope you will get to see them soon and introduce your new baby to them.

If you really feel you have to send thank-you cards or you are getting lots of pressure from parents and in-laws to do so, then choose one of the many websites on offer. We are so lucky that we have this option available to us now. Just upload a photo of your baby, type in some general words of thanks and print a stack. You can ask a friend or relative to write the names and addresses on each envelope.

Think of going to the post office as a great way to get out of the house for some much needed fresh air and a change of environment.

What the dads say

'I'm not an expert by any means, and I'm learning on the job. I don't get wound up about there being a 'correct method' or what the latest parenting fad is. I think there are solid basics like spending quality time with your kids, being consistent (individually and with your partner), encouraging good behaviour and being a role model. I think most of what I try to do as a parent is based on my own experience growing up with my own parents. I think they did a good job, so I'm trying to be similar to them.'

Paul, Christchurch, one daughter aged 2 years

'My main pieces of advice would be:
1. Being able to let go of personal needs and to support the "new" family. Give yourself over to the new and changing needs of your wife and the situation. It doesn't last for ever.
2. Don't get too absorbed by the process of being a new parent. Stand back and observe "Is this working?"
3. Create space for mum and dad to have quality time without baby. Even 30 minutes can be great.
4. Let go of your (male) needs and issues and realise the sacrifice your wife has made to have your children!'

Mark, Motueka, two daughters
aged 3 and 6 years

What the mums say

'You cannot spoil a baby! A baby needs to know that they can trust their parents to meet their needs/wants for anything in the first year (or beyond, depending on the child's personality). This creates an independent, confident, happy child who doesn't need to attention seek, doesn't have insecurities and has high self-esteem. We are already reaping the benefits of this with our happy, confident, not-overly-demanding 3-year-old.'

Anna, Dunedin, one son aged 3 years

'I felt very strongly about not leaving the baby to cry herself to sleep. When my partner wanted to try it I felt really angry and misunderstood. I wanted to run off with the baby and protect her. Lots of strong feelings.'

Jane, Dunedin, one daughter aged 3 months

IOTTM top tips for new parents

- ◉ Get as much advice from the experts as possible.
- ◉ Get the midwife or nurse to show you the correct latch for breastfeeding. And ask them to teach you a swaddle technique.
- ◉ It's OK to cry.
- ◉ Baby blues may hit you around days 3–5 or you may experience post-natal depression. People want to help and support you, so let them.
- ◉ Give your body time to heal.
- ◉ Don't go out for a run two weeks after having baby. Your body needs to recover. Rest when you can.
- ◉ Make your relationship a priority. It's easy to get so busy with baby that you forget to invest time and effort into you as a couple. Set time aside to have dessert together once baby's in bed or go for a walk together when baby is sleeping in the stroller.

- Murphy's Law: Adjust your state of mind to expect Murphy's Law. You will be much happier!
- Adjust your expectations of yourself and each other. Babies take time, love and energy. Lower your daily expectations of what you will achieve and enjoy the moment. Accept that you both have different job descriptions for now. Don't expect it to feel the same and do things the same way (or same amount).
- Nap when you can. Put a sign on the door, take the phone off the hook, forget the washing, stonewall the visitors and *go to bed*. Even if you don't manage to actually get any sleep, at least lie down on the bed and rest for a while. It will recharge your batteries and allow you to face the rest of the day with more energy.
- Appreciate each other and your baby. Instead of dwelling on how much sleep you didn't get last night, revel in the wonder of your new baby and your hubby in his new role as parent.

CHAPTER FOUR

The new you and home, sweet home

The new you

When you become a parent (especially a 'mother'), your identity is thrown up in the air. You meet new 'mother' friends and are inevitably appraised (or judged) on how you look and act as well as how your children look and behave.

Here are some candid thoughts from new parents around the world:

> 'I have less time to be the person I used to be, and have struggled with the transition of being a mum, and all the things that go along with that. I don't like being classified as a mum.'
>
> Anonymous, Christchurch, one daughter aged 3 years

> 'Sometimes I feel like I've lost myself and I miss who I used to be. I still struggle with that. My children are everything to me and they give me so much joy but sometimes, when I'm feeling a bit low or tired, I think about who I "was" a lot. I know that my kids won't be small for ever and I can get "me" back again someday. On the positive side, being a parent has made me way less selfish and much more responsible. I surprise myself with how much I'm capable of with these two and I wouldn't swap it for anything.'
>
> Anonymous, Terrigal, one son aged 6 years, one daughter aged 18 months

As a parent, there will be times when you will suddenly stop and look around and think 'Is this my life?' For me, it happened when I was vacuuming the carpet for the fourth time that week and thought 'I have done nine years of tertiary education for this?'

Just getting on top of the day-to-day chores takes a lot longer and everything suddenly seems harder, to the point that one day you think, 'Now, when exactly did I lose my confidence?' Most women work for years before embarking on a family, women are used to running the finances, running businesses and being well-respected and recognised in their careers. When baby comes along we swear it won't change us and spend much of the first year of baby's life trying desperately to hang on to our previous lives. I used to visit my old work weekly when I had my first-born, determined they wouldn't forget me and sure that the business couldn't go on without me. Of course it could, and it did. And, although at first my old workmates would crowd around cooing and all wanting to take turns to hold the baby, they eventually lost interest and barely looked up when I sauntered in for my weekly visits, wanting to know what was happening with different clients and begging someone to come for coffee with me.

In my case, I was so determined to hang on to my old life that I went back to work full time when baby was just 8 months old. I missed the sociability of work, the lunches, the drinks, the friendships as well as work itself. I missed having my own income, being able to afford nice things and having my own identity, being regarded as being good at my job. At home, I didn't feel good at my job. The fact that my baby cried so often was surely testament to that.

Five years on I don't feel like that. But that is because over the last few years following the birth of my second child I have embraced my new life as a stay-at-home mum. But, let's face it, most first-time mums are not confident at first. Usually babyhood is such a change that it takes us a good 12 months to get used to our new lives and to change our attitudes and lifestyles accordingly.

Years on, my life has changed again. I am now back in full-time employment and instead of struggling to hold on to my 'work' identity, it is the opposite. I miss my time at home with the children and try desperately to hold on to friendships with the school and kindy mums, despite my busy schedule never allowing me the time to do so.

Get me outta here

 Once hubby has gone back to work, there will come a time when you realise that you cannot hide at home a moment longer. It is time to get up the nerve to leave the house. The first time you do so will be fraught. You will spend much of your morning trying to figure out what to dress baby in for his first outing. You will start to panic a little as you don't want him to be too cold or too hot and you will phone around all your mummy friends to ask them how many layers they put on their newborn when they first left the house. Once you have realised that those phone calls have been no help whatsoever, you will bundle him into the capsule and start to overpack the nappy bag with nappies, wipes, scented nappy bags, changes of clothes, more hats, more coats, bibs, muslins, until you can barely manage to carry it.

You are just about to leave the house when a quick glance at your watch tells you that it is almost time for baby's feed. Maybe it's best to feed baby and then go to the shops. You feed baby, burp him, bundle him up again and grab yourself a quick bite, oh and a cup of tea while you're at it. Actually, you may as well change his nappy again. Hang on a minute, it's time to feed him again, isn't it? Then, eventually you will walk out of the house, shut the door and realise you have forgotten something. Ah, that's right, you've forgotten baby!

On my very first outing alone with baby, I tried leaving the house at 10.30 a.m. — I finally got out of the house at 4 p.m.

Rest assured, it does get better. The second time I left the house with him, I was only 40 minutes late for the 'baby and you' course. The course itself was only one hour long so I missed most of it, but at least I got there. Part of the reason I was so late was that I parked outside the building where the course was and cried for 10 minutes. It was the trauma of leaving the house. I thought my life was over and I would never again be able to get out of the house in under an hour. I asked one of my girlfriends how she did it. She told me to pre-pack the nappy bags and lay out the clothes you want baby to wear the night before and start putting things in the car at least 30 minutes before you are due to leave. I took her advice to heart and it did get easier.

Tips for getting out of the house with a new baby

⊙ Pack the nappy bag the night before: two nappies, cream, bags, wipes, two outfits, two bibs, one muslin (for draping over you when feeding/breastfeeding, mopping up spills etc.), hat, cotton blanket that can also be used to put on the floor as a 'mat' for baby to lie on.

- When you arrive back home from your outing, replenish and repack the nappy bag straight away so you are ready for next time.
- Lay out the outfit you are going to put baby in the night before.
- Put capsule, blankets and coats by the door.
- Start trying to leave the house half an hour before you really have to leave.
- Plan to leave the house directly after you have finished a feed. Lay everything out, ready to go, then feed then pack baby into capsule after burping and checking the nappy.

One of your first outings with your baby in those first couple of months will probably be a trip to the supermarket. It is a confusing time. How do you go to the supermarket with a newborn? The first time I rocked up, I unbuckled baby from his capsule, carefully carried him into the supermarket then looked with horror at the trolleys lined up. 'Where do you put a baby?' I asked my mum, who luckily was visiting from England at the time.

We tried sitting him in the children's seat but, of course he was too little and we were worried he would fall through the gaps. I studied the other 'baby' chairs on some of the other trolleys and even those looked too upright, hard plastic and uncomfortable. Mum and I even looked at wrapping him in blankets and lying him down in the trolley but that was a no-go too. Eventually, Mum held baby while I went back to the car to retrieve the capsule, we re-buckled him in and put the whole capsule in the trolley. I later learned that there is a way of clicking baby capsules directly onto the front of the trolley. My advice would be to hang around outside the supermarket on your first visit with baby and wait for another mother to come by. Chances are she will have been through exactly the same as the above and will be able to help show you how to click the capsule on properly.

One thing a day

'I washed my hair today,' I announced proudly to my husband as he came in the door from work in answer to his question about how my day had gone. I was sitting on the living room floor, playing trains with my just-turned-2-year-old while bouncing my 4-month-old in the bouncinette.

He looked at me blankly. 'Erm, don't you usually?' he asked, inspecting my head.

'Not any more,' I shrugged. 'I don't normally have the time. Besides, Jack screams every time I turn the hairdryer on. It's just not worth it.'

Hubby looked pretty disbelieving. 'Right,' he nodded.

It was true, Jack had some sort of aversion to hairdryers, vacuum cleaners, food processors and just about anything that made any sort of loud noise.

When the cleaners would come around (lucky me!), he would cling on to my legs every time, sobbing his little heart out and refusing to come out until the vacuum cleaner had been safely turned off. With the blender he would just shout 'No! No! No!' at the top of his voice and for some reason. His *pièce de résistance* was the hairdryer. Perhaps he thought it was hurting my head. He would fling himself on the floor screaming and sobbing his little heart out until it finished, then as soon as it was turned off he would pick himself up and sort of shrug as though he knew it was fine really. (We later learned that extreme sensitivity to sound is an indication of possible ear problems.)

Sighing, I realised that it was pointless to explain all this to hubby. He, who could wash his hair in two seconds flat in the shower and with a couple of shakes of the head have it dry again, could not possibly understand how much I would give to have a nice long shower and be able to wash and dry my hair in peace without having to entertain the children by singing 'The Wheels on the Bus' in the bathroom.

'And then what happened?' hubby asked.

'I just kept going.'

'What, through the screaming?'

'Yep. I thought, I'm going to ignore it today and see what happens.'

'And what did happen?'

'He screamed the entire time. But as soon as I turned it off he just looked me straight in the eye and said "All done?" When I said yes, he just nodded, picked himself up off the floor and went back to his book.'

I could see hubby thinking this through and wondering if I exaggerated the whole thing.

No matter how many things you used to be able to achieve in your typical day prior to having children, once you are a parent, everything gets completely thrown out of the window. It takes so much longer to get anything done. However, it is in those first few months of having a new baby that you really realise how little you are able to achieve within your day. Don't beat yourself up about this but just set yourself one daily goal. At the beginning, this could be as simple as having a shower, washing your hair or perhaps returning a phone call or two. As you get through those early sleep-deprived days then you can start to add more things on your list of what to achieve that day such as going out to get some milk, visiting a friend or even getting to the supermarket. Remember, you are not alone — all other mums have been through what you are going through and it will get easier as time goes on and your confidence increases.

The witching hours

 People talk about the witching hour (or more accurately hours), where not only are baby and kids at the end of their rope, it's also Mum who, after holding it together all day, gets to the end of her tether just before Dad walks through the door. I seriously feel the world would be a happier place if dads arrived home every day at 4.30 p.m.! Honestly, that's the time when I am constantly glancing at the clock as it oh-so-slowly inches towards 5.30. I know, I'm pretty spoiled as my hubby gets home usually before 6 p.m. and he is super helpful. I remember saying to hubby once, 'I wish you could have seen me earlier today. I was so awesome and happy and fun with the kids but now I'm a bit over it.'

The witching hour has a variety of different looks depending on what stage of the parental journey you are on. Trying to cook dinner while doing the 'baby dance' (bouncing a baby on your hip or dragging a toddler around on your leg) can have a negative effect on your posture as well as your mood.

 I remember not wanting to go home in the evenings, literally dragging my feet because I wanted to 'delay' the witching hour for as long as humanly possible. For example, I would pick my child up from kindy at 3.15 p.m. daily and still be hanging around the kindergarten playground until 4.15 p.m. when the teachers would be shaking their keys and threatening to lock me in if I didn't leave. Reluctantly I would head home, dreading what was to come. I knew I wasn't the only one feeling this way, as there were two other mums there at the kindy playground too, scared of what was about to hit them when they returned to the house. We would reassure each other that it wouldn't be that bad, and give each other tips and advice, while at the same time acknowledging that we had to go through the same thing again the next night. You hope that hubby will be home early that night so you don't have to go through it alone.

I make it sound like a horror story — it's only the feeding-bathtime-bedtime routine. Perhaps all children are at their absolute worst at that time of day, or perhaps you're just desperate for some adult company, I really don't know.

Even more recently when I returned to work I used to dread going home from a hard day at the office to face the music at home. It made me appreciate how working dads feel when they walk through the door at the end of the day and we mums thrust our children at them, demanding they help.

What do dads really think when they walk through the door at the end of the day greeted by hyper children and a busy, stressed and 'over it' wife? One of my male NBFs is convinced dads stay at work longer than needed just to avoid going home to the chaos.

In the movie *Marley and Me*, the father cannot face going home to the screaming baby and unhappy wife and sits outside his house in his car, crying quietly as he surveys the chaos of his home.

Scott Haltzman, author of *The Secrets of Happily Married Men*, warns 'none of us want to go home when we know we'll be walking on landmines. At home men often get accused of doing wrong/not enough with the kids.' He also notes that in many men's magazines the underlying message values freedom and adventure. This may contribute to men staying away from home, the place that reminds them of their real responsibilities.

Even when the children are past the baby stage, getting the children to bed is full of challenges. For example, don't get me wrong — I love my husband very much — but there is something about that 7 o'clock chime that tests even the most patient mum in the world.

It's 7 o'clock, now go to sleep!

 Picture this. It is 6.45 p.m. The children are snuggled peacefully in their beds. It's quiet. It's calm. Eyes are fluttering softly to sleep. Then all of a sudden, *wham bam!* Dad's home from work and party central has hit suburban Auckland. Kids are lifted onto shoulders, music is on, dancing has begun and it's all going off.

By 7.10 p.m. Dad's lost his juice. He's had enough of the fun and decides it's time for bed. The only problem is the children are now wired. Surprise, surprise, the switch isn't easily turned off. The kids are past it, hyper, giggly. Mum's hard work calming them down has gone out the window. Damage done. Mum and Dad try to calm them down again but they are now in silly mode. Mum loses her temper with Dad. Dad loses his temper with the kids. The kids burst into tears.

By 7.40 p.m. Mum is throwing up her hands, refusing to deal with it any more and pouring herself a generous glass of wine. Nobody's talking. Nobody's happy. Everybody's tired.

Eventually, of course, they do fall asleep and Mum and Dad make up again. But then the next day begins and it happens again...

Attitude is everything

In the movie *The Hangover*, one of the characters, Phil, refers to his life with his wife and child. He warns his friend that each day is closer to death. That sense of freedom and independence definitely shifts when you welcome a baby into your life. This magnifies with each successive child. The mum is immersed in it and the dad wakes up, looks in the mirror and thinks 'Is this my life?'

 I definitely feel aged by the experience — drained of energy, more 'smile lines' — but I feel like my life is enriched rather than depleted. It sounds cheesy but think about the language you use with your kids and partner. Your tone, choice of words and body language all matter. For a few years after I first listened to a Tony Robbins CD my mantra was 'attitude is everything'. Tony hit a chord with me as the key message was that the words you choose to use determine how you feel. Like a broken record I would greet hubby's morning enquiry about my night with a range of different responses all with negative undertones. My usual responses included 'Crap, a complete joke, two times for Ruby, one for Jojo and one for the dog.' According to Tony, if I replace my usual 'I had a horrendous night' with 'my night was far from fabulous' it doesn't seem quite so bad. This, however, takes vigilance and constant self-reminding.

> *'I'm at the end of my wick when you (finally) walk through the door sometime after 6 p.m. but you should've seen me two hours ago — I was dancing around and singing ABBA with the kids. I was **awesome**!'*

Seeing each other primarily in the high-stress times of the day (early morning and the 5 p.m. witching hour) is really not conducive to marital bliss. I'm puffy-eyed and a bit disgruntled in the morning then slightly frazzled by the time he walks through the door at the end of the day. Your partner misses seeing you when you're in the zone of positive parenting. If only work started at 10 a.m. or finished at 4 p.m. In an ideal world, what would your family's work arrangement be?

We have now introduced a more family-friendly work-life balance into our family lives to enable each of us to spend more quality time with the children and family. It works really well and is easier than you think. Take a look at how we do it:

Nat and Matt's nine-day fortnight

Matt and I recently decided to tweak our lifestyle to try to get more balance. A bit of scheduled writing time for me and a bit more kid-time for him. Not just hectic breakfast and dinner but 'real quality' kid time where he gets the experience of walking and talking with Ruby on her way to school and the thrill of Jonah rushing into his arms after a fun afternoon at kindy.

Here's how it works: Matt has negotiated with his work to do a 'nine-day fortnight'. This means he takes every second Thursday off work. While this means less income for us as a family, it means enriched involvement in the kids' lives and a bit of focused writing time for me. I love those Thursdays! I love seeing Matt do his thing with the kids without me hovering over him and I love being able to really get 'stuck in' to my writing knowing the kids are happy and safe.

Jacqui and John restructure their work-life balance to suit their family

John and I recently reassessed how we would live our lives and earn a crust going forward. We worked out that if we both took short-term but higher paid (and therefore slightly more stressful) contracting jobs then we could work like beavers for a few months, earn some money then take a few months off with the family over summer to 'hang out', go to the beach and other fun stuff.

This is the first year we have done something like this and so far it is going well. Yes, when you have children and are both working long hours it is pretty full on and stressful, but at the end of this contract I will have done six months of paid full-time employment and therefore be able to take six months off to spend time with the children and to do all the other stuff that is so important to them: helping at the kindy and on school trips, organising playdates and just generally spending quality time with them.

It wouldn't work for everyone and you definitely need a good support network or an extra-obliging nanny to make it work but knowing that there is a prize at the end makes all the hard work worthwhile.

Do something or get things done?

 When I started writing this book, I anticipated that one of the most frustrating things for mothers is that feeling of not getting ahead, merely 'treading water' rather than GTD — getting things done!

I needed to be reminded that GTD isn't everything when our third baby was born. I automatically lapsed into GTD mode once baby was down for a nap, to the extent that I got grumpy and impatient with the other kids (or anyone) who impeded my efforts to 'achieve something'! My setting automatically swaps into 'don't slow me down, don't get in my way'. People standing in doorways is a big pet peeve for me.

I used to be quite rude if anybody phoned me on what I classed as *my* time (baby's big middle-of-the-day nap). I would curse anyone who phoned me during that 'precious time,' as I found it was the only time I could really get on top of things I needed to.

Prior to having children I had no concept of the preciousness of my time. Suddenly you have a child and your time is gone. Smashed to smithereens.

When your children are babies you might have a little bit of time while they nap. But, as they grow and nap time reduces, then any non-child time you do have, you guard jealously. Now my children are older they rarely nap at all. It means that the little bit of time I have when both are at kindy, I hold on to for all I'm worth. If anything or anyone interrupts that precious me-time then I lose all sense of civility.

Recently I was grabbing some 'me/writing time' and there was a knock at the door. Both children were at kindy and I had one hour to get my thoughts together and do some writing. I cursed and pretended I hadn't heard it. The person knocked again. Grumbling, I went to answer it. It was a girlfriend popping in to say hi and have a quick cuppa. 'You've got to be kidding me,' I thought. I was ungracious and uninviting. She, in turn, was affronted.

She lives alone, and had no concept of how precious my time was and couldn't understand why I couldn't spare 20 minutes to have a chat with her. I was so ungracious that in the end she left. I then immediately felt guilty.

When the weekend finally comes, there's often a discrepancy between what he wants and what she wants. I was thrilled when my hubby said he was taking the morning off work for my birthday. I had to laugh when he suggested we just have a quiet morning at home. I was so often at home (housebound by a napping child or domestic duties), and on weekends want to go out as a family (or by myself) and 'do something'.

The domestic grind

 With little ones, your life as a mother very much revolves around the kitchen, laundry and the grocery store. It's the constant catering and cleaning that leave you feeling like you're just treading water and not actually 'achieving' anything. You are chief caterer, not to mention dishwasher and laundry maid extraordinaire. You tidy up the kitchen only to turn around and find it messy again. And the laundry — did you ever imagine having kids would create so much washing?

I recently asked a bunch of girlfriends to complete this sentence: 'Motherhood would be so much easier if not for the . . . ' Responses ranged from 'fighting' to 'afterschool activities' but for me, the constant catering is a killer. I know meals are supposed to be cooked or rather 'created' with love but sometimes at 5 p.m. there is not a lot of lovin' going into my food prep. More like a cup of frustration and a hint of bitterness. I don't mind cooking, it's the kids wanting my attention and trying to cook with a baby glued to my leg that makes it a bit challenging. My solution for staying sane is to have hubby cook dinner twice a week if possible. I don't care what we have, as long as I'm not making it!

When my first child was 3, I decided I wanted to make a conscious effort to be 'in the present' more, instead of trying to keep her occupied while the baby was napping so that I could get things done. Sure the dishes need doing, but I'm never going to look back and say 'Ah, remember that time when the sink really sparkled?'.

My daughter was constantly asking me to play shoe shops or restaurants. I realised that her frequent requests for my attention were consistently met with phrases like 'I'll just tidy this' or 'I'll just put this away, then I'll play with you'. So one day I decided to have a domestic-free day, to just let the domestic stuff slide and whenever she wanted me I would be there.

Sadly it didn't last long before I'd fallen into my old habits of striving to 'achieve' something. Now two years and another baby later, I still have to adjust my expectations of what I'll achieve in a day. And more importantly remind myself that playing with them, teaching them stuff and living in the moment *is* real achievement.

The domestic divide

 A friend rang me up one day with a bit of tension in her voice. 'Can I ask your advice? How do you stay such a positive and supportive partner when your husband gets to go out and have fun while you are home looking after the kids *again*?' I responded, 'I definitely have my moments.' I think that being out of the dinner or bedtime routine at least once a week is key!

I definitely found that the domestic gender stereotypes magnified with baby number two. Couples have different systems for divvying up who's in charge of what around the house. One (male) friend even goes so far as to call them 'pink job' or 'blue job'. Pre-children, many couples share the domestic duties, somewhere between 50:50 and 60:40. When the first baby comes along, the dad sometimes will step up particularly in the early days and help with the washing and cooking. With baby number two Dad is so busy entertaining the toddler and working that the domestic ratio takes a shift and Mum is left with the majority. Upon surveying my coffee group girls the averages ranged from 80:20 to 99:1.

Here's an activity to help make the domestic divide more manageable:

Choose your chores

Have a chart with different chores written up on the chart or written up on magnets. Put them on the fridge and you and hubby choose which chores you prefer doing. That way you each discover more about what the other likes doing and you focus your energy on the chores you enjoy the most and spend less stress and energy lamenting that your partner 'never' does them. Otherwise how is my hubby meant to know that I would much rather wash the dishes than bring the washing in from the line or give the kids a bath? This is also something you can do with the children as they get older to help them learn to take responsibility for chores around the house.

Find out what your partner values and tweak things accordingly. If you both value dining together as a family most nights then it's worth the effort to have the meal prepared by the time Dad walks through the door but maybe establish a 'set' night when hubby is in charge of the hosting.

> *'Dan cooks Friday through Sunday so that's a great help.'*
> **Maria, New Zealand, two children**

While some couples may discuss (or debate) the division of domestic jobs, others fall into patterns.

My friend Tania is one of those mothers whose kids always look stylish yet comfortable. Hair brushed, shoes on the correct feet and so on. She often arrives with baking and her house is always clean. After exclaiming with admiration to Tania how calm and non-frazzled she always seemed, she let me in on her secret. 'At five o'clock Friday I am off kitchen duty.' Her husband Tim arrives with fish and chips every Friday and then he is 'in charge' of meals (and snacks, oh the endless snacks) for the remainder of the weekend. Brilliant!

While some mothers may scoff at this as they 'have trouble getting their husband to put his socks in the laundry basket let alone cook a meal', I make a conscious effort to thank my husband for acts such as tidying the kitchen, giving me time out at home etc. My motive is partly to genuinely make him feel good and partly positive reinforcement. However, part of me feels like thanking him acknowledges that he is helping me out or doing me a favour rather than doing his job as a dad.

Domestic dad

My husband is awesome in the kitchen, and the lounge and the bedroom! Mind out of the gutter, please — I'm talking about domestic stuff. Keeping the house tidy, cooking meals, making snacks, doing the washing … But how greedy am I? I still want more!

My sisters sigh and say 'He's like a girl — he just knows what needs to be done and does it.'

I remember watching hubby get disheartened seeing the kitchen bench and lounge that he'd cleared and cleaned go from gorgeous to ghastly in a matter of hours. 'Welcome to my world,' I would think. I'm a confident mum, I don't feel threatened by the fact that the only things I do better than him are make rice and stack the dishwasher. OK, I'm being harsh on myself, but while I'm no domestic goddess, I do keep the kids entertained, happy and safe day after day, year after year, so all is well.

I was a little put out when I returned from a weekend away (my first one ever) and there was no mention about 'how tough it is' or 'how amazing you are for doing it all the time'. When hubby does have extended sole-charge time with the kids, you hope that he has a great time but also that he finds it challenging so he appreciates you, right? Oh well, at least he had fun and is keen on doing it again!

Modern-day dads definitely do have higher expectations from us mums to help with kids and around the house than in previous generations. My mum who is now a grandparent often comments on how things have changed and how rare it was to see dads pushing babies in strollers when she was a young mum.

My hubby loves hanging out with the kids and is great at encouraging me to 'take some time out' while he cares for the kids for half a day now and then. He is not, however, interested in being a stay-at-home dad. He's made that quite clear many times over the years as our family has grown.

Other friends of ours have done things like mum at home for baby's first year then dad is at home with baby for the second year! Pretty amazing if you can swing it but my hubby always maintained that he had the 'easy job' (going out to work) and that was the way he liked it. He would make an awesome home dad but I certainly prefer to be home than at work full time. As they get older I'd love us to find a balance of both doing a bit of work and being actively involved in the kids' lives.

As mentioned previously, we decided to tweak our lifestyle and take a slight pay cut in order to allow Matt to pick up and drop the kids at school and kindy now and then. Ask yourself, what would your ideal lifestyle look like if you were to make a few changes? Would you or spouse work more or less? How did you and your partner decide who would stay home and for how long? How can you divvy up the domestic duties and keep everyone happy? How do you show your partner or hubby that you appreciate him?

'I think it's fair to say that I have got a long way to go to be a better man but I never thought I would be as challenged as I have in trying to be a good husband. This topic is a biggie for me because being a good dad is something I have thought about for most of my life. I never thought that it would become more about being a good partner.'

Cam, New Zealand, one child

Do's and don'ts for dads

Do:

- help with the 'morning madness' by making kids' lunches, unloading the dishwasher or getting the kids' breakfasts so Mum can have a shower!
- take baby/kids 'away' to give mum some child-free time and arrange for her to do the same for you.
- make arrangements so that you can drop off or pick up kid(s) from childcare/school now and then.
- help with the housework. A 'domestic dad' is sexy and you'll likely get more action.
- know that you are loved, appreciated and desired. We mums are just too flustered to show you sometimes.
- consider ordering some home-cooked meals or getting a subscription to a local maternity or baby concierge service if you're going away on business or working really long hours.

Don't:

- offer to get takeaways if it's *your* night to cook dinner! Save that for when it's one of Mum's (many) cooking nights.
- say things like 'Why is the house so messy? What do you do all day?' or anything remotely similar.
- rev the kids up when you walk through the door just before bedtime.

Jacqui: Confessions of a neat freak

 Pre-children I was the most organised person you could ever meet. I knew exactly where to lay my hand on anything I needed. Diaries were synchronised with my hubby, life was beautifully planned and my home was neat and ordered.

I struggled to maintain order with our first baby, but when our second child came along, I found the demands of a baby and a toddler threw my well-ordered systems out of the window. Washing piled up, the fridge was often bare, you would trip over toys and it would just drive me mad. Try selling a house with a baby and toddler! I would no sooner put away the toys and clear one room and another would have been trashed. Spontaneous home viewings used to give me heart palpitations. I have worked hard to get myself into a routine and on track, and have since developed new systems to help and it's definitely easier now the children are older.

Nat: Organised chaos

 All people have an acceptable level of cleanliness but I'm sure most parents get perturbed by the ongoing pursuit of keeping things tidy. Some people just go with the chaos of having kids, others let it rile them. Remember the 80:20 rule, and do whatever works for you.

Though I'm a bit chaotic by nature, I still love the Montessori philosophy of 'a place for everything and everything in its place'. I love the idea of my house being tidy and organised; I just find it hard to make it a reality (for more than one day). When it comes to clothes I'm a bit of a hoarder, and I struggle to throw away any type of memorabilia (letters, photos etc.).

I popped in to visit a former neighbour with a newborn. (I know you're not meant to just pop in unannounced but the baby was four weeks early and I didn't even know she'd had it!) Anyway, after oohing and aahing over the gorgeous tiny darling I couldn't help but acknowledge how tidy her house was. I expect to be surrounded by stacks of washing and piled plates of food but maybe that's just me.

So much of motherhood revolves around cooking and cleaning. I honestly feel that motherhood would be 'easy' if the catering was taken out of the equation. Then I could actually sit and play with the kids without feeling like I had to sneak away to prepare a meal or clean up the kitchen.

I remember walking in on a discussion between my mother-in-law and my mum. My mum was mid-sentence about how she has one tidy daughter and two messy ones. I knew without asking that I was one of the messy girls. I did that thing where you carry on as usual and pretend you didn't hear but it was then that I thought maybe messy is just the way that I am. Should I embrace it rather than fight it?

I do get flustered now and then by the state of the house or slightly embarrassed when people pop in, but friends know that I'm not a 'tidy' person. It warms my heart when I visit friends and they too have a messy house.

I do go through phases of getting inspired and want to be tidy and organised. I've tried to incorporate systems into my week: fresh sheets on Friday, sweet treats on Sunday (baking), but these routine methods often give way to a more higgledy-piggledy approach.

I visited a friend with a 15-month-old baby and admired the string and seven wooden clothes pegs she had along the top of a blackboard in her kitchen. Each peg had a square piece of paper with salmon steaks, spaghetti Bolognese and so on written on each one. 'Is that your weekly menu?' I asked in amazement. She has a stack of the square paper notes with a different meal written on each. Every Sunday her husband flips through them like a deck of cards and selects the weekly menu!

I'm definitely a planner in terms of social events, doctor's appointments and so on but not so much for the domestic stuff. In efforts to become more tidy and organised I called upon my friend, 'organisation and style consultant', Clara. You should have seen her face when I showed her my 'drawer of doom', the pile of clothes by my bed and the *pièce de résistance* — my pantry! Her house looks like it's out of a magazine, mine looks like we've just been robbed.

But for me, it's the moments and the memories that matter. I want to be able to close my eyes and recall teaching Ruby how to snip and glue bits of paper into animal shapes on a sunny afternoon, instead of worrying about them messing up the carpet.

Thanks Clara for some of your tips included in this list below.

 Top Tips for a Tidy Home: ifonlytheytoldme.com/6

Top tips for domestic bliss

- ⊙ Meal planning. There is a list on my fridge of what we are eating every day of the week. I plan my meals in advance and shop for each of those meals.
- ⊙ Online shopping. Online shopping is a great system for all families. Not only is it much less stressful to sit at home with a glass of wine, watching *The X Factor* while doing your shopping, but it is a better way of sticking to a budget as you don't put extra items in your trolley, you don't have to shop with the kids, and there are often delivery vouchers and other specials on offer too.

- Packing bags. Pack nappy, school and kindy bags the night before. Check the clothes in bags are clean, and include clean knickers/fresh nappies, drink bottles, hats, warm cardies and so on.
- Packed lunches. Plan lunches and pack non-perishables in lunchboxes the night before.
- Laundry. Put a wash on the night before so all you need to do is hang it out in the morning. Or, put your washing machine on a timer (if you have one) so it automatically starts the washing at 6 a.m. That way you can hang out the first load before the school drop-off.
- Linen. Wash linen on a sunny, breezy day!
- Dishes. Try to get the dishes done and kitchen cleared at night before you go to bed. You may be tired but you'll be sick and tired in the morning if you don't do it the night before. Load, wash and (here's the key) *unload* the dishwasher before you go to bed.
- Organising files and bills. Introduce an in-tray and a good filing system for bills, correspondence etc. Bin everything else.
- Downscale your 'stuff'. Too many items make for clutter and a busy look.
- Categorise. One place for everything. I tend to have a few places for the same type of items. Cluster and categorise everything. For example, instead of having the markers, pencils and crayons in a big plastic container, try using a kitchen utensil tray and grouping them. They'll be easier to use.
- Cleaning products. Use eco-friendly cleaning products and soak kitchen sponges, toothbrushes, drink bottles etc. in a baby-friendly anti-bacterial tablet solution. Good staple cleaning products include chamois leather and vinegar, which are great for wiping down windows, TV, tables and so on.
- Keeping playdates tidy. When you have other children over for playdates, encourage everybody to play in the toy room/lounge or outside. This helps to keep the bedrooms clean.
- Ban the bags. You know how you save all those plastic bags that you seem to collect when you forget your cloth eco bags? Well, try keeping a smaller collection of bags for reusing. Apparently Toronto has banned plastic bags in grocery stores. Go, Toronto!
- Clean and clear. After every meal, clear and wipe the table and benches, and sweep under the table. I am now much better at fully clearing my kitchen bench and it does look way better!
- Good storage. Keep a cute plastic box or wicker basket outside each bedroom for you to put stuff in during the day or at night when they're in bed. Looks tidier than a pile!

- Having areas of responsibility can be a great approach to divvying up the domestic duties.
- Check out our recommended reads and websites: Recommended Reading: ifonlytheytoldme.com/recommendations and our boards on Pinterest: Pinterest.com/IOTTM.

 Despite all this, our household is still chaotic in the morning. Sometimes you have to let things go. I'd prefer to ensure all curtains are open, all beds are made and everyone has teeth and hair brushed before leaving the house, but I find it hard to do this when trying to get out the door in time for school. It may just mean that I have to leave the dishes in the sink unwashed, and maybe, just maybe, the curtains in the bedroom won't be opened until 11 a.m. and, goodness gracious, I might even have to forgo the mascara sometimes. Life is chaotic, life with children even more so. I am trying hard to put the vacuum cleaner away and to pull out the jigsaws a lot more with the kids and spend some quality time with them.

Supermarket dramas

 My husband is a strong man. It's not often you see him moved to tears. But, the other day, his children managed to do just that.

Usually I am in charge of domestic chores, including supermarket shopping. Although I don't particularly enjoy shopping with the children, I have firm systems and rules in place that allow me to escape relatively unscathed from most of my supermarket visits:

- Sasha, the youngest, must sit in the trolley (or the supermarket police will appear).
- Jack needs to hold on firmly to the trolley unless I give him a specific item to go and find.
- If they are good they get to choose one item each to go in the trolley (they normally choose chocolate-covered cornflakes or some other item that they know Mum won't buy).

This particular week, I couldn't manage the shop. Hubby sprang to the rescue. 'I'll go,' he offered. 'You can leave the children here,' I responded. He rolled his eyes, obviously thinking I was making a big deal of it and 'how hard can it be, after all?'

Fast forward two hours. I was ready to send out a search party when he finally drove up the driveway, red-faced and mouth set in a firm grim line. I knew they had broken him.

'I am *never* taking them to the supermarket again!' he screeched. 'Jack ran off in one direction and Sasha ran in the opposite direction. I couldn't find them for half an hour. Then I finally found them sitting on the floor, eating sweets out of the value bins.'

Despite myself, I laughed. 'Why didn't you put Sasha in the trolley?' I asked. He looked confused. 'I didn't think of that.'

Needless to say, I think I'll be taking over that particular domestic chore from now on.

Tips for successful supermarket shopping with children

- ◉ Keep them in the trolley/ tied to you with reins
- ◉ Do *not* be tempted to put them in the Wiggles car. It is a pain to push around the supermarket, it hardly holds any groceries and the kids can get in and out whenever they want and cause chaos.
- ◉ Promise them *one* treat at the end *if* they are well-behaved.
- ◉ Tell them the supermarket police are watching.
- ◉ If your child is slightly older, give them their own trolley to push, even if it is one of those plastic or wooden ones they normally push their blocks around in. They can put their things in the trolley and it makes them feel they have made choices.
- ◉ Avoid the sweetie aisle, biscuit aisle and toy aisle (although supermarkets often will put the essential items next to these harmful, chaos-causing items).
- ◉ Pack snacks to feed them all the way around to keep their mouths full and their hands busy. Raisins are a great idea.
- ◉ Be strong and prepared for battle at all times.
- ◉ Leave the kids at home.

IOTTM tips for The New You and Home, Sweet Home

- ◉ Try to embrace who you are now as a parent rather than clinging to the person you used to be.
- ◉ OTAD — One Thing A Day — is a realistic goal when you have a newborn.
- ◉ The domestic grind is relentless. Balance getting things done with enjoying the moment.

- ☉ Consider 'lifestyle design' and tweak your life to get more balance.
- ☉ Whether you are organised chaos (like Nat) or a neat freak (like Jacqui) make sure you focus on what is important to *you* rather than judging yourself by others' standards or expectations.

CHAPTER FIVE

Keeping the love alive

When our children were 5, 3 and 10 months old we went to Australia to celebrate their great-grandparents' seventieth wedding anniversary. This was quite a momentous event as both of them were in their nineties. Even with the room full of people and the congratulatory cards from the Queen and the Governor General on display, it was hard to fully appreciate the magnitude of the event. Seventy years (and five children) with the same person.

So how do you keep the love alive for all those years? Let's get one thing straight. Having kids is tough on a marriage, really tough. It's so easy to lose yourselves in the day to day and forget about each other. I suppose it's easier to talk about toilet training and fussy eaters than about 'us', but really the 'us' is inseparable from all that day-to-day stuff. It takes a lot of work to keep a 'thriving', not just 'surviving', relationship in those early years of parenthood.

> 'I could never in my wildest dreams have imagined how much effort it would take to keep my relationship positive after having a child. I know it has helped to "walk in my partner's shoes" every now and then to truly appreciate how hard it is to be a mum.'
>
> Wayne, Dunedin, married two years, one son aged 3 years, baby on the way

I've said it before and I'll say it again. I really and truly don't think that the husbands get just how tired we are.

Recipe for a thriving, not just surviving, marriage in the baby years:

1. Take one exhausted mother.
2. Add a dash of romance.
3. Look her in the eye and give her a hug, kiss and snuggle and tell her that you really love her and that she's doing an amazing job.
4. Let her sleep until she wakes up naturally. No baby crying. No toddler saying 'Mummmmmmmy'. No rubbish or recycling truck. No husband sneaking out early to go to work, swimming or running. No dog barking.
5. Just sleep…

As well as sleep, fun is a key but often elusive ingredient in a marriage. My husband and I have a lot of fun times with the kids, exchanging smiles or laughs at the things they say and do. There's definitely less laughter when the little darlings are tucked up in bed. A lot of the time it feels like you are reporting back to each other and updating each other on what went on at work or with the kids.

'Sexiness wears thin after a while and beauty fades, but to be married to a man who makes you laugh every day, ah, now that's a real treat.'

Joanne Woodward, married to Paul Newman

When asked, 'What makes you feel happy?' Tim, father of two, replied: 'The laughter of our kids. And spending a romantic evening away from the kids (the former happens more often than the latter)!'

'My advice for parents is simple. If you want to be good parents, you need to care for each other first.'

Willard Harley, author

'I am very aware of how lucky I am to have someone like Stu — he is fabulous. We're very united. Our rules are: no games get played, be honest and no sulking.'

Jude, Christchurch, two daughters aged 2 and 4 years

Marriage is a multisport event without a finish line. You don't necessarily want the finish line but at times you do long for the transition area so you can refuel and rest your feet. In parenting there is no awards ceremony and there are no winners and losers. People are their own harshest critics and appreciate applause or acknowledgement from the sidelines.

Perhaps the key is to treat our partners more like we treat our children. Complete admiration (most of the time), detailed and animated explanation and enquiry, lots of cuddles and snuggles. I tell my kids I love them and how smart and amazing they are multiple times a day but probably only say this to my husband a few times a month. It's so easy for the romance to fade among the chaos and logistics of family life. You have to make a real effort to refuel your romance.

Refuelling your romance

 When you have children, it's more important than ever to spend quality time with your partner and put even more effort into your relationship. When you are DINKs (double income no kids) you can get away with putting in long hours at work and you still have oodles of time to spend with other friends, your partner, and your own 'me time'. You can afford to play golf all day Saturday and then have some beers with the boys afterwards, knowing your wife is doing something equally fun with her girlfriends and won't miss you for a few hours. You can have leisurely mornings with the paper, watch movies on a lazy Sunday afternoon, have a nice glass of wine together on the deck and generally life is pretty nice, albeit rather self-absorbed.

When you have children, this stuff does tend to stop for a while. You're tired, you have much more to fit into your day, and it is easy to stop making an effort with your partner.

Initially you can be excused. There is nothing more off-putting to sex than walking around with cabbage leaves stuffed into your bra, and chances are you haven't had much sleep and are feeling pretty grumpy. That's the 'don't even think about it' phase.

This is the time when, more than ever, you need to really put the effort into your partner. It is too easy to slip down the non-intimacy road. So, whether you're tired or not, make an effort to sit down and have dinner at the table, rather than slouch in front of the TV, at the very least a couple of times a week.

If you have family nearby then put it in your diary to have a regular date night and ask a family member over to babysit. Start off by doing it once a month and putting it in as a non-moveable date. As time goes on and your baby grows older, move it to every two weeks and then weekly thereafter. Even if your date is for you both to go for a nice walk together, do a class together, a quick meal, a movie you both want to see, or even just dessert — make the effort to do it. You might not feel like getting dressed up and going out before you go but, I promise, you will enjoy it more than you think.

If you don't have a family member nearby that you can sign on for regular date nights then set up a reciprocal arrangement with a girlfriend or neighbour. I had a swapsie arrangement with my friend, Jo, for a while. Every Thursday it was one couple's turn to go out for the night and one person from the other couple would babysit. It was great because not only was it fun to have your 'date night' treat every other week, but it is actually quite nice to go to someone else's house and watch a movie or read a book too. When you are babysitting for someone else's kids it is much more relaxing as you don't have to fold the washing, do the dishes or the other chores you tend to do at your own home.

Dating again

Your first date (after baby)

 The first date will be a big deal. You'll be nervous about leaving the baby. What if he cries? What if he wakes hungry? What if he won't settle? Allow yourself to be pushed out the door for just a couple of hours, and believe that all will be calm at home.

Our first date after baby was a disaster. My mother-in-law was babysitting and Jack was just 6 weeks old. We normally wouldn't have gone out but my parents were visiting from the UK and it was their last night in New Zealand. We hadn't been out once since they had been here and it had been my dad's sixtieth birthday the month before. We wanted to shout them dinner and so off we went with much worrying on my part. We had just finished our starters when the restaurant brought the phone to our table. Unfortunately Jack had woken up five minutes after we had left and had been screaming nonstop ever since. My poor mother-in-law had tried desperately to soothe him and after an hour-and-a-half, couldn't take the crying any more and phoned.

We had ordered our mains and gulped them down quickly but pudding wasn't even a thought and we raced back home. Ironically the moment we walked in the door he stopped crying and went to sleep.

It couldn't get any worse than that so after that we became a lot better about making the effort to go out together. When baby is a newborn, they are quite portable and will often fall asleep in the capsule or a Moses basket under the table if you take them out with you. As they get older it becomes a bit trickier to tote them along and possibly more relaxing to leave them at home. If finding a babysitter is hard or expensive, then book the kids into a shopping centre crèche for a couple of hours. Mooch around the shops together like you used to, go to a daytime movie, get a pedicure together, grab something to eat or just sit and have coffee. A friend of mine did just this recently for Mother's Day. She popped the children into the shopping centre crèche and she and her hubby went to one of the many eateries in the shopping centre and had lunch together.

My husband and I have done the same on multiple occasions. We have been to a Saturday afternoon movie together while the children were in the shopping centre crèche and we also went out for lunch together once when the children were at kindy. You can't beat it. Most shopping centre crèches either are free or just want a gold coin donation as they are often funded by the shops in the centre, so it really is an excellent option for all budgets.

A regular date night

Why do we find it so hard to have a regular date night? The hassle factor? The money? Perhaps those with in-laws or parents in town feel like they're burdening them by asking too often or is it just that it's easier to stay home?

It doesn't always have to be dinner or a movie. Here are some things you can do as a couple.

Out-of-the-house date ideas:

⊙ walk around the neighbourhood
⊙ go out for lunch (rather than dinner) as it's cheaper and you'll possibly have more energy for good conversation
⊙ get takeaway (take-out) Thai or Indian food at lunchtime and reheat it for dinner
⊙ hike up a hill and watch the sunset
⊙ book your children into a shopping centre crèche while you catch up with your partner over coffee, lunch or even a movie
⊙ swap 'date night babysitting' with a friend or neighbour
⊙ do a cooking or dance class together
⊙ go to the gym, swim or play tennis together
⊙ fish and chips at the beach or local park.

You don't have to leave the house for it to count as a date! Sometimes you like the idea of a date but the thought of having to get dressed up or spend money puts you off.

At-home date ideas:

- ⊚ turn off the TV and just talk
- ⊚ romantic dinner at the table when kids are in bed
- ⊚ create a mind-map or goal/dream poster
- ⊚ board games/cards
- ⊚ glass of wine on the deck
- ⊚ bath together with bubbles
- ⊚ flip through cookbooks and find new recipes for your weekly menu
- ⊚ massage.

Theme nights: sex for dinner and night off

 Another way to revitalise your love as a couple is to have 'theme nights'. I'm not talking about kinky theme dress-up nights (though you could do that too, come to think of it). I'm talking about nights where you do the domestic things a little differently than usual, like a 'walk away' night once a week for example, where instead of spending hours folding washing and getting the kitchen spotless you literally 'walk away' and deal with it in the morning. Instead you could curl up on the couch for a movie with your spouse or, better yet, go to your bedroom for some pre-sleep playtime.

Once a month, save on grocery bills and tidy-up time by having 'sex for dinner'. That's right, skip dinner altogether and once the kids are in bed move straight on to dessert!

Another 'theme night' is taking turns having a 'night off' doing the bath-books-bed routine. Each family does this differently but in my family it's me who makes the dinner (a kid version and more gourmet variation for adults). Then we collectively tidy the kitchen, bath the kids, read stories and put them to bed. Once a week, give one of you a 'night off' where you either go out of the house (for a walk or a movie with a friend) or retire to another part of the house (if possible) and have a relaxing bubble bath, read a book or do whatever feels indulgent to you.

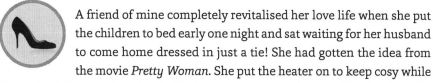 A friend of mine completely revitalised her love life when she put the children to bed early one night and sat waiting for her husband to come home dressed in just a tie! She had gotten the idea from the movie *Pretty Woman*. She put the heater on to keep cosy while she waited. You can imagine hubby's reaction when he walked in the door. He was *thrilled*! Samantha from *Sex and the City* famously dressed herself in nothing but sushi waiting for her boyfriend to come home from work one night. That one didn't turn out quite so well ... but you get the idea.

Personally I once sent hubby out for wine. When he came back I had laid out a little picnic on a rug on the floor and was wearing a very sexy nightie he had given me. Let's just say that dinner was a little late that night ...

Here are some comments from other parents on relationship and romance in the early years:

'(Having children) has surely deepened our bond as husband and wife. We have made it through the chaos together after a lot of ups, downs and hard work. We have created this beautiful family. On the other side, some days it is sad to reflect how our marriage has lost the carefree spontaneity that it once had before we had kids. I am hopeful that there will be a day when we can revisit such a dreamy lifestyle.'

SLC, Richmond Hill, two sons aged 2 and 5 years

'When I am tired and overworked, creating romance is not in the forefront of my mind. It's actually nowhere in my mind. I just need to be reminded that what I do is just as important to our family unit as Dad's outside job. Reminded of that and that I am still the love of his life after birthing his son.'

Katie, Bozeman, one son aged 8 months

'Look after yourself. Look after your marriage. It is important for kids to see that their parents or caregivers are happy and healthy. This will seem the "right" way for people to be and behave. You do yourself and your kids a disservice if you don't look after your own physical, mental and spiritual well-being, if you run yourself down so much and diminish your own healthy parenting input. Help your wife. You know deep down that you "escape" to work some days. Give your wife a break when you get home sometimes. Do some dishes, help with a meal, do some cleaning. Yes, you still have to do the lawns, the rubbish and all the other "man" stuff. Don't moan, that's life, make your house a "no-moan zone", for both kids and parents.'

Vaughan, married 8 years, three kids aged 2, 4 and 6 years

You owe me!

It's easy to lapse into 'you owe me' mode. When our baby Jonah was 10 months old I told hubby that I was taking the afternoon off for me (to write this book actually). Granted he had floated the concept a few weeks earlier, but I felt that it was up to me to make it happen.

When I notice that I'm slipping into 'you owe me' mode, I realise that asking for what I want while also working towards making him happy are key to keeping things positive rather than reactive.

A great way to start is to identify what you each value and what makes you happy. Then you can work to incorporate that into your life. Here's a list to start you off:

What mums value:
- Dad letting Mum have a sleep-in
- a peaceful and uninterrupted shower (Dad can help by keeping any crying babies or fighting toddlers out of earshot)
- intangible gifts — a lie-in in the morning, a cup of tea in bed, a massage
- tangible gifts — gifts to remind her that she's still a woman, i.e. luxury shower gel, flowers, hand-cream
- what not to give — anti-wrinkle cream.

I don't think guys get just how tired we mums really are and how much of a complete gift it is when they come home from work early. Dad walking through the door *before* 5 p.m. is a great way to show love, right up there with a shoulder massage or a Sunday sleep-in.

What dads value:

- guilt-free Child-Free Time (CFT) to do whatever they want, for example, go for a run, play a round of golf, have a beer with the boys
- relaxing in front of a movie or TV show
- time at home alone without the children
- wife initiating sex or making the effort in the bedroom
- seeing wife happy and relaxed.

Appreciation and thanks

How frequently do you express your appreciation to your spouse for the great job they do? Try saying things like 'Honey, you're doing a great job with the kids' or 'Thanks for working so hard.'

I definitely acknowledge my appreciation for help with domestic stuff or school drop-offs. Sometimes I'll send hubby a text in the morning like 'Thanks for tidying the kitchen' but I'm less likely to tackle the big stuff and say 'You're doing a great job at balancing work and family.'

'Appreciation is a biggie! It is amazing how my day changes when my husband shows appreciation, especially for the small things. Motherhood is a somewhat thankless job at times and it is wonderful when someone says "thank you", or "I appreciate". Self-confidence was a big issue right after the birth of both of our babies. I really needed a lot of reassurance in many ways. Thankfully my husband was sensitive to this and on the days that he wasn't I was sure to remind him. It is such a big transition for women, especially with their first-born.'

SLC, Richmond Hill, two sons aged 2 and 5 years

Ask yourself 'how loved do you feel by your spouse right now?' Take a look at the questions below and fill it in with your immediate and honest responses.

How loved do you feel by your partner right now?

How much love do you feel towards your partner right now?

What makes you feel loved by your partner?

How do you show your partner you love them?

> 'We have a very honest and open relationship. Becoming parents has not changed that. We know how to cope with stress and lack of sleep. We know how to give each other time-out and listen to each other's advice.'
>
> **Ellen, Christchurch, two daughters aged 18 months and 3 weeks**

In their book *Eight Lessons for a Happier Marriage*, Glasser and Glasser warn against the seven deadly habits: criticising, blaming, complaining, nagging, threatening, punishing and bribing. Instead actively make your interactions reflective of what they call the 'caring habits': supporting, encouraging, listening, accepting, trusting, respecting and negotiating differences. If you feel critical or resentful towards your partner, ask yourself why.

Do any of these statements 'ring true' for you?

- I feel like the baby/kids have replaced me as number one in my spouse's affection.
- I feel uncomfortable about my body because of the weight that I have gained.
- I feel more self-conscious about my body now because of my post-breastfeeding boobs.
- My big boobs make me feel better about my body.
- It is sometimes more enjoyable to be at work than at home.
- I sometimes stay at work longer just to avoid going home to my grumpy partner.
- I want to give my spouse more frequent and better sex but when I get into bed I just want to sleep!

Once you have thought about and answered those questions, start thinking about how you can articulate and resolve those feelings. For example, if Dad really feels it is more enjoyable to be at work than at home, ask him what makes him feel that way and what you can do to make him want to come home. Is it simply that he comes home to a chaotic house, screaming children and a miserable wife? Or is he finding it difficult to cope? Does he want to help but doesn't know how? Maybe you can make an effort to start feeding and bathing the children earlier by bringing their mealtime forward by half an hour to 4.30 p.m. to ensure that by the time Dad gets home at 6 p.m., the house is relatively calm, the children are in their pyjamas having stories and he isn't walking in on witching-hour terrors. If it's the latter, maybe you can help him by giving him specific jobs to do in the evening so he feels he has a purpose such as bathtime or stories with Dad.

Give the boys a break

It's important that we appreciate that dads these days have two jobs and two 'worlds' in which they live, both with high levels of expectation.

When they're at work, they (hopefully) feel successful, admired and that they are achieving something. Then they come home to a disgruntled mum and crying child. Their wife or partner is annoyed at their lateness and jumps on them as soon as they walk through the door, not appreciating the other stresses and strains they may have faced through the day. Nothing they do is good enough. They are 'scolded' for putting children in the wrong pyjamas, reading the wrong story or getting the children worked up. They go to help with some other chore, only to be told they are being more of a hindrance than a help. It is little wonder that they feel deflated, useless and underappreciated. The following night it becomes easier to stay late at work... and the drift apart begins.

Gary Neuman, author of *The Truth about Cheating*, identifies this feeling of 'not being good enough' and 'just can't win' as a leading cause of cheating.

On the flipside, sometimes Dad swoops in with the best intentions to help but completely misreads the situation and things take a turn for the worse. When Dad comes home at night, the best thing he can do or say is 'What can I do to help?' That way, he can help out by doing what needs to be done instead of feeling like he's doing the wrong thing or getting in the way.

What to do when hubby walks out

 What do you do when your hubby's best friend walks out on his wife? We tried to support them both. While most friends encouraged her to 'move on, she was better off without him', I found myself telling her she wasn't crazy for hoping he would come back. And hope she did. She rose above the pain and anger, even when after much denial it came out that there was 'another woman'. While others would be throwing rocks at the window, she kept calm and kept things as 'normal' as possible for the sake of the boys.

In a podcast interview, I chatted with long-time friend Pip, who also went through separation and divorce. We talked about what to do when your husband walks out and how to avoid it happening. She talked about how friends can help, how to keep a relationship positive in the baby years and the importance of making things 'fun'.

It was an emotional and monumental interview for me as the break-up of these friends was pivotal to me starting to write my book. There I was with a toddler and a 5-month-old, planning a massive home renovation while my hubby was on business trips with a female colleague. It made me wonder and worry. We were both stressed and it made me think 'I can totally see how that could happen. How the relationship can be pushed aside and start to crumble.' Not long after, another friend's husband announced he was having an affair. They tried to make it work but to no avail.

Fast forward four years and Pip has fallen in love again and has remarried. She is thriving after separating. The new couple are gushing with love for each other and their 8-month-old baby. Pip's boys adore the baby and all is well. Her ex-husband has also made great efforts to be very involved in the boys' lives despite a geographic distance. He, too, has now remarried the 'other woman'.

 Thriving After Separation: ifonlytheytoldme.com/46

Happy blended family

Here are some of Pip's tips for keeping a relationship and family happy:
- ⊙ Don't let your relationship slip to standby.
- ⊙ Try not to let motherhood 'consume' you.
- ⊙ Keep the fun alive as a family and a couple.
- ⊙ If you're a dad, don't give up. The baby years are hard. Hang in there.
- ⊙ If you are attracted to someone else you can make a choice to avoid temptation or you can give in to it.
- ⊙ Seek counselling and work through your problems.
- ⊙ Friends can help by coming over to watch TV and just being there. Offers to take the kids away are kind but in that emotional time you just want to keep them close.
- ⊙ If you do separate, keep your relationship with the ex as positive as you can. Bad-mouthing your partner doesn't help the kids.

The book (and Facebook page) *Babyproofing Your Marriage* also has some great tips about how to keep the love alive in those early years.

Gary Neuman, author of *Cheating*, points out that men stray when they feel they 'just can't win' or they're 'not good enough'. So being appreciative and not nagging can help him to feel loved. He claims that 'Most affairs occur because people are emotionally lonely.' Also if men hang around other men who have cheated it becomes more 'acceptable' to them — 77 per cent of cheating men interviewed had a friend who had cheated. He recommends a 'marriage-centred lifestyle' where you actively try to make each other feel happy. Isn't that what we all used to do in the dating years?

Different types of families

In researching for this book, I met psychologist Nigel Latta and had the pleasure of chatting with him about his book, *The Modern Family Survival Guide*. It's funny when someone's on TV, you kind of feel like you already know them. He was just as I'd expected: friendly, entertaining and wise.

A 'modern family', in Nigel's book, refers to blended families, step-families, single parents, adoptive parents, same-sex parents and grandparents raising grandchildren. Whatever your situation, Nigel is passionate about his message that 'your family is not broken'; bruised but certainly not broken. As he says in his book, 'Families have been forming, falling apart and reforming since the very beginning. Far from being broken, the modern blended family is actually very normal.'

One other thing that Nigel acknowledges in this book is the role of the step-mum. 'There is no more difficult job than being a stepmother. It's like being a mother, but without any real power, both hands tied painfully behind your back, and a choice of options which often seem to range from crap to even more crap.' (*The Modern Family Survival Guide*, p. 205.)

 Nigel Latta: ifonlytheytoldme.com/75

Striving to thrive

We asked a bunch of dads about how to have a thriving (not just surviving) marriage/relationship once you become parents. The responses ranged from cynical to serious. Here are some of the responses they gave:

- Don't do it!
- Keep the dog.
- White lies are OK to keep the peace.

- Write about your sex life pre-children to reread post-children so you can remember what it was.
- When we talk, things get resolved.
- I just had to get over myself. Life is so much bigger now ... and better!
- I was never really selfish before I had a partner and child because no one really depended on me. At times I really want to be selfish now ... but I'm not and it isn't always easy!
- I have had to work on being humble, to say I'm sorry even if it doesn't seem 'fair'.
- When things get hard I remind myself of my first thought after my child was born, the feeling that life finally has a purpose.
- Make time for each other and remember to give as much as you can, and not just to the baby. It is easy to forget about each other but these are the times when you need more support than ever.

Describe what a 'thriving' marriage would look like to you?

'Good communication. Still having the ability to laugh and not take life too seriously.'

Nick, New Zealand, two children and a baby on the way

How do you and your spouse/partner make life easier/happier for each other?

'I think we play to each other's strengths, try to ensure each has time doing what they like doing. Being at work during the week, I try to let my spouse have a break away from the kids when I get home and during the weekend.'

Tim, Christchurch, two children aged 1½ and 3½ years

'Giving each other sleep-ins or guilt-free time to do our own things.'

Nick, New Zealand, two children and a baby on the way

Love language and personality types

Understanding you and your spouse's love language and personality type can have a huge impact on your relationship. Gary Chapman discusses the idea of 'Love Languages' and encourages couples to work with their partners to discover how each of you prefers to express your love. It may sound a bit heavy but it does make sense. There are six love styles: do, be, give, encourage, talk and touch.

- do (things for me)
- be (time with me)
- give (things to me)
- encourage (encourage me)
- talk (with me)
- touch (physical touch)

As Chapman says: 'Learning to identify the emotional need that is behind your spouse's behaviour is a major step in being a positive influence in an otherwise desperate marriage. Don't curse the behaviour. Address the need.'

He identifies that one of our deepest emotional needs is the need for freedom. In a marriage, we want to be free to express our feelings, thoughts, and desires. We want the freedom to make choices. We often do things for each other, but we don't want to be manipulated or forced to do things. If we feel like we are being controlled we get defensive and angry. My friend talked about how she had to 'strongly suggest' that her husband tidy up, rather than ask him directly as he would get offended and not help.

How do I express love?

It's good to identify both how you express your love and how your partner expresses their love, as this can turn confusion and frustration into understanding and happiness. For example, my husband expresses his love through 'acts of service' such as doing domestic duties around the house, bringing me food and drinks. However, all I want is words of love and physical affection.

Many men show love through doing things like tidying up the backyard or fixing the car (or doing the dishes and washing). 'Men want to feel like capable, strong and valuable assets whom you could not live without.' Women often show love through words and affection. While a bit of a generalisation, they do have a point.

Sometimes it's daunting to start a heavy conversation with your partner and it's easier just to 'get on with things'. However, you will feel much better and closer once you know where each other is at.

Here is a selection of 'Dear Husband' letters that I wrote, as much to myself as to my hubby. Write your own 'dear husband' or 'dear wife' letter. It's a great way to get things off your chest and let your partner know how you're feeling. You could also write the letter as a way of clarifying your own feelings, but choose not to show it to your partner.

Dear Husband,

I don't know who you are any more and I certainly don't know who I've become. I see you walk through the door at the end of the long work day but I don't look you in the eyes. Instead my glance goes to the clock. How late are you and how many hours has my solo shift been today?

I don't like resentment. The 'old me' would have never allowed such hollow sentiments on board. But I'm a new girl now and I seem to keep count of points like a soccer fan. You nil, me one zillion. It's not healthy I know and the funny thing is that it's so easy to wipe away my frustration with words of love and affectionate embraces. These are few and far between these days and I know I don't invite them even though it's what I crave the most. Not sex, just love.

Dear Husband,

Thank you for all that you do. For navigating the crucial divide between work and us. For still seeing me as a person even when all I can see is a muted version of a girl I once knew. Thank you for the rough and tumble times that you have with the kids. They make me warm inside even though I have no desire to join in.

Dear Husband,

Thank you for encouraging me to take time for myself. For bringing me water during my endless hours of feeding the baby. For asking the children to 'give me space' when they're clambering all over me as I try to eat more than a few mouthfuls at a time. I need someone to stand up for me. I'm often too busy or tired to stand up for myself.

Dear Husband,

I like it when we talk to each other directly, instead of through the children. I'm sorry I'm often half distracted by their animated interjections. I want to drown you with the attention that you deserve when all too often a cold shoulder is the best you get. And most of all I want you to know that a loving hug and words of affection can wipe away any discontentment that builds up in me.

Dear Husband,

It's a shame you only see me at the 'crazy' times of day. Morning when I'm haggard from interrupted sleep and trying to get kids ready for school, then again at dinner time when I'm exhausted from the day and frantically trying to put a decent meal on the table with a toddler clinging to my leg. I've been meaning to tell you about the 'waves of sheer joy' that come over me at various points every day. The delight in Jonah's eyes when he builds something out of Lego or Ruby rushing into my arms at school pick-up. I tell them I love them countless times a day but I need to tell *you* more. I do love you and I feel so lucky to have our family healthy and safe. We need to make more time for 'us'.

Woo me again

 I've heard lots of wives comment how they want their hubby to initiate or suggest dates, outings and time together. 'His idea of time together is me doing dishes while he works on the computer in the same room.' Even though you're married and the courtship days may be a distant memory, they are still worth revitalising now and then. Wives still crave romantic gestures. Dinners where we don't cook or clean up and we actually sit down for more than 10 minutes without 'bobbing' up and down getting this spoon and that cup. We love it when our partners make the plans, don't we? Take us out for dinner or a romantic walk in the moonlight. When I started back at work, my husband surprised me by taking me out for lunch. It was a Friday and one child was at school, while he had organised the other to go to a friend's house for a playdate. He told me to keep Friday lunch free and organised a half-day for himself. He came via the house to 'pick me up' and whisked me off to a little local restaurant for lunch. It wasn't expensive or flash but the sun was shining and, although there was a cool bite in the air, we sat outside the café. It's a memory that always brings a smile to my face because it reminds me of the 'us' we used to be before kids.

In his book *The Proper Care and Feeding of Marriage*, Schlessinger comments: 'I think the biggest mistake people make in a marriage is forgetting that you can still be boyfriend and girlfriend. We tend to treat each other more like roommates because we get comfortable. We don't give enough compliments and praise. We stop experimenting with new things together and settle into the same old routines.'

Get that new-relationship buzz back again by making an effort to really feel that thrill and attraction. I vividly recall climbing back into bed after yet another wake-up to one of the kids in the wee hours of the morning. I noticed the silhouette of my husband sleeping. The curves of his body looked like a mountain range against the curtain backdrop. To keep love and attraction alive you need to actively look for these things or at least stop and appreciate them. Recall and create intimate moments. Even things like stopping doing the dishes to look my husband in the eye and give him a hug when he walks into the kitchen.

Speaking of kitchen, for years I've daydreamed about 'seducing' my husband on the kitchen table but never worked up the guts to make it happen. What stopped me? Fear of rejection? Afraid I'd feel silly. Yes, but also I think it's just easier not to. I'm often bemused by a common scene in movies where the new couple passionately burst through the door, knocking over lampshades and stripping clothes off each other as they make their way towards the couch, bed or nearest horizontal surface. Who does that? I think to myself but if I'm honest I like the thought of having that level of passion resurface now and then. But how do you create that or bring it back?

I like to feel loved and desired out of the bed as well as in. I love it when my husband says to me 'You looked great in that top tonight' or 'Ooh, you're wearing a skirt!'. That kind of positive reinforcement will ensure repeat performances.

> '*It is great when my husband plays hooky from work and we sneak in a lunch date when kids are at school! Now that the kids are a bit older, we try to take short trips together.*'
>
> **Daria, Toronto, three sons aged 4, 7 and 9 years**

How do you get the sizzle back into your relationship when you feel like you're just too tired or too busy to shower your spouse with love? Reigniting your romance will definitely help to heat things up between the sheets.

Between the sheets

 Sometimes it's tough to tell what your partner wants in bed. I'm not talking about the details (sorry), I'm talking about the 'will we or won't we?'. Like most mothers, I cherish my sleep, so generally the later it is by the time we hit the sack, the less likely it is that there will be any action.

Sometimes it's a bit of a calculated decision, often based around sleep. Look at the clock, see the time (10.14 p.m.), think if we have quick sex then allow for fall-asleep time I can be asleep before 11. Alternatively remain quiet, feign sleep and hope he gives up. Pretty sad, isn't it? Is this a familiar scenario? You've just finished feeding baby. It's 1 a.m. and you creep back into bed. Your husband spoons into you. You welcome his warmth and the feeling of love. Then he does a slight pelvic move. You think he's just getting comfortable. You feel a prod in the back followed by a more enthusiastic pelvic move and think *you have got to be kidding me*! The hilarious book *Babyproofing Your Marriage* calls this 'the 10 o'clock shoulder tap' but as many of you know it can happen at any time.

He initiates sex but I wish he would also initiate more honest, heartfelt conversation about us. It's usually me who brings something up if there's any tension between us. Maybe he doesn't ask because he doesn't want to open a can of worms. 'How was your day?' is not the same as 'How are you doing?' You're going get a totally different answer.

Our lack of enthusiasm is not just about being 'exhausted' though. And sorry, lads, it's not only in the newborn months but please don't take it personally! When kids clamber on you and you're 'needed' all day, by the time you're off duty you almost crave just being in your own space. No more groping or being needed! Don't get me wrong, we like to be wanted and loved but there is a big difference between affection and sex. But if you do want a bit of action, boys, don't save all your loving for the bedroom. A hug here and a kiss there during the day could lead to more frisky business at night.

Apparently men need to feel 'needed' and sometimes feel rejected if we don't 'want them'. Talk about more pressure and guilt for Mamma! It's not that we don't desire you, hubbies, it's just that we desire sleep more! Throw in a bit of post-baby body consciousness and no wonder she's not initiating! We do need to make the first move now and then though.

Here are some tactics if you find the 'will we or won't we' guessing stressful or time consuming. You could try my 'SMS' system (Sex, Massage and Sleep on alternate nights) so there's no 'guessing', or another favourite, the 'be in bed by 10 on weeknights and 11 on the weekend if you want any action' rule.

We often assume that the man is ever-wanting and the woman is the decider but the tables turned for me when I was pregnant. There I was in all my preggie glory and he was just reading his book. Wow, I thought, that better be one *%@! good book!

Us women are hard to please, aren't we? I felt empathy for the feeling of rejection that husbands sometimes have when the wife never initiates or doesn't respond to their advances in the bedroom. When my husband was going through a very low stage at work he stopped paying attention to me in the bedroom. I understood though — at work he was feeling underappreciated and unmotivated. He's not feeling the love at work so naturally he's not giving out the love at home, right?

'For me, sex is like going to the beach. Sometimes it feels like too much effort to get everything ready but when we get there I think it was so worth it! The more I do it, the more I think we should do this more often.'

'Sometimes I want to snuggle with my husband in bed but I don't want to give him the wrong idea. I love feeling close to him but then he gets offended when he realises that that's all I want.'

Here are some ideas of how you can re-introduce the passion and romance back into your relationship:

The seven-second rule

Don't rush the hello or goodbye kiss. Kissing is one of the most intimate things you can do. Enjoy it. Kiss often and throughout the day. Don't rush a fleeting graze on the cheek. Hold the kiss for at least seven seconds so it really means something. So it really matters.

Daytime sneaky sex

Take each other unawares. Pop a DVD on for the kids and sneak off to the bedroom for some intimate time out. Sex and a snuggle during the day means no one is tired and it makes it more exciting.

You can initiate too

It shouldn't always be left to the man to initiate intimacy. Men love it when you make the effort.

Love notes

Leave a note for your partner in their briefcase or lunchbox or in other unexpected places, telling how much you love and desire them.

Just a tie

Imagine how sexy your husband would find it if you packed the children off to bed early, set the table and sat waiting for him in just a tie? My girlfriend did exactly that and their passion is still strong today.

Sweet and sexy texts

Send texts to each other throughout the day telling each other you cannot wait to see each other that night.

Don't just save it for the bedroom

Where is the rule that says sex needs to be saved just for the bedroom? Mixing things up may make a big difference.

SMS

To avoid the awkward '10 o'clock shoulder tap' and him feeling rejected, indicate in advance what the night holds. For example, you could agree what certain language might mean. Honey, I'm going to sleep (translation: don't expect any action) or Honey, I'm going to bed (translation: don't dally I'm good to go!)

Try this simple solution to the 'will we or won't we' (have sex tonight) dilemma. It's what I like to call SMS (Sex, Massage, Sleep).

As a couple you get into a pattern of expectations as to when and how often you have sex. I had an idea to take away the guesswork (and possibly, though hopefully, not the romance). There is a different theme on a three-night cycle of 'SMS'. One night you have 'sex', the next night 'massage' and the third night 'sleep', then the cycle repeats. This way you know what to expect and you can anticipate it. It takes out the guesswork from the guy's perspective too. For the girls you get a massage (or give a massage depending on whose turn it is). If I'm getting a relaxing massage then I can enjoy it and drift off to sleep or whatever. On the sleep night you can drift off to sleep without anyone feeling rejected, knowing that a snuggle is just a snuggle.

Work out a clear and fun way to communicate your evening intentions to your partner. Maybe hang a double-sided happy face on your door (like room service) with open excited eyes on one side and sleeping eyes on the other. Or have a certain pair of sexy pyjamas that you put on when you're ready for some action, and save the flannel frog jammies for when you simply want to slumber.

Words of wisdom

Sex in the baby years is an interesting thing. For some couples you were surprised how quickly you became pregnant and for others it has been a long time coming and sex may have become a bit of a chore. In the book *The Stay-at-Home Martyr*, Kimes and Worley discuss the concept of 'choreplay' — getting turned on at the sight of your hubby sweeping the floor!

Sex after baby

There are things that normally you'd love as part of sex but in the baby and breastfeeding years they're not so desirable. For example, any sort of sucking or nibbling on breasts (as your boobs get their fair share of action during the day). Your nipples just want a bit of time to themselves!

When your hubby joins you in the shower this is a Catch 22. Finally you get five minutes to yourself to relax without having one eye on the baby behind the glass or toddler watching you from the sanctity of their potty. Yet you crave the attention and physical closeness with your spouse.

Top tips on sex after children
- When she's breastfeeding adopt a 'look but don't touch' mindset.
- Don't expect action when your wife has her period. Cramps and a pad between her legs are not a recipe for arousal. Instead give her a spontaneous massage (just a massage) so that she can relax and drift off to sleep.
- Having a shower immediately before bed means you're also more likely to get downstairs action.

⊙ Be clear about how often you'd like sex. Talk about it or set up a system like the double-sided smiley face or sexy pyjamas.

Attraction and distraction

Though they may not admit it, many people have had an experience where someone else catches their eye and creates an excited flutter of attraction. Acknowledging attraction is one thing, but doing something about it is a whole other thing entirely. There are three doors before you:

Door 1: Do nothing, say nothing.

Door 2: Tell your spouse (it may or may not be related to an issue between you).

Door 3: Act on it.

Which door will you open and step through?

Honey, we need to talk

 A few months after I started writing this book, a friend's husband told her that he had cheated and was unhappy but was willing to make it work for the child's sake. Perhaps if men chatted more among themselves about the joys and stresses of marriage and parenting, they would realise how 'normal' it is to feel overly domesticated and underappreciated.

One time when hubby and I were feeling distant I suggested that when we feel like there's a wall between us or we're not close, let's have a buzzword like 'we're drifting'. No one really likes saying 'we need to talk'.

There are heaps of marriage habits that are so helpful but invariably involve a bit of effort, so they often fall into the category of 'easier not to'. These include weekly check-ins and date nights.

Scott Haltzman, author of *The Secrets of Happily Married Men*, points out that marriage is like a career that you build throughout your life, not a job that you change when you don't like it any more. It needs determination and staying power.

Dr Ellen Wachtel, author of *We Love Each Other But*, suggests couples appease the negative cycle of criticism by making an effort to warm the heart of their partner. The biggest complaint from couples is that they feel constantly scrutinised and evaluated.

We use positive reinforcement with our children and parenting style but not with our partner. They're usually privy to our grumpy, unedited thoughts. It's easy to criticise with phrases like 'you never do this' (washing, planning social events). Ask yourself, am I wanting him to make an effort to lighten my load or to be more like me? For me, initiating time together is important as it shows he *wants* to spend time together.

Sometimes I wish he'd just ask me what's wrong. It's like they can sense from our body language (emotionless cheek kiss, lack of eye contact, rigid hug) that something is amiss but are they going to open that can of worms? No way!

An 'I love' list

Relationships seem to go in waves — sometimes you feel close and other times it feels like there is a wall between you. During a 'wall' time for hubby and me, I suggested we do this activity. He was doing dishes at the sink and I was at the table. I said 'how about we each make a list of what the other loves'.

I did a brainstorm then read out my list. My 'hubby loves' list included: going for a long run and beating your time; reading instruction manuals; watching *Myth Busters*; talking to your dad on the phone without your mum interrupting; play-wrestling with Ruby; when I don't leave dishes in the sink. His list for me accurately included: reading a book in the sun; talking to friends on the phone; taking photos; eating a cooked breakfast. The cool thing about this activity is that it actually shows both of you how aware you are of what each other loves (and possibly craves and needs) in their life. It made us feel closer and inspired us each to create more opportunities for those things to happen. It was a great alternative to highlighting our spouse's flaws or telling them that they 'never do this or that…'

Take turns making a list (written or verbal) of 15–20 things you believe that your spouse loves, including physical pursuits, foods and behaviours. Think about how you can include more of these things in your lives.

Marriage mentors

Think of one or two couples whose relationship you admire. What is it about that couple that makes them work? Is it the way they treat each other? The way they communicate to and about each other? Is it respect, admiration, affection? What can you do as a couple to capture that feeling in your own relationship?

We're drifting apart

Gottman et al, in their book *10 Lessons to Transform Your Marriage,* warn against getting gridlocked over perpetual conflicts. Conflicts that frequently reoccur are often linked to one's dreams and aspirations. Try to discover the dream behind the conflict.

Friends of ours visited a counsellor where they practised a communication technique based on values. They picked an issue that had been creating conflict in the relationship and were invited to look past the defensive reaction and determine what personal *value* was being compromised. (This would be different for each person.) In this scenario her value was kindness and generosity and his was trust.

I know people who get in fights with their hubby and literally don't speak to each other for two to three days. I'm not sure how healthy the 'silent treatment' is as I'm more inclined to talk it out. In fact I sometimes wish for hubby to raise an issue for discussion. I will occasionally try to 'not speak until spoken to' if I feel like I'm the only one driving the conversation. At other times I say nothing in attempt to keep cynical or sarcastic thoughts to myself.

Most of the time it doesn't take much to get you and your spouse back on track. A bit of time together or actually addressing that issue or incident that's been bugging you will help. Other times it takes much more and a real effort and commitment from both of you.

How has having a baby affected your relationship as a couple?

'Both of us now place more importance on our values. As we are quite different people this has led to conflict. Whereas in the past we might have simply appreciated our differences, now we take things very seriously and stand up more assertively for the things we believe in. Stress through added financial pressures, lack of sleep, post-natal depression and work responsibilities has led to an environment where our views become polarised and we fight for control over the situation.

'When I reflect on our disagreements it now seems that it is more how we express our values or how our values manifest themselves in our behaviours that is the difference between us. For example, my partner would get annoyed that when I arrived home from work I would initially wash my hands before playing with my son. To my partner this behaviour signalled that I did not value giving time to my son. For me, spending time with my son was the very reason I would rush to my car *from work so that I could get home five minutes sooner to be with him.*

'Some of our differences of opinion since becoming parents have had such a big impact on our relationship because they have been about differing values. When values are involved they touch a deep part of who we are and what is truly important in life. Such arguments tend to lead to soul-searching questions about the whole future and purpose of the partnership. It is sad but also encouraging to realise that poor communication is a big part of the problem. Guilt, blame and contempt are also end results of such values differences.

'After several years of this cycle of disagreement it seems harder to find the energy to resolve conflict. Being in a state of constant tiredness makes clear communication very hard to achieve, particularly with the added stress factors that filter every communication. I have observed males in other relationships choose to withdraw from communicating and ultimately allow the slow death of their relationship. I can see how this feels like the only option when nothing else seems to work. I think it's a survival strategy, a final attempt to protect the male from breaking down, committing acts of violence or having an affair. It's a way of retaining some self-dignity and direction in a situation that is spiralling out of control.'

Cam, one son aged 2½ years

Who cares wins

In relationships, and particularly 'parenting' relationships, there are a lot of decisions to be made. These can range from relatively simple decisions such as 'where should we go for our holiday?' or 'which curtain fabric do we like?' to more complex decisions around discipline or childcare. We've stumbled upon a decision-making technique called 'who cares wins'. The concept is that the partner who 'cares the most' or is most passionate about the decision gets the final say. My hubby and I have used this many times and it makes things quicker and less stressful than they might otherwise have been.

Marriage maintenance

Isn't it crazy that we get a warrant of fitness for our cars every six months, go to the doctor only when we're sick and go to the marriage doctor only when our marriage is really, really sick? We earn degrees and diplomas for our careers but don't do any training for one of the toughest and most important roles that we'll ever take on: parenthood!

Holding an 'annual review' of your marriage/relationship and family may sound full on, but it's a great thing to do! Rather than just living day to day and year to year, hold a conscious check-in on a significant date each year, such as your anniversary maybe or perhaps your first-born's birthday (because let's face it, that's when your marriage took you on a new, wonderful and challenging journey). You could buy a journal to record 'favourite memories' and 'goals for the year ahead'. You could even dig out your wedding vows if you are married and write some new 'parenthood vows'.

Make a commitment to do something once a year together, just the two of you. Book grandparents or friends to have the kids for the weekend and go away by yourselves for one or two nights. You'll rediscover what you found attractive in each other in the first place, laugh and talk again. Not only is it great for you as a couple, but it's wonderful for you as a family too. In a family, if the marriage is strong, the family is strong.

Create a mission statement

In her book, *Advice for the Newly Engaged: Prepare for an Awesome Marriage*, the Reverend Laurie Sue Brockway suggests that the first step of any new enterprise is to create a mission statement. This applies to your marriage as well. Brainstorm, discuss, process and bat around ideas until you come up with a marriage mission statement. This is your mutual intention for marriage; it is what you want to be and build together. It can have one sentence or reflect a number of ideas. For example:

> *'Our union gives us strength, power and fortitude to deal with all of life's ups and downs, and it empowers us to contribute to others and the world. We are best friends, confidantes and partners, and we have many close relationships with friends and family. We are a couple who inspire others with our love and who model what it is to be in a great relationship.'*

A marriage mission statement can be another good tool for decision-making. If you're at a crossroad when making a decision, look at your mission statement and ask, 'Will this help us to fulfil our marriage mission?' That often helps to point you in a particular direction.

Relationship traditions

I call these 'traditions' but they don't have to be an annual event. I'm talking about little rituals or habits that you have as a couple to help keep life running smoothly and the love alive. A wine together after the kids are in bed, a dip in the spa once a week, date night once a month, a night in a hotel once every six months and so on.

Hubby and I are currently trying to get back into the habit of our Sunday night 'check-in' for the week ahead, where we plan and discuss our various appointments, evenings out and things we need to achieve that week.

What traditions or habits do you have that keep your marriage and family thriving?

Here are some other ideas for positive habits from other parents:
- make the school lunches together
- make a special dinner together
- date night once a month, and a weekend away once a year to talk about the future together
- spa once kids in bed each night
- takeaways, a glass of wine and a DVD on the weekend
- wine and a chat after the children are tucked up in bed
- exercise together once a month, e.g. a walk, a run or a swim
- go out for coffee on the weekends
- dinner together at the table after the children are in bed
- a cup of tea and some chocolate when the kids are all in bed, catching up and watching a movie or reading
- a hot bath together once every two weeks
- hire a babysitter once a week and go out for dinner either on your own or with friends.

I was especially wowed by this comment:

> *'We employ a nanny three days a week and we always use one day a month for a "date day".'*
>
> **Amy, Vancouver, two daughters aged 7 and 12 years and a boy aged 8 months**

Imagine a whole day together every month! (Or in my case ever!)

> *'Work it out every day. Don't let things lapse.'*
>
> **Great advice from my grandfather on our wedding day**

IOTTM tips for keeping the love alive

- ☉ Get rid of the TV in the bedroom.
- ☉ Put a CD player or iPod player in the bedroom and listen to a range of music while you 'snuggle' in bed.
- ☉ Take the time to notice how attractive and wonderful your partner is *out* of the bedroom. Make this attraction and appreciation known through physical affection or words.
- ☉ Remember why you fell in love. It's so easy to get caught up in the day to day and forget about why you were besotted in the first place.
- ☉ Remember that you're on the same team, instead of falling into the 'exhausted contest' with your partner about who's the most tired!
- ☉ Focus on making your partner's life easier and better instead of letting bitterness and resentment creep in.
- ☉ Sex or snuggle? The big S-E-X is a huge part of marriage. Avoid awkward conversations by agreeing beforehand whether sex is on tonight's agenda.
- ☉ Quality couple time. It's great to have fabulous family moments but make sure you arrange some quality couple time as well. Try having a 'walk away' night every few weeks where you literally 'walk away' from the dirty dishes and spend some quality time on the couch with a glass of wine, the TV off and some distraction-free conversation.
- ☉ Write an 'I love' list. Not only will this activity show you and your partner that you know what makes them happy, but it will remind you to include more of what each other loves to do into your lives.
- ☉ Share the domestic duties. The domestic grind can really wear a mother down. Conflict can arise if we mums feel like hubby isn't 'pulling his weight'. Let your partner know what 'domestic duties' you love and loathe and, most importantly, share the load!
- ☉ Know each other's 'love language': it makes it so much easier to understand your partner's actions.
- ☉ Invest in regular 'marriage maintenance'. It's important for the whole family, not just for you as a couple.

CHAPTER SIX

Changing friendships

Non-baby friends

Before I had children, I remember thinking it totally ridiculous when a girlfriend with two children under the age of 2 told me that she hardly ever managed to go to the loo by herself any more. How can she not go the loo? Surely she just closes the door and goes?

Another girlfriend said she never had time to do anything around the house. 'But what do you do all day?' I remember asking. I never understood what mothers at home actually did. I was under the preposterous illusion that babies slept all day, leaving mum to sit in front of daytime TV, drinking endless cups of tea with biscuits.

I suddenly recognised all the years I had been a terrible NBF (Non-Baby Friend) to all my MFs (Mummy Friends).

Ah, our NBFs. These are the people who turn up to view the new baby at completely inappropriate times of the day, with totally inappropriate gifts like a newborn outfit with domes up the back. They turn up or phone when you are in the middle of the bathing and bedtime routine and seem unfazed by the screaming child in the background as they describe their highly stressful day at work and how they need to go out to the local cool bar for a stiff pinot gris to recover. Meanwhile, you have a new baby perched on one boob, sucking you dry, and your toddler running around with no nappy on pulling out all the DVDs and CDs from their cases.

You still need to cook dinner for your toddler, cook and prepare dinner for you and your husband, bathe both your baby and toddler, give the baby one more feed, try to settle the baby while reading stories to your toddler and giving them their bottle of milk in tandem… while the NBF perches with a glass of wine nattering on about work, men, parties, fashion and everything else you are now so far removed from.

Let's not pretend that things don't change between friends when a baby is added to the mix.

Things do change. You often re-appreciate friends who had babies before you, and become drawn to people with babies at the same age and stage as you. It can feel like there's a growing void between you and your friends without kids.

The minute you have kids, all those stereotypical things that your Mummy Friends, siblings and parents have been saying for years start coming true. Nat remembers her sister saying things like 'I'm so busy ... it's 11 a.m. and I haven't had breakfast yet.' Simple pleasures like having an uninterrupted shower become pure bliss.

If you are a NBF, you probably don't have a clue about what a mum at home does all day. She doesn't go out for coffee or laze around the house watching *Oprah*, eating chocolate and reading magazines. You're not trying to be cruel, but you really don't get it. And we women at home feel resentful. Not only have we lost our identities and our freedom but we are now tied to this little bundle, unable to leave the house without it. Not for us those peaceful car journeys any more. It's no longer possible to watch the news quietly. Our lives have changed.

I was one of those women who didn't have a clue about children. In fact, prior to having my own children, I was probably the one who bought the baby-grow with the domes up the back.

I'll give you an example of how totally and utterly useless I was. I've already told you about my friend Sarah and my disastrous visit to see her first-born up in Yorkshire.

Well, fast-forward 17 months later. Sarah had just had her second child — a boy, Jack. Again I had popped up to Yorkshire to visit and to meet the new addition. I phoned her on a Saturday morning to invite her out for lunch that day.

'I can't, Jacqui,' she stated, 'the children sleep at lunchtime.'

'Well, can't they sleep at another time today?' I asked.

'It's their routine,' she stated. 'It would put everything out if they don't sleep at lunchtime. It's when they have their big sleep of the day.'

'Well, can they sleep in their pram?' I asked innocently.

Sarah sighed, clearly exasperated.

'OK, OK,' I said, getting the message. 'Well, shall I just pop over and see you at lunchtime when they're asleep?'

'No, that's when I sleep,' she said.

'You?' I was stunned. 'Why?'

'Why?' she repeated slowly. 'Well, probably because I only manage to get around four hours' sleep a night.'

'I thought babies slept all the time?' I said.

She laughed. 'Oh Jacqui, you can really tell you don't have children.'

I took this in good humour — everything I'd just heard was fast putting me off. And besides I just wanted to catch up with my friend. I really wasn't that bothered about anything else. 'When can we meet up then?' I asked. I was only there for a weekend. Looking back I realise how totally selfish I was being but to be completely honest, at the time I had no concept of Sarah's fraught and tiring world and how she had to schedule her whole day.

'They sleep until around 2 p.m. then I need to feed Jack and give Ellen her afternoon tea. I can meet you around 3 p.m. but I need to be home by 4.30 p.m. at the latest.'

'Why do you need to be home by 4.30 p.m.?' I asked, wondering if an hour and a half would be enough for a catch-up.

'I have to be home to feed Jack,' Sarah explained.

'But you just said you were feeding him at 2 p.m.?' I was now perplexed.

Sarah spoke slowly. 'He is a newborn, and I need to feed him every three hours.'

'OK, 3 p.m. it is, at Betty's.'

Betty's was our favourite tea haunt. It was an old-fashioned tea room in central Harrogate, Yorkshire, and served the most delicious, warm, buttery cinnamon toast with a pot of tea. Many Saturday and Sunday afternoons had been spent there together analysing the latest boyfriend.

This time Sarah hesitated. 'I don't have that long for Betty's,' she said, then relented. 'Oh OK.'

'Great! See you there.' I hung up before she could change her mind.

A few hours later I sat waiting for her at Betty's. It was 3.20 p.m. and there was still no sign of her. If she had to be home by 4.30 p.m. then she wasn't going to have much time at all. I tapped my feet impatiently and then I saw her. Harassed, pushing a big double pram and trying to squeeze it towards me, knocking people's elbows and legs as she passed by. One child was crying and the other one was trying to get down from the pram.

I stood up. Clearly Betty's was not a good idea. 'Erm, are you OK?' I asked.

'Ellen needs to go to the toilet,' she said, picking up the crying baby as Ellen hopped down from the pram and started dancing around. 'Can you take her?'

'What do I do?' I asked, worried. This was completely new territory for me.

'Oh never mind,' she snapped, thrusting baby Jack at me as she took Ellen by the hand and marched her to the toilet. Jack's crying reached a new level I never thought possible. I held him at arm's length, willing Sarah to return. Several minutes later she returned, scooping him from me and sitting herself down in the chair while signalling for a waitress.

'I'll have the pikelets, please, plus a plate of scrambled eggs, toast and bacon,' she ordered. 'I'm starving,' she announced to me, nodding at Jack. 'He just drains everything out of me. I find I'm eating constantly.'

'Right,' I nodded. 'Just cinnamon toast and tea, please, for me,' I ordered, not needing to look at the menu. 'So, how have you been?'

'Just peachy,' she replied sarcastically. 'Oh, let's see now, I spend my nights soothing and feeding, my nipples are bleeding, everything is aching and I just want to be able to wash my hair.'

Her hair was definitely looking ropey. 'Right,' I said again.

She sighed. 'Tell me about your life, Jacqui. It's got to be more exciting than mine.'

She wasn't wrong. My life was going swimmingly. Working for an advertising agency in London and engaged to a gorgeous New Zealand man, life was definitely looking rosy. My work life was going from strength to strength. Hubby and I ate out five nights out of seven, usually at the latest restaurant. We spent everything we earned but had a fabulous life.

I looked at her closely and knew that I had to be careful not to overdo it so I started telling her about our wedding plans. It wasn't an easy conversation. Every time I started a sentence, Ellen would interrupt to ask Sarah something trivial.

'Muuuummmmy, why's that man got something on his head? What's that lady doing? Who's that, Mummy? What they say, Mummy? Why they eating that, Mummy? Why? Why? *Why*?'

If Sarah tried to ignore her, Ellen's questioning would escalate into a louder, more intrusive question so it was much easier to just answer straight away. At the same time Sarah was standing up, rocking a crying Jack and trying to eat her meal. It was really very off-putting and I was quite relieved when she announced that she really had to go.

'I'll get it,' I offered. It was really the least I could do. 'Poor girl,' I thought to myself, swearing it would never ever happen to me...

Sarah's side of the story

Jacqui is my best friend. We grew up together, went to school together, went on holiday together and she was my bridesmaid when I got married.

When I had my first child, however, Jacqui was useless. We had always been so close and suddenly she seemed so far away.

By the time I'd had my third child, Jacqui was pregnant with her first. I was thrilled she was finally going to be in the same stage of life as me. I can never forget when she phoned long-distance to tell me her news.

'Sarah, please be honest with me, is having kids really all it's cut out to be?' she asked.

I had two children very close together, just 18 months apart, and to be honest I was the last person she should have been consulting. Jack, my second child, was still only 9 months old. He had been a particularly difficult baby. I had just moved house and my husband was working away from home five days a week, which meant Monday to Friday I felt like a single mum. I was going through one of the toughest periods in my life.

I tried to make my response to her question sound as positive as I could. 'Yes, of course it's great. It's the best thing that ever happened to me!' I lied.

What else could I say? I couldn't say, 'Don't go there, it's the hardest job that ever existed, it's physically and emotionally draining, you'll lose your life as you know it, you'll have no time for yourself any more, life as a couple will be over, you'll be constantly sleep deprived...'

No, of course not. I knew these feelings were momentary, brought on from exhaustion. I also wanted Jacqui to experience some of my life too, not so she would have a hard time, but so that our worlds wouldn't drift too far apart.

I now have four children and of course there are still plenty of hard days, but there are also many good days. If you were to ask me the same question again, I would reply as I did in 2003, but this time I would mean it, for it is true.

Having said that, Jacqui was a useless NBF, that's for sure. It was even more amusing when she finally had children herself. From being the person who was always firmly in control, always well turned out and taking pride in her organisation and appearance, my best friend turned into someone else overnight.

In 2007, I met up with Jacqui as she was in transit in Hong Kong airport. I had just moved to Hong Kong from Yorkshire with my husband and our three children, aged 6, 5 and 18 months. Not long after moving, Jacqui announced that she would be travelling to England to visit family and friends for the first time since having her first child, and would be transiting through Hong Kong on their return flight home.

So here I was, three children and a helper in tow, about to meet my best friend for the first time since she'd first announced her pregnancy.

Nothing could really have prepared me for the sight I was about to witness. My glamorous, high-flying, Mulberry-bag-swinging, manicured, dining and wining, socialite friend lumbered towards me. Instead of swinging the latest Mulberry bag, she was pushing the latest model pushchair. Her hair was lank from the stresses of the long journey, her nose was bright red, and she looked absolutely exhausted, stretched to the extreme. Her equally harassed, usually unflappable, husband at her side was trying hard to smile politely and look like he hadn't a care in the world, but was failing miserably. A red-faced, rather large baby thrashed in the pushchair, strapped in, screaming, tears and snot mingling and running steadily in a slow stream down his face. This must be Jack. (We both named our children Jack).

We greeted each other warmly with hugs and kisses and exchanged pleasantries. Meanwhile, little Jack, or rather not so little, was beside himself, distraught, angry, annoyed, wrestling with his straps, trying to escape his prison. 'Let's find somewhere for a drink and a bite to eat,' I urged, hoping this would help dispel some of the stress. 'How was the flight?'

'Awful. Jack has been a nightmare the whole journey, and he just needs to crawl around somewhere and let off steam. Can we go somewhere he can do that?' Jacqui asked almost tearfully.

The tables had indeed turned. In stark contrast to this poor creature facing me, I was tanned, relaxed, hair neatly tied back, fingers and toenails recently manicured. My petite 18-month-old sat serenely. My two older children stood calmly by my side, smiling sweetly. The all-important Filipino helper, an essential asset to any ex-pat mother in Hong Kong, was a quiet presence in the background.

We opted for a quiet Chinese restaurant. It was about 3 p.m. so they had finished lunch service and not yet started dinner and therefore we found ourselves a quiet little spot in which to relax and catch up.

I quickly ordered some rather lovely Chinese delicacies, dumplings, noodles, sticky ribs and jasmine tea. We positioned baby Jack and my youngest, Anna-Marie, next to each other in their prams and hoped they would keep each other entertained. Anna-Marie was quick to identify Jack as her peer and reached out to try to make friends. However, Jack was having none of it, and more yells and screams ensued.

His parents, clearly distressed, looked at each other for a solution. They searched through a bottomless bag of toys, and finally Jack was appeased with a toy train and a noisy, colourful rattle. A few minutes of calm followed and Jacqui was able to announce the great news that she was three months pregnant and they would soon be expecting their second child!

Differences between Baby Friends (BFs) and Non-Baby Friends (NBFs)

Baby Friends	Non-Baby Friends
They understand it will take you at least an hour to be able to leave the house to meet you for coffee. So, they will come to *you*.	They're free *now* for the next 10 minutes and expect you to leg it across town to meet them.
They give you nappies, hand-me-down clothes and useful presents.	They give you gorgeous but entirely inappropriate outfits with domes up the back.
They make and drop off meals.	They want to know if you fancy coming out for dinner Friday night with the girls to the latest restaurant.
They know and get what you 'do' all day.	They go on about how busy their day has been and how stressed they are.
They don't expect you to return calls, write thank-you cards or even to put your head above water.	They turn up at your doorstep between 5 and 7 p.m. when everything is going pear-shaped, help themselves to your wine, want to know why you haven't returned their 15 messages as they've been dying to talk to you about what your old boss has gone and done now…and did you get the card and flowers they sent as they haven't received a thank-you card?
You don't need to explain anything. They just know.	You can't explain anything. They're just not interested.

I'm sure there are some really wonderful NBFs around, as well as friends who are dying to become Mummy Friends but haven't managed to get there for one reason or another.

Nat was one of those NBFs who really got it. Here she talks about her own experience as a NBF.

Nat's NBF experience

Matt and I were pretty awesome NBFs, if I do say so myself. We had lots of friends and siblings who 'paved the way' and it just seemed natural to us to enjoy their children and to 'help' them as parents where we could. My friend Wendy had a 2-year-old and was keen to enter a women's team adventure race, so we looked after her daughter Khyla for the weekend. Other friends were going camping with their kids that weekend so we went along too with our temporary 2-year-old. We had a great time! We also offered to babysit for other friends with kids as it was no drama for us both to go and watch TV at their place while they had some coveted 'couple time'. We must have had a sixth sense about parenting as I would *love* for someone to spontaneously offer to babysit for us these days!

That being said, I do vividly remember Wendy putting me on the phone with Khyla *every time* I called her, or having to wait while she responded to a question or got Khyla something she needed. 'I can call back later,' I would say, thinking impatiently 'if you're that busy just call me when it suits.' Little did I know that it never really suits.

What NBFs *really* think

Before having children, I remember getting very annoyed with mums pushing buggies into cafes and shops. The buggies would knock the back of my legs or scrape or catch my tights. I use to think how selfish they were; couldn't they just leave their buggies outside or eat at one of the outside tables? Now I recognise how frustrating it is trying to push a buggy through a crowded room, especially when nobody moves out of your way. I used to get so annoyed if they didn't move, after asking politely for people to 'excuse me, please'. I would just jam the pram through the small gap, not caring whose knees I knocked in the process.

To be fair, I think as mums we do try to justify how hard we work, even though we are at home. We probably do go on a bit about what we do all day and how busy we are, as we are desperate for what we do to be acknowledged. We want our NBFs to know and understand how hard it is and so, without realising it, we probably portray ourselves as martyrs. It is good to understand how we come across to our NBFs so we can be more considerate in the future. So sit yourself down and prepare for a reality check about what NBFs really think:

'The childbirth details are boring (and makes me cross my legs), breastfeeding sounds awful, the sleep patterns of the baby are boring and then everything revolves around feeding, burping and sleeping, the loss of sleep for Mum sounds like torture, the solids and food stages are boring, and the high maintenance of a baby totally dependent on you would have me running for the hills. My pet hate is when you are on the phone and are constantly been asked to 'hang on' while the child interrupts Mum.'

Julie, Auckland

'The most annoying thing is trying to catch up with "Mummy Friends" on the phone and constantly being told to "hang on", especially when I'm ringing on my mobile. And then, after "hanging on" for minutes at a time, getting a full run-down on why I had to "hang on". I don't care that little Johnny just tipped his bowl of Rice Bubbles all over the cat. The same applies when you're visiting MFs' houses and you really want a proper girlie catch-up — too many interruptions and incessant noise. And don't even think about bringing your children to my house. I am not, and never will be, childproof, and I don't care if Emma prefers to eat her mushed-up veges directly off the dining table while wandering around — put the bloody food on a plate and sit down!

'I now opt to meet MFs on neutral territory only. Even then, the first 10 minutes of these wine-bar meetings consist of hearing all about how great it is for the MF to have actually escaped from the house, how long it's been since she had five minutes to herself and how she was going to wear her new top, but the baby threw up on it just before she left the house and sorry, that's why she's so late.

'Then there's the "judging". Please don't feel sorry for me — I have chosen not to have children — I don't want any. Really. Please don't look at me with that I-know-you're-just-saying-that-but-gosh-your-life-must-be-so-empty-and-what-are-you-going-to-do-when-you-get-old? sympathetic stare . . . you know the one, with the head slightly tilted to one side and the concerned little frown/half smile . . . and then comes the pat on the knee, or the stroke on the arm. Seriously?

'The whole process of childbirth turns my stomach. I don't want to know the details. I prefer to keep my private bits for fun, not for function. I can't even imagine the horrors of the episiotomy and the chapped nipples. I think I just threw up a little bit in my mouth.

'I need my sleep. And I don't need anyone interrupting it, unless they're popping a bottle of champagne and handing me two plane tickets to a tropical paradise on the way out to the taxi which will take us to the airport. How on earth do you go on holiday with children? Actually, don't tell me, I don't want to know!

'I am selfish. I don't want to put someone else's needs before my own. Especially when their needs more often than not involve involuntary bodily functions.

'And, no, I don't want to see the video on your iPhone of little Carly saying "poo".'

Sam, Auckland

'My rather harsh comment is "It's not a miracle birth — other people have children too." I find it so annoying, all the cooing, the kit parents haul with them, the fact that they want the world to move around them.

'I often think that it would be nice to have some reciprocal arrangement in place for an element of flexible leave for those without kids. It's also annoying when parents go on about the routine, cost and stress of it all. If you didn't take that into consideration, should you have had kids?'

Melisa, England

'To quote Homer Simpson: "It's not that I don't care, it's just that I am not interested". What about children who are place-friendly rather than finding child-friendly places to meet up? And don't get me started on mother-baby parking zones in supermarkets!'

Craig, England

As new parents, we also make quite a few mistakes as friends. Let's face it, we are the ones who have changed. Our old friends are the same. It's good to keep this in mind when chatting with NBFs, describing our labour or showing off baby pics. It's easy to forget that those without young ones may feel awkward, irritated or offended by things we consider adorable. Here are a few:

Things that are awkward or annoying for NBFs

- nudey rudey
- food face is neither cute nor clever
- talking to kids while you're on the phone (just call them back when your child is quiet)
- don't immediately thrust your baby on friends or visiting family
- poos and wees — spare the graphic details
- labour experience — spare the graphic details (and the photos)
- snotty noses are never appealing
- eating leftovers off your child's plate is not a good look

How to be a better friend to NBFs (by Melisa, an NBF)

- Be proactive planning a catch-up. NBFs aren't sure when to ask to meet up. We fear we are guilt-tripping those with babies by asking to go out.
- Don't go into gory detail about the colour of your baby's poo or the strength or otherwise of your pelvic floor muscles!
- Agree in advance that you will talk about other stuff or plan a gathering where there is an activity (the races, a spa) rather than just chatting over a coffee.
- Leave the child with Dad or someone else! The baby doesn't always have to be attached to Mum's hip. I get the impression from a lot of mums that they somehow like being a bit of a martyr.
- Enough of the physical guilt trips! I often hear 'You are so fit, Mel, but then again you haven't had kids.'
- Accept your body's changes. Lots of mums become obsessive about getting back to how they were before baby, and seem to take it to extremes.
- Often NBFs seem to be excluded from certain social groups. Not all people without children have tried to have them and failed. Some, like me, have chosen not to have them, and don't need to be 'protected' from social occasions with children.

The high-school factor

 Motherhood sometimes feels like returning to high school. You find yourself asking your friends for advice. You question your decisions, compare yourself to others and are bombarded by well-intentioned friends and strangers. Suddenly you're ringing your own mother in tears because you don't know what you're doing or you want to suddenly tell her that you love her (or in other cases to give you your space).

Meeting new mummy friends is almost like dating again. You meet other mothers at playgroups, music class, during the frantic drop-off and pick-up times for kindy or school. Some mothers you click with, and you'd like to get together with the kids sometime. Some mothers have no qualms about chatting to others and suggesting this while others may wish it but never act on it. I am by nature a very social person and I enjoy introducing like-minded people to one another. If I meet a mother who I click with I'll happily suggest we get together for a playdate. But what do you do when your effort feels unreciprocated?

 I was surprised by how 'high school' the world of parenthood can feel. This time, however, it's other mothers rather than pubescent boys that you're dithering over whether to call or wait for them to make the first move. You're wondering 'Does she like me? Should I text her again or just let it go?' Is it just that some people are initiators and others are not or should I casually let those who haven't made an effort or returned my calls slip off my radar? Once I decided that I wasn't calling anyone for a whole week; I would only make plans with people who contacted *me*. Ironically the invites started coming in.

Perhaps I'm hyper-sensitive after an out-of-the-blue and full-on phone call that I received from a friend highlighted to me how one person's interpretation of a situation can be so different to another's. One person can be mortally offended yet the other may have absolutely no idea.

Here's the story: Claire moved back to New Zealand with her husband and baby after a stint in the UK. I knew her from college and being the friendly networker that I am, I took it upon myself to make an effort and introduce her to some other mums. I babysat for her while she went for a run, we went round to their place for curry one night, all was well. She invited us to her baby's naming day ceremony and while I initially wrote back with an enthusiastic 'yes' RSVP email, I later followed it up with 'we will likely not make it to the beach ceremony but we will be at the after party at your house'. The day came and went and our baby Ruby had an extra-long nap and my husband wasn't feeling well so we didn't end up going — at all. I know ... I 'should have' gone to the after party. But you know what it's like with a newborn ...

Fast forward six months. Claire calls me on the phone and in a calm but intense tone says, 'I was so embarrassed when you didn't turn up to Sienna's naming-day ceremony. I know you have fleeting friendships here and there but I only have a few friends and I treat them right. You didn't turn up and I made them wait because I thought you would come. I have never felt so embarrassed. I don't think we can be friends any more.' I was stunned! My initial thought was 'Oh my gosh, are you breaking up with me? No one has broken up with me since Mark Lewis in Grade 10!' But then I collected myself and said with a shaky voice, 'I am so sorry. I didn't realise that it was such a big event. It's hard to remember as it was six months ago but I think I sent an email saying we wouldn't be at the beach. Wow, why didn't you tell me about this sooner?'

The conversation went on for a while but she had processed the situation and had obviously made up her mind. We were officially no longer friends. I called a mutual friend for advice as to whether I should try to make it up to her or did she think Claire genuinely did not want to be friends and I should just let it go. 'Claire's stubborn and very hurt,' she advised, 'just let it go.' So I did.

I called Claire when her second child was born — a boy, like mine, but the conversation hit a brick wall. I invited her to be my friend on Facebook but to no avail. Now, five years later, I still think about that phone call. I still find it strange that she never phoned me the day after to find out why I didn't come. To enquire whether maybe there was something wrong and see if everything was OK. Ruby or I could have been ill. I could have been having a horrible time and needed help for a change.

Just like at work or with extended family, some people you will 'click with' and others ... not so much. But what do you do when a mummy friendship goes from awesome to awkward? When someone who was previously your friend suddenly stops calling or starts acting funny when you meet up? This awkwardness may be brought on by something you know about — perhaps one of your children did something to cause some upset or maybe one of the mums did. Hopefully you can address it and move on.

But what if there was no 'event'? No uncalled-for outburst, no conflicting parenting philosophies? How do you respond? Do you enquire casually while watching the kids in the playground? Do you ignore it and pretend all is normal? Or do you move on and spend your time and energy on friends who 'give back'?

A friend, Sandra, commented to me that one of her friends, Lucy, started giving her the cold shoulder and it was weird between them for a while. Two months later she discovered that Lucy's sister had been terribly ill and it had nothing to do with Sandra at all! Sometimes you can be totally off the mark with these things. Don't assume it's you when really it's a turn of events in their life and they need you as a friend more than ever.

But what if it is you?

 After receiving a few curt texts from someone who I'd considered a friend, I sent her an email and asked her what was up. Perhaps my mistake was using the term 'I appreciate your honesty' in my message because she really let rip! There was no padding, no fluff, no 'I know you have the best intentions' or 'it's great that you want to help people'. It was all instead about how I was too full on and exhausting as a friend as well as comments about my son's personality and how she was 'surprised that I was surprised to hear this'. I did appreciate her honesty but there is a difference between being upfront and being hurtful.

How do you move on from that? It's fine if the family lives on the other side of town so you don't see them much or if the kids have also outgrown each other but what if they haven't? What if the awkwardness waits for you at the school gates on a daily basis? The kids are in the same class or do ballet together? You scan the schoolyard as you near the door hoping you've staggered your timing enough to miss crossing paths. They ignore you or give a wide-eyed over-enthusiastic 'hello' followed by silence. What if your child constantly pleads for you to arrange play-dates with child of said awkward mum? Do you cringe, set your humility aside and make the call? Or do you make up some excuse about them being busy and suggest another friend instead?

These are the trials and tribulations of parenthood.

If you do have 'awkwardness' with another parent there are generally three paths to go down:

1. **Let it go.**
   If it's not really affecting you or your child then you can just let it go and focus your friendship on friends who give back to you.

2. **Say something and address it.**
   Talk in person or on the phone (but not in an email or text, unless it's to arrange meeting for a drink or a get-together without the kids) and ask them about it. Often it's tricky to have personal conversations with the kids around. This will

hopefully clear the air but if they didn't realise anything was wrong it could make things more uncomfortable.

3. **Say nothing and live with it.**
   Be aware that it may magnify and you might one day 'burst out' and say something you didn't mean to.

 Mummy/Mommy Friends: ifonlytheytoldme.com/28

It can be a bit of a minefield out there with all of the communication, miscommunication and potential awkwardness that comes with friendships once you have a family. When you have a baby you often spend time with your own friends but when your baby grows older you start to become friends with their friends' parents and that's when it can get interesting. Different personality types and parenting styles may mean that even though little Chloe and Sophie may be best buddies, their mums Rachel and Bec might not see eye to eye.

> 'I have made a lot of new friends through pregnancy and birth: at preggy yoga, mums 'n' bubs Swiss ball class, antenatal, Plunket and now (horror of horrors) an older mothers group (OMG!). They are a diverse mix of people that I would never have met otherwise, but we all have the wee bubs in common.
>
> 'It has been easy to make all these new friends. I think all us new mums must be open-minded to new friendships with women going through similar experiences to our own so that we can feel supported and know that we are not alone. It's important to hear that we are not bad mothers for doing xyz and yes, that is normal behaviour for a six-week-old. Another thing I noticed is that we are sharing quite intimate details with women that were total strangers until very recently.
>
> 'Existing friendships have lapsed somewhat unless said friends also happen to be new mums or expecting, as the battle for time management and squeezing time out of a not-so-juicy orange (as one new friend put it) takes its toll and we have to prioritise who we share our time with. Email and social media are fantastic as we can communicate in those rare five

minutes that we get when bub is napping and the chores are done, or Daddy is having some quality playtime, when it suits both parties with differing windows of opportunity, i.e. time to write or read rather than chat when one or other baby is screaming!'

Sarah, Auckland, one daughter aged 4 months

I had a great friend, Theresa, for years. When we both became pregnant at the same time we were thrilled. We went through pregnancy together and when we had our babies just a few weeks apart we would do everything together. We were excited about our children growing up together and planned their futures together. They would be best friends for life, we declared!

Unfortunately 18 months later it became apparent we wouldn't. It wasn't that the children didn't get on — far from it. It was that in becoming mummies, we had changed in different ways. Our parenting styles were very different. Our philosophies about what was important for our children and families were different and things started to become tense. When Theresa called me one day to tell me that I needed to change the way I parented, it was the final straw.

I cried for days afterwards, truly believing I was a bad mother. But I later came to realise that I was just a *different* mother to her. Whereas she would happily stay at home all day with the children, I couldn't bear to be stuck inside and would be off for walks and to the park or visiting friends or nana with the children in tow. In her eyes, I did too much. In my eyes, she did too little. She felt I didn't control my children. I felt she was too strict. Rather than thinking about why I always needed to get out of the house (I wasn't coping and couldn't bear to be by myself with the children), she assumed that I was being a bad parent.

What had once been a wonderful friendship began to shift like sand between my fingers. Although we are still friendly and we never actually went as far as falling out, our priorities and different styles drove a wedge between us and although we do still see each other, our friendship definitely changed since becoming parents.

On the other hand, another good friend who also had a child close in age to me has become a better and closer friend through us having children so close together. We both struggled, particularly when our second children came along so soon after our first children. We were able to struggle together. We would take it in turns to go to each other's houses and spend the day there as we couldn't bear to be by ourselves with the children. (I later learned we were both likely suffering from post-natal depression. If you're in this situation, see a doctor.)

We would cry on each other's shoulders, but at the same time we supported each other. One could leave all four children with the other and go and get some milk and other supplies (mind you, the one who was left behind with four babies would be literally counting the minutes until the other returned). We would drop our children at the other one's house for baths and stories so we could take it in turn to get our hair cut. We suffered together and got through it together and, as a result, we have an incredibly close friendship today.

Even though this dear friend has moved totally away from my own circle — she is now fully immersed in her local Steiner school and completely follows their philosophy with wooden toys, no television, home-grown cuisine and hand-knitted clothes, while I am Mrs Traditional all the way — we love and respect each other's differences and love spending time together and also bringing the children together. The children also still get on, despite the fact that they are being raised so differently. It is probably due to a deep bond between us. We will be there for each other even when we haven't set eyes on each other for months.

Playground Mummy Mafia

Just because you're all 'mummies' together in the playground, it doesn't mean you are necessarily going to be friends. Some women can be notoriously catty and being a mum isn't going to change that — it just gives them different things to be mean about.

There are a number of 'types' of mummy around and very quickly you learn to fall in with the group you feel most comfortable with. It's just like being at school again yourself!

For instance, there's the mummy 'in' crowd — I call them the Playground Mummy Mafia. They are glamorous, while the rest of us are frazzled. They are the ones who arrive at the kindergarten calm and collected, sporting Versace sunnies, driving large black trucks, baby accessory on one hip, Prada handbag flopped over an arm, while the rest of us race in late, hair stuck to our heads, mascara smudged under our eyes, wet patches from breastfeeding on our T-shirts.

Quite frankly, I don't mind these people — I just don't know how they do it. For some reason I am always running late, which means that no matter how neat and tidy my children and I are when we leave the house, by the time we arrive at kindy or school we are a mess.

Then, of course, you have the Mummy Do-Gooder. You know the type. She is on every committee going, including secretary for the PTA, relentlessly baking cakes for fundraisers, giving up her weekends to shake tins at shoppers or do working bees at the local kindy, school or old people's home. She's always on the look-out for new recruits to join her circle. Her children seem to always win the 'star tidy-upper of the day' badge and she is always volunteering to help the teachers.

Then there's the Sporty Mum. These mums turn up at school every day in their gym gear and are always off running with the pram or dropping the younger sibling in crèche so they can go and pump iron at the gym.

Don't forget Super Mum. She works part time, and yet somehow runs the home and family without batting an eyelid. Her work is under control, her children are happy and content, freshly packed lunches include home-baked muffins. Her iPhone is always beeping and she uses it to know exactly where she has to be and when. She doesn't miss a school sports day and homework is always in on time and in order.

Finally there is Pushy Mum. You know the type. She was the one at antenatal class who played classical music to her stomach. When baby was 6 months old, she tried to get him to walk. Now her child is older, she is convinced that he is a genius and the poor wee thing is enrolled at every activity going — he's only 5 years old but is currently going to piano, judo, soccer, tennis, French lessons and hip hop. Her conversation tends to focus solely on her children. She lives her life through them and her interests are their interests, her friends are her children's friends' mothers.

Whatever category of mummy you fall into, you will eventually find your own group of mummy friends, even if it is a bit of a stumble in the beginning.

A friend of mine recently arrived from the UK and started her children at a local private kindergarten, and was astonished that nobody took the time to talk to her. She had hoped she would soon meet lots of other mums through her children and playdates but she was left out of the clique of the Mummy Playground.

The other mummies used playdates as a way of networking among their peers and, as she didn't fit into the right category, her daughter was never invited over for a play.

She's not alone. Other mums have been ignored — just completely left out of the playground chatter — just because they haven't been to the right school or are not dressed correctly. It may be hurtful but it can hopefully be put to one side, unless of course it extends to how your child is treated. In that case, take action. If you or your child are finding playground politics have gone too far, then make sure you talk to the teacher immediately. The sooner this sort of bullying can be nipped in the bud, the better.

In my own experience, I picked up the importance of the different 'mummy types' early on. When Jack was younger, I had him enrolled in a local private kindergarten that had been recommended by a friend. I didn't realise that it was the most expensive kindergarten in Auckland at the time. All I knew was it was much cleaner and nicer than the other kindies I had visited. Initially I would turn up to drop Jack off in my oldest clothes with my newborn baby in her capsule. Sometimes I hadn't even showered. It took me just one week to recognise that every other mother at the kindergarten was dressed like they had just walked out of Karen Walker. Most of them were blonde. Pretty much all of them drove Range Rovers (parking was a complete nightmare with my Mitsubishi!) and they had all been to private schools together. I realised that I had to start getting dressed up to go to kindergarten! Crazy! And still no one spoke to me.

I took Jack out after less than a year and enrolled him at the local public kindergarten. It wasn't full of new toys and it certainly wasn't as clean or as well kept as the private one but it was friendly and encouraging and I soon made friends with the other mums. Mind you, I hardly ever pick up my children wearing my old clothes any more!

Coffee groups

 Once you have a baby you are suddenly thrust into a network of other mothers with whom you might actually have absolutely nothing in common. Your coffee group is an example of this — you might strike gold or you might attend countless get-togethers and wonder how you can extract yourself. Just because you're all mums doesn't mean you need to be friends.

My own coffee group was made up of a lovely group of girls with whom I had absolutely no common ground, save for babies born a few weeks apart. However, they were so caring and helpful to one another it made everything else irrelevant. When one of the girls suffered from post-natal depression with both her babies, the group rallied around her and her family, putting together meal schedules, taking it in turns to supermarket shop for her, picking up the older child and taking him on playdates as mum literally couldn't get out of bed. And likewise, when I had health issues which involved a minor operation, they looked after my youngest for me, dropped meals in and generally made me feel loved. How can you beat a support system like that?

Funnily enough, I nearly dropped out of the group before it even really got going. I had been put off after going to the very first coffee group, after our antenatal class had finished. The lady who hosted it had had her baby just a few days earlier. Then she invited us strangers around to meet the baby and for coffee. None of us had had our babies at that time so we all assumed it was perfectly normal to have a baby and then invite people over to view them. Her house was pristine and her home baking sat on the table beside us. Her baby was perfect and cooed quietly in the corner. I was excited, looking forward to hosting my own coffee group when my baby arrived, believing it would be as serene and calm as this one was.

Of course it was a complete disaster. After I had my baby, I could hardly find the time or energy to clean myself up, let alone the house. And I certainly hadn't time to do baking as I was barely able to shovel enough food in my mouth to produce milk. I refused to go to the first few gatherings, ignoring emails and phone calls, feeling overwhelmed. The girls didn't give up and with reluctance I finally offered my own home reasoning that surely it was easier to have people come to me as opposed to having to get myself together enough to leave the house.

I assumed that my coffee group meeting had to be like first one and so I scrubbed and cleaned and baked until I could barely stand. When the girls came over I was so exhausted I could hardly make tea and after they left I collapsed into tears feeling it was all too hard.

I later realised that the first hostess was actually superwoman (although a very nice one!), and none of the others could be as natural a hostess as she was. When I started going to the other mums' places, I was thrilled to see messy houses, unwashed dishes and unmade beds, dishevelled-looking mums and Homebrand shortbread, and realised that it was OK and that nobody gave a monkey's anyway.

Meeting other mums with children the same age as you, and who live in your neighbourhood, is crucial to helping you get through that first year. If you live close to each other then you are more likely to see each other as your 'windows of opportunity' are so small between naps and feeds. If you are within walking distance from each other it is even better as you will be able to wheel the pram over to each other's houses and later on, as the kids get older, you'll be able to take it in turns to do kindy and school drop-offs.

Join the local playgroup, your local Plunket group, baby gymnastics or even go to the local park. These are all good ways to meet other mums who live within your community, and who will make your life easier and more enjoyable. I was lucky enough to have a very good friend who moved one street away from me. We did everything together and would often 'camp out' at each other's houses for the day. We would look after each other's babies while the other did her shopping or other appointments. We completely looked out for each other.

I also met some girls through the local Plunket fundraiser, knocking on doors

153

to ask for donations. They had children roughly the same age as mine and as our paths crossed several times at toy libraries, playgroups and Plunket volunteering, we decided to get together for coffee one day. We now have become firm friends and coffee on a Monday morning has turned into wine on a Friday afternoon. We reasoned that our husbands had a drinks trolley at their workplaces every Friday afternoon. The home was our workplace and we would do the same. And so our wine group was born. We would take it in turns to wheel our babies (who were no longer being breastfed, in case anyone decides to throw up their arms in horror) in their prams to each other's houses — we were only a few houses apart from each other — and sip Chardonnay and munch cheese and crackers while our babies rolled around quite happily on the floor. When we started wine group there were only four of us, each with one baby. Now there are eight of us in the group and between us are 18 children. Phew! The Chardonnay is no longer as relaxing now, but we still do get together, at the park or the zoo or at some brave mum's house. And our friendship has developed outside of the children — we have been on cocktail-making and cupcake-making courses, out for dinners with our partners, pot-luck dinners without partners and, despite the fact that many of us have moved away from the original street where we all met, we are all still a great support to each other.

Putting yourself out there

 You definitely have to 'put yourself out there' when you're in a new social group and you don't know anyone. I went to preggie yoga when I was pregnant with my second child. I remember hearing some of the mums that were already friends planning to go for a coffee and hoping that they would invite me — so high school! I was walking out behind them and an inclusive mum invited me to join them. Now four years later we are still fabulous friends!

I met two of my best friends at antenatal class and I loved my coffee groups. I met a great group of 10 mums who I'm still friends with six years later. Unfortunately due to the massive earthquake in Christchurch we ended up moving cities so I essentially had to 'start again'. New neighbourhood, new friends, new life.

Kids are a great conversation starter so a little bit of effort can break the ice. It doesn't take long. I was lucky when Ruby started kindergarten as I became friends with three mums who had three kids the exact same age as mine: 4, 2 and a baby. It was so wonderful to be able to help each other out, whether it be sleeping advice or kindy pick-up. Mary and I lived around the corner from each other so each morning we would just text each other to see whose baby was sleeping and decide who would do the kindy drop.

When Ruby started school and Jonah started kindy there was a whole new dynamic and a whole new group of people to meet. Not only are friendships valuable for helping each other out and helping the children to settle at school but also for a bit of 'mummy time'. We have a 'Stitch 'n' Bitch' group that I started up a year ago. It's made up of kindy and school mums who meet on a Wednesday night every two weeks. We have a wine or coffee and a dessert of some sort. We bring along anything 'crafty' that we've been meaning to do at home but never seem to find the time for. We take turns hosting and it is so much fun! It's just so nice to have a bit of child-free time! Once every few months we will have a special 'theme night'. We've had a 'clothing swap' where we each bring along three quality items and lay them out in the host's living room. Then we 'browse' and are allowed to select three items to try. It was like we were teenagers again! Six mums in my bedroom stripping off tops, trying on outfits and tossing them to one another if they didn't get the sisterly approval. Then we did a bit of a fashion show and gave tribute to the previous owner: 'This is from the Tanya Evans collection.' We've since followed this up with an 'accessories swap', a 'kids' stuff swap' and a 'style night' where we got a personal stylist to enlighten us about the colours and styles that suit us best! S'n'B, as we like to call it, has become such a hit that the dads have recently started up an Ales 'n' Tales group. They meet once a month and alternate between the local pub and taking turns hosting. Brilliant!

IOTTM top tips for making new mummy friends

- ☺ Start your own Stitch 'n' Bitch group — simply send on an invite to like-minded mums who live close by and take it in turns to host each other for coffee/wine, some craft and a chat.
- ☺ Likewise, if Stitch 'n' Bitch ain't your thing, try a book club, supper club, pot-luck dinner night, wine group or some other regular group gathering.
- ☺ Join local music groups or playgroups with your children — not only will your children get a fun outing with other kids but you get to have coffee and a chat with other mums too.
- ☺ Become a member of the local Plunket, NCT or parenting centre group and help out at fundraising events by shaking tins in shopping centres, baking cakes or manning stalls at garage sales.
- ☺ If your child is old enough, join a local kindergarten and, if you have the energy, make yourself known to the committee. These are usually the mums

who know everything about the local area and will be able to introduce you to other mums. (Our kindergarten used to host a new parent coffee afternoon every term, which was a great way to meet the other mums.)

⊙ Find out when the local library holds their weekly story time. The library is a great place to meet other parents.

⊙ Parks are a great meeting place. Bite the bullet, smile and make conversation with another mum. Sometimes that's all that is needed.

CHAPTER SEVEN

What about you?

You time

You know you need a bit of 'you time' or 'time out' when:
- ⊙ you finish vacuuming and declare 'the end'
- ⊙ you come out of a doctor's appointment and say to the receptionist in a proud cheery voice, 'all done'.

> 'I used to be very good at looking after myself before I had kids. Now I am at the bottom of the list. This is somewhat upsetting. Every day I think about it and try to work on it. I go to yoga, for a run, meet a friend for lunch, or stay at a hotel on my own overnight. It just doesn't seem to be enough somehow. I hate that feeling. I tell myself that there will be a time when it will be all about me again, but the boys need me now.'
>
> **Daria, Toronto, three sons aged 4, 7 and 9 years**

Before having children, did you believe that things wouldn't change? That you would hang on to your old life? That your child would fit in with you, accompanying you to dinners out, movies, visits to friends? How's it going so far, huh?

If you are anything like most of us, you will have now realised that you had been living in Dreamland, that reality is not quite living up to your expectations.

When your baby is young, you are probably feeling pretty tired. You may not have had that much sleep since the arrival of your prince or princess. You may have tried to squeeze in the odd social outing here and there but reality is that you haven't had any time to yourself since his or her arrival (unless you count nipping to the supermarket while someone looks after your angel for 10 minutes). And as for one-on-one time with your husband or spouse — it feels like a thing of the past. You did have intentions to make a date night but on the night in question you were so exhausted that you cancelled your babysitter and just hit the sack. To sleep.

The problem is that mums aren't great at taking time out. As mums we are constantly asking the kids and our husband to do things for us. 'Sweetheart, please bring your bowl across from the table', 'Honey, can you please get some milk on your way home from work?' and so on.

It's a strange balance, making sure everyone is contributing and feeling cared for. Sometimes it's not so much 'time out' that we mothers desire, but for him to have more 'time in'. This would help you to feel appreciated and, if you're anything like me, to curb your growing resentment about being 'on duty' all the time.

Prior to having children you have no concept of the preciousness of your time. You waste it, fritter it away on nothing. Suddenly you have a child and your time is gone.

What about you?

A video produced by a US maternity bra company, Nummies Nursing Bras, featured advice, tips and reflections from mums around the world. This is what they shared about things they wish they'd known earlier:

- ⊙ you are beautiful
- ⊙ meet other mums
- ⊙ it's OK to be scared
- ⊙ it's OK to want a break
- ⊙ your mum was right
- ⊙ you will miss your mum
- ⊙ she will have your eyes
- ⊙ you will make mistakes
- ⊙ forgive yourself
- ⊙ no one knows what they're doing
- ⊙ you're the expert
- ⊙ this will pass
- ⊙ Google doesn't have children
- ⊙ take time for yourself
- ⊙ take time to fall in love with yourself and your body
- ⊙ let Grandma spoil him
- ⊙ be brave

- ☉ sleep *now*
- ☉ imperfect is the new perfect
- ☉ trust your instincts
- ☉ breathe.

We asked parents how becoming a parent has affected them as a person. Here are a selection of their thoughts:

'It brings out the best and worst in me. On a good day I am an amazing project manager and creative genius with the patience of a saint. On a bad day I am a short-tempered, unsympathetic and hypocritical menial worker!'

Rebecca, Christchurch, one daughter aged 4 years

'I think I instantly became more mature. Although I have found parenting easy and enjoyable I have found other areas of my life harder to deal with, e.g. maintaining relationships and finding the motivation to work from home. I think I have become less tolerant of things I may have tolerated before I had a baby. In the beginning I felt a little invisible — people only see your baby and forget about you. I have also found that some people have forgotten the type of person I was before and treat me differently. Suddenly people only ask you questions about children and babies and you wonder why they can't just talk to you like they used to. So it's not so much that I've changed, it's more that people treat me differently and their attitude towards me has changed.'

Lauren, Wellington, girl aged 1 year

'I am learning to put myself and my child first. I used to make sure everyone else had things their way, or they were happy, before thinking about my own happiness. I am learning to prioritise. I am learning to be more assertive, to make sure I take care of the needs of my family.'

Ruth, Christchurch, daughter aged 10 months

'I have become more introverted. I find myself less social, with energy going into looking after my child. I find I'd rather spend time doing my own thing.'

Rob, Christchurch, daughter aged 3 years

Sometimes it can be hard to make the time for yourself. Like anything, only you can make it happen. If you have nearby family support then it is easier of course — although you still need to learn to let go and let someone else look after baby while you enjoy a bit of 'you' time.

For those without family support it is even more important to make that effort. Although 'time for you' often falls in the too hard basket, you are the only person who can change that. Start by telling your husband that it is important that you have a 'you date' once a week. Perhaps you might have your nails done weekly, or maybe it's a long run or walk, or joining a Pilates class, mooching around the shops, or even going to the library by yourself and browsing.

Don't you just love that word 'browsing'? How often do you get to 'browse' now that you're a mum? Not a lot, I expect, so make the time.

You can also do 'swapsies' with friends. I have a girlfriend with two children similar ages to mine and we have often taken it in turns to have both lots of children for a morning while the other goes off to do whatever she wants to do. It works for everyone. The children are happy as they have playmates and we are happy as we have breaks!

You might also have neighbours with teenagers living in the street who want to earn a little pocket money for a couple of hours looking after your children. Or, the shopping centre crèche is a great option. One of my girlfriends books her children into a crèche every Monday morning and has a coffee and gets her nails done. Every Monday without fail. Everyone who knows her knows that this is her date with herself and she is out of bounds on Mondays.

Until my self-imposed writing retreat my book was an exciting yet distant dream; a drawer full of scribbled notes (plus about 10 pages on the computer). After all, as a mother there's always something else on our eternal 'to do' list and we're experts at looking after others before ourselves. Putting peppermint foot-cream on our feet once every few months feels like luxury. We are so much better for it (and nicer to our husbands) when we do 'something for ourselves'. We need to incorporate it into our week and write it down in our calendar! For some this may be tag-teaming with hubby and heading out the door when he gets home at 6 p.m. to run or meet a friend for a drink/movie/late-night shopping. For others a weekly Pilates class or working on another goal or hobby does the trick. Although it's not entirely for 'me', I found relaxing on the couch and updating my kids' journals to be a therapeutic and creatively fulfilling time out.

Why is it that I can't seem to go to bed before 10 p.m.? Knowledge and experience go hand in hand and tell me that I need to. But when the kids are in bed I switch into slow mode. I'll wash my face without a child clinging to my leg or have a shower without making baby talk.

Hubby has a way of diffusing my frustration. At various stress-provoking points of the day I think to myself, 'the minute he gets home I'm going to take some time out!' (go for a walk, clean our room etc. ...) but then he gets home and responds so genuinely to my daughter's detailed yet slightly indecipherable overview of the day I don't want to miss out.

It's a dichotomy. When you're with the kids you crave a bit of time to yourself now and then (oh, to go to the toilet in peace) and when you're without them you wonder what they're up to and if they're OK (or if the person caring for them is OK). Like relishing your freedom when you go to the grocery store without the kids, but then you smile at another mother and baby and fight off the desire to tell her that 'I'm a mum too'. You force yourself not to baby-talk to her kids as you suddenly start missing yours.

> 'We have loads of family time and I get to spend lots of time with my kids, being a stay-at-home mum. I would like to have more quiet time with my husband so we could actually have a conversation. I would love to have some 'me' time. I would love to go shopping on my own.'
>
> **Anon, Terrigal, one son aged 6 years, one daughter aged 18 months**

Do something for you!

 After eight years as a give-it-all-you've-got stay-at-home mother, having had four kids by the time she was 30, my sister took up running again. She'd been a talented runner in her university years but since then had traded in her track spikes for sensible shoes and strollers. Now she's looking sleek and feeling fab. Happiness emanates from her.

It's so easy to lose yourself in parenting. Goals become forgotten or pushed to the sidelines.

> *'A family member of the same age and situation as us became very ill and it reminded us that life is short, so we have made a yearly "to do" list, with 20 personal things and 20 things to do as a family. It has worked a treat so far and life is exciting.'*
>
> **Sonya, Marlborough, one son aged 3½ years, one daughter aged 16 months**

Things that I do for me include sleeping, catching up with friends, writing and exercising.

On my first 'writing retreat' the pace was so different from my usual pace where I'm constantly racing the clock trying to get things done while the baby sleeps or while Ruby's independently engaged in an activity. Even when I'm away from them I constantly have that sands-through-the-hourglass feeling.

Now and then it becomes clear that I need a little bit of 'me time'. Sometimes it's time away from the kids that I crave but more often it's just time to do something for me, at my pace. Other times it's real 'us' time that I desire to get us back on track or to feel more connected. It's amazing what a bit of uninterrupted conversation and eye contact can do!

I get grumpy if we get to the end of the weekend and we haven't had any fun 'family time', if it's just been a series of hubby and me tagging in and out with each other and looking after the kids while the other tries to get things done. Now we book family time into the diary on Friday night.

A friend lamented to me that her husband had recently started looking after their 3-year-old and 1-year-old in the house for an hour or so but had never taken them out on his own. I 'made' hubby take both of ours grocery shopping when Jonah was 2 weeks old. I think it's completely a win-win situation when the dad is empowered by the experience of taking both kids out on his own, maybe even just to the nearby park. It will give mum some 'me time', show trust and give Dad some confidence.

Taking care of Number One

There are tweaks that we mums can make in our daily patterns to make sure that we take care of ourselves.

It's the simple things: drinking a glass of water, sitting down for five minutes, having a shower in peace (no baby crying or toddler banging on the door) or going to the toilet without an audience.

When I get frazzled with the kids I react by feeling resentment towards my husband. I look at the clock and get frustrated that he's not home from work yet. I know that he's got pressures of his own at work and he's absolutely incredible with the kids but I just can't help myself! These are all indicators that a little bit of 'me time' is in order.

'You seem overwhelmed'

 I went to see a naturopath when Jonah was just over 1 year old. It makes me smile now but at the time I was a blithering mess. The reason for my visit was to discuss Jonah's eczema. I was fine when talking about his diet, introduction of solids, love of yoghurt and so on but when she asked about me I completely fell to pieces! Perhaps it was her ultra-calm nature highlighted by her musical Scottish accent or the fact that I had my period, hubby was away on a business trip and we'd had a small tiff the previous night. But when she asked 'And how are *you*? You seem overwhelmed', I responded with a flood of tears. It really surprised me as I hadn't realised just how low I'd felt at the time. So often as mothers we find ourselves responding to the 'how are you?' question with a plural 'we're good'. Later that day I texted hubby and said 'I'm a mess.' That was *huge* for me! How many mothers want to acknowledge and then admit that they are a mess? In need of some serious loving and a bit of help?

We may want the guys to offer us 'me time' but often you'll just have to announce that you're having some. Let them know a day or so ahead and generally how long you'll be gone for. Don't faff around making meals and laying out clothes. Not only will this make them feel incompetent but it will magnify your role as the primary carer.

I've stumbled upon a cool way to give yourself 'me time' while helping out a friend (and her marriage). Offer to babysit for a friend to give her and her spouse a date night. Now here's the key: leave your house one to two hours before you are due to babysit and give yourself some 'me time' on the way. Walk in the hills, meet a friend for a leisurely coffee and some uninterrupted conversation, go to the art gallery... you'll find it's a win-win-win as you'll get a chance to recharge, your spouse will get the kids to himself for the dinner-bath-bed routine (depending on what time you're babysitting) and your friend will get a date night and a free babysitter. I find that babysitting for friends gives me a 'night off' in a way because I'm away from my house and no longer surrounded by all the things that need doing. It's guilt-free TV watching or lying on the couch reading once the kids are asleep.

Most of the dads that I interviewed felt that their wives needed more 'me time' and commented that the trouble was 'getting her out the door'. Are guys offended that we have such a hard time prying ourselves away from our kids? Do they feel we don't trust them? Many of the mothers advised that you don't *wait* for him to offer time off, you have to make it happen!

Post-natal depression (PND)

Post-natal depression, also known as PND, affects up to 20 per cent of mothers worldwide. Not to be confused with the baby blues, which often occur just days after childbirth, PND can make you feel overwhelmed and that you just can't cope. Unfortunately, in those first few months of hazy sleeplessness, PND can often be overlooked or mistaken for tiredness.

If you are feeling overloaded and under-rested, try to get some sleep and some help around the house and wait for it to pass. But if you feel that you are completely losing track of reality, if you have stopped being able to make rational, sensible decisions, if you cannot get through a day without wishing it were over, if you have stopped living in a normal, safe way or if your moods or behaviour frighten you, then you need to get some help.

'I felt like I hit a wall around three months post-baby. It has made things very challenging. I asked for help from friends and family, had counselling and took anti-depressants. I talked to my partner honestly about everything I was feeling. I hate to think how things would have been if it had dragged on any longer. Take it seriously and find treatment and/or management that works.'

Anon

'I don't think my partner really understood that I had PND until I went on medication and turned back into a rational person! I totally recommend Plunket's post-natal adjustment programme which uses a peer group setting to work through the changes a baby brings to your life and relationship. We had some very useful exercises and discussions around managing our expectations of our partners, communicating better with them, and finding a more positive view of ourselves and our partners. Following one of the sessions I made two lists — one of things my partner was doing that I appreciated and one of things I wanted him to do — and gave them to him. That was really helpful.'

Anne, Christchurch, one daughter aged 4 years

'We've had some rough patches but we always get through it. When my son was 2, I had a bit of a breakdown. I was suffering with depression and my husband had to step in and be the main caregiver to my son for a while. It was a really tough time but we really pulled together and got through it. My husband is an amazing support. We expected it would be difficult, we just didn't know in what way.'

Anon, Terrigal, one son aged 6 years, one daughter aged 18 months

Liz Fraser, mother of three and author of *The Yummy Mummy's Survival Guide*, writes frankly about PND and how taking anti-depressant medication changed her world: 'From the moment I started taking the stuff our lives changed drastically. I was happier and less volatile; we started spending more time as a family doing fun things; I was less rushed, obsessive and hyperactive; I didn't mind all the hitherto frustrating aspects of motherhood and I could feel my whole body and mind slowing down and becoming more balanced.'

She also highlights these points:

- Most doctors recommend you take medication for at least a year
- They can have some unpleasant side effects
- They may make you feel worse
- They may not work
- They can be hard to come off unless you do it carefully and slowly
- It's wise to use them in conjunction with some psychotherapy or counselling.

Post-natal depression doesn't only strike just when you have a new baby. In some instances it can happen six weeks, six months or even a year or more after your children are born. Dads can also experience post-natal depression.

> 'I don't know if my depression was technically "post-natal" as my son was 2 when it hit me. It was awful. I look back on that period of my life and I don't even recognise who I was. I was so miserable and just wanted to run away and hide.'
>
> Anon, Terrigal, one son aged 6 years, one daughter aged 18 months

A post-natal depression case study

Meet Jenny and Bill. Jenny had post-natal depression with her second baby. Her first child was 2½ and her second child was 12 months old when it hit. Jenny had survived moving house, moving country and her second child being severely ill in hospital for the first months of her life. There was just 15 months between her children. She felt tearful often but hadn't realised how she was spiralling downhill fast until it all came to a climax one day. Jenny and her husband both describe her descent into the dark pit and how it almost cost them their marriage.

Jenny's story

When I had my first child, Mary, it was a piece of cake. My pregnancy had gone really well all the way through and I felt really great. I remember thinking that I couldn't understand all those other mums moaning about how hard it was. Mary had slept through from 5 weeks and she fed on demand. She was perfect.

However, I got pregnant again very quickly and my second daughter was born just 15 months after my first.

We were living in Australia at the time, away from friends and family in New Zealand. That in itself was fine. We had coped with that with the first relatively easily. However, my second daughter got severely ill from just 3 weeks of age and that was when things started to go wrong.

Our midwife had visited and was concerned that at 20 days old Lilly was sleeping for seven hours without waking up for a feed. When we weighed her, we realised that actually Lilly was losing weight so we were sent to hospital and it was discovered that Lilly had a urine infection.

She was in hospital for three nights. It was a horrible experience. The children's wards were sterile and Lilly was in a stainless steel cot with curtains drawn around her. Not where any mum wants to be with their new baby. When the hospital re-leased her and we returned home it became apparent that just one week later, Lilly was losing weight again.

She was just 6 weeks old and was limp and skeleton-like. When we returned to hospital we were advised that our baby was severely malnourished and that she was unlikely to survive. She had contracted rotavirus while in the hospital and that was the cause of her weight loss. She weighed less at 6 weeks than she had when she was born.

She was quickly re-admitted to hospital and before we knew it, weeks had gone by. I didn't leave her side, sleeping on a fold-out bed every night beside the steel cot in the isolation unit. My husband Bill had to stay at home to look after our toddler so we were separated. If we had been together supporting each other, I think things would have been better but for us that was the beginning of the downward spiral.

Unfortunately, because my daughter had been so sick and had lost so much weight, she was struggling to feed. I persevered with the breastfeeding as much as I could, often force-feeding her my breast every two hours during the day and then putting her on a nasal-gastric tube at night. I would pump after every feed so I was able to top her up whenever I could. Having breastfed my eldest until she was 12 months, I couldn't see how Lilly couldn't be putting on weight, but as the days went by and her weight barely inched up, a doctor finally intervened, telling

WHAT ABOUT YOU?

167

us that unless we introduced her to the bottle, she would be unlikely to put on enough weight to survive. That night we gave her my breast milk in a bottle. She finished it and then looked at us for more. We never looked back and eventually introduced formula.

We had got through it. Lilly was finally putting on weight and I was fine — or so I thought.

Six months later my husband was offered a job back home in New Zealand. It was a great opportunity and the shock of what we had gone through with Lilly made us realise we wanted to be close to family again. My husband went over to start the new job and I was left in Adelaide to pack up and sell the house with two very young children, and to move over and join him when I was done. It was exhausting but I did it and I couldn't wait to get on the plane to get back home to New Zealand.

Those first few months at home were awful. We were living in a furnished rental far from town and I knew nobody. Then the rain came, in the form of a New Zealand winter, and a very dark cloud over me too.

I had been cushioned before, as we had spent so long just coping with Lilly and then the move that I hadn't even had time to think or talk about everything we had gone through. But then when I finally let some of those feelings in, everything suddenly felt so black.

I hated everything. I hated the house. I hated the rain. I hated not having my own things around me. I found problems with everything and I spent most of my days in tears. I had survived huge stresses but I felt empty. I would feel so overwhelmed and hated it when Bill went off to work. I would literally clock-watch until his return and felt jealous of his new role and of the fact that he seemed to be settling back into New Zealand easily. I expected Bill home every night at 6 p.m. and every minute after that I would feel angrier and angrier and hate him even more. I would lose my temper or burst into tears over the smallest things and it just seemed harder and harder to leave the house and much easier to stay at home. I was so tired all of the time and very, very negative. My job as a mum suddenly felt so hard.

Bill tried to be supportive. He pushed me to go out with friends, to have a haircut, to go to the movies. But I always felt it was just too hard. I felt so tired all of the time and would go to bed during the daytime. When my children woke up crying after their naps I would lie in bed listening and resenting them and thinking how horrible they were.

It came to a head one day when Bill was off work sick. He had gone back to bed and was feeling awful. I resented the fact that he could go back to bed while I was still up looking after the kids. I became hysterical, boiling mad that he was asleep while I was dealing with everything. When I shouted at him, he replied: 'You only needed to ask. I will look after the children for a while. You go and have a lie down.'

I got the duvet and climbed into a cupboard and sat there in the darkness, with the door shut, curled into a ball. When Bill found me he was angry.

He said, 'What are you doing?'

I replied, 'Leave me alone.'

He looked at me and said, 'Get up. Don't be so pathetic. These children did not ask for this.' He was so angry with me for letting it get to that stage. I was hysterical, sobbing. He made me come out of the cupboard and we bundled the girls in the pram and went for a family walk. My anxiety returned the moment we came home. It was almost overwhelming. That feeling of, 'The routine starts again. Every day for the rest of my life.' I became hysterical again and Bill had enough. He told me I wasn't coming into the house until I had written down what I wanted out of life. Until I sorted myself out and wrote myself a list.

He was serious. He took the girls into the house and locked me out. No amount of screaming or banging on the door helped. I finally realised that this was his way of helping. I wrote down a list of what would make me happy and shouted that I had the list to show him. He looked carefully at me and said: 'I don't need to see the list. The list isn't for me. It's for you. So that you can learn what you want.'

Finally I saw what he was trying to show me. I had a real problem and I needed professional help. The next day I went to see a doctor. Boom. The floodgates finally opened when I told the doctor, 'I can't stop crying. I don't have the energy to be happy any more.'

Although I didn't want to go on the pills, I realised it was the only way forward for me. I was on medication for two years and it was hard to come off them but I have done it now. I have also realised something. Being a stay-at-home mother is not for everyone. I still find it hard being home with the children and I am much happier having the balance and the feeling of importance of work in my life.

Bill's story

I didn't pick up on Jenny's depression that early on. It was a really busy time when Lilly was in hospital. Not only were we contending with all that Lilly was going through but we had a little baby girl at home too. So really we were just on auto-pilot, in survival mode and doing what we had to do to get through it.

Even when we moved to New Zealand we were still on autopilot, just pushing through until we got to the other side. Having suffered from depression before, I do understand what it is like. It is like a grey cloud. It just creeps up. You're not that worried about it if there's still sunshine around then suddenly you look around and it's black. When we got to New Zealand it was almost as if that black cloud suddenly came up from behind.

I would just think 'oh, she's having a bad day' then, 'she's having a bad week' and then it just gets worse and worse and nothing you do can cheer her up.

You go through the sexual desert and you think, is it me? Is she just not into me any more? Human nature makes you question yourself.

You try everything and nothing works. As a man, whether you're into computers or cars, you can press different buttons to try to get something to work, to reboot whatever is broken. You look at the tyres, the engine and go through all the procedures. As a man, you think you can fix everything. And so, you buy flowers, you take her out for dinner, you get someone to look after the kids. But nothing fixes it.

By this time you have a floppy, unresponsive person whose only conversation with you is to tell you not to be late home from work. And you sit there thinking, 'Why would I want to be early?'

You think, I'll take the kids and give her a break. And you go out with the kids to the park and McDonald's and you're having fun. And then you go home to Mrs Glum. And the whole family's down again.

Now what do you do? Trade in Mrs Glum? I'd think, I've tried everything. Nothing fixes it.

Then I realised there was nothing I could do. And it was awful. I've always been able to fix things. Even between us. With love, flowers, wine, underwear, a facial. It had always worked before. This time, all the old tricks hadn't worked.

I'd been understanding, caring, loving, giving. Nothing had worked. I'm a salesman and I use 'closes'. There was one final one to try. The 'No, I'm afraid we can no longer do business any more' close. The 'I don't want you to be my client any more' close. It was ballsy, but I went with it.

I told her: 'You need to fix this because these children didn't ask to be born. These children didn't ask for this and this wasn't part of the deal. You're opting out and you can't just quit.'

I called her bluff. I told her that we (me and the kids) weren't interested any more. I told her she was making them sad and it had to stop. I told her, I don't want you around them any more.

I locked her out of the house and told her 'Go and sort yourself out. I can't fix this. You need to.' I made her write a list of what she wanted. She thought she would give me the list and I would fix it. I said: 'No, there's no point. I can't fix it. You need to.'

She started crying and crying and I knew we had finally got there. And then we were away...

Her parents had a different approach. They would mollycoddle her but I'm a great believer that sympathy doesn't help. It just feeds the misery. The problem with depression is that it just creeps up so the faster you recognise it for what it is, the better. The longer you stay in it, the worse it becomes. It just gets darker and colder.

That day, when she went into the cupboard — that was her cry for help. It was her way of saying, 'I need you to notice that I'm not right.'

Is it right to go on the pills? Definitely. It's like, by the time you're too drunk to drive, you're also too drunk to realise that you need a taxi. You have to get the medical help because, when you're depressed, you haven't got the right judgement. Your judgement is gone.

Signs of post-natal depression

- ☺ uncontrollable crying
- ☺ loss of interest in things that used to interest you
- ☺ negative thoughts and self-blame
- ☺ severe mood swings
- ☺ feeling numb inside
- ☺ feelings of isolation
- ☺ trouble sleeping
- ☺ thinking about harming yourself or your baby
- ☺ feeling like you just can't cope.

If you feel or experience any of the above, or think a friend may be feeling this way, get help straight away. Post-natal depression will not go away by itself and you need help to combat it.

 Post Natal Depression: ifonlytheytoldme.com/44

Getting your body back

'It's amazing how many rundown, overweight mothers will spend countless hours and hundreds of dollars carting their children to competitive sporting events, beauty pageants, and auditions, but will do absolutely nothing for themselves.'

The Stay-at-Home Martyr, Kimes and Worley

If you feel good about yourself, that goes a long way to contribute to marital happiness. It's cliché but only because it's true — so many mums are unhappy about their post-baby body and long to get their body back. It's easy to say you'll join a gym or a class or go for a run/bike/swim but it's harder to find the time to do it. Instead you need to *make* the time to integrate it into your regular domestic routine, especially if you view exercise as a chore. Perhaps shift your perspective and consider it as a time to focus on your health and well-being, rather than a mission to lose weight.

It could be about getting your body back or just about finding time for exercise. Find someone local who is keen to go with you if you can. Alternatively, you can help a friend out by taking it turns to babysit each other's children to allow you to fit in your daily exercise.

 Exercise has always been crucial to me and I was lucky enough to meet a mum who lived on the other side of the local park who craved her exercise too. We decided to join forces to help each other out. I would wheel my baby over to her house and leave him with her while I went for a run. She would do the same. We even decided to do a Stroke 'n' Stride duathlon together to enable us to get back into our fitness. We would meet at the local beach and one of us would look after the babies in the buggies while the other would don their wetsuit, go for a swim and then a run, and then we would swap. It was great fun!

You don't necessarily need to be totally into fitness. It could just be a stroll and some fresh air — and that's all anyone needs to feel better about themselves. A 10-minute walk will work wonders. If you are feeling 'over it' then just tag out with hubby when he gets home and walk it out. It's amazing what a bit of fresh air and walking at your own pace can do for the soul!

Try this:

- ⚬ A walk by the river or in the hills (at your own pace rather than toddler pace).
- ⚬ Joining another mum for a walk with strollers while your toddler is at kindy.
- ⚬ Try a couple of chin-ups or stretches in the playground while your kids play or leg lunges while pushing the baby on a swing.
- ⚬ Get down on the ground and do exercises or stretches with the kids (a straddle stretch is a lot tougher after having kids).
- ⚬ Magazines are full of good fitness regimes. Why not try investing in some low weights and a Swiss ball and try exercising in front of the news in the morning or the evening?
- ⚬ When the children are older and don't need you in the water with them while they are having swimming lessons, jump in alongside them and do some laps. I book our children in for a swimming lesson together every week. We play together in the pool before the lesson and they go to their lesson and once they are settled into it, I do a few laps and come back for the last five minutes of their lesson.
- ⚬ Walk to kindy or school with the pram. It's great for the heart, arms and legs.

Finding time for fitness

Here's some advice from personal trainer Nicola Merrilees of Next Level Personal Training:

Getting Fit After Baby
www.ifonlytheytoldme.com

 Keeping Fit Through Pregnancy: ifonlytheytoldme.com/18

Sport New Zealand (formerly SPARC) recommends that we include at least 30 minutes of moderate-intensity exercise into our day. I can hear the collective gasp from here: 'How on earth can I possibly fit that in?' Fitting exercise into your day *is* possible, and you don't need to turn your life upside down to do it. Here are some simple ideas to make sure you keep active:

1. **Do your chores!**

   Your daily exercise goal can be tackled simply by completing your household chores. Tasks such as vacuuming, cleaning windows, gardening or mopping floors all activate large muscle groups, get your heart rate going and (even better) burn calories. Thirty minutes of housework at a moderate effort is comparable to a 30-minute workout. If you get interrupted, don't worry; you can space it out over the day and still get the benefits. Try to think about other ways to get your body moving: take the stairs, get up some pace in the supermarket aisles or walk the long way home after school drop-off. It all counts.

2. **Walk it out**

   Don't underestimate the power of a walk, be it 10 minutes or an hour. If you can fit it in then put your shoes on. Walking is a great exercise which moves your entire body and gets your heart rate up, and it can be completed at any time of day and with your baby or children. Pop baby in the pram and get yourself out into the fresh air. To make it really count, challenge yourself with some hills or try to walk at a slightly faster pace. Another great idea is to chat to other mums and see if anyone else will join you at a mutually convenient time for a brisk walk. You will feel so much better for it and get to have a good social catch-up as well.

3. **Play**

   Ever noticed that kids move a lot? I once tried to follow my 4-year-old son around a playground and copy everything he did. After five minutes I was exhausted! Children are your best personal trainers. Accept their requests to play with you. Kick a ball, have running races, play hide and seek, skip and jump. Try to copy them swinging on the monkey bars (good luck with that one!) and get your heart rate up — not only will you have a great time with your little person, you will get your recommended daily dose of exercise.

4. **Plan, prioritise and make it sacred**

   If you want to tackle some more serious exercise then plan to make it happen. Too often, mums defer their exercise time for other engagements and then miss out on that precious time. Make a sacred appointment that is strictly for exercise. Make sure it is at the time of day that suits you best — for example, 6 a.m. is my favoured time and the time I know is my own. I have friends who could in no way exercise at that time and prefer 7 p.m. slots. For you it may be 20 minutes after school drop-off, lunchtimes or nap times. Either way, make it a regular appointment that is not negotiable.

5. **Negotiate and get support**

   Talk to your partner, husband or support person about how they can support you to exercise. My husband and I sit down and divide up the week and work out when we can both fit in some exercise. Not only does this ensure that our exercise time is planned, it also helps to know that you are supporting and encouraging each other. Other mums can also be your supporters. Take turns babysitting so that each of you can get out for a little bit of exercise. Or, while the children play, work out together. I often train coffee groups and the children come too. The kids love it and often try to do the exercises with us as well as having a fabulous playdate.

6. **Have a goal**

   There is nothing like having a goal to suddenly boost exercise to the top of your 'to do' list. Whether it is to walk for half an hour, complete a Zumba class or to tackle a 21 km run, having a goal is motivating and gives you that extra impetus to get going. Choose a goal that is realistic, specific and time bound so that you make sure are committed to it. I also encourage my clients to tell people about their goal so that it is public and friends and family are able to support and encourage their efforts. There is no better feeling than completing a goal, especially one that benefits your health.

7. **Make it fun**

   You will only be motivated to exercise if it is something you enjoy. Look for an exercise that you get a kick out of and then you will not have a problem fitting it in. I have a friend who loves to dance. Every so often during the day she will turn on the radio and have a good 10-minute boogie. She and her husband have now signed up to a dance class one night a week. What a fantastic way to exercise — doing something they enjoy and spending time together. It may take some looking and experimenting, but if you can find an exercise that 'spins your wheels' then inevitably you will make a point of scheduling it into your day.

   So there you have it, give it a go. Although it sometimes may seem difficult and time consuming, including exercise in your day will make a difference to you both physically and mentally. You will never regret making space in your day for exercise.

Drawing the line

 Sometimes you have to 'draw the line' and stand up for yourself as our little darlings tend to take all we have to give. Often when I get upset or shouty it's not really the kids but *myself* that I'm upset with. I get frustrated for not 'standing up for myself' enough and for being 'too soft'. Hubby is great at standing up for me by stepping in and telling the kids to give me respect or some space.

Here are some things that keep me from losing myself in motherhood:

Some things are sacred

With children, the constant negotiation is draining and sure, you've got to 'pick your battles', but you also need to draw the line. They climb on your knee (cute) and eat your meal (annoying). They rifle through your purse for treasures like lipstick or money to play shops. I'm trying to enforce a 'some things are sacred' rule. My wallet, keys and camera are officially off limits — always.

Non-negotiables

As silly as it may seem, I do not eat from plastic (kids') plates. In fact the whole 'eating' thing is huge for me as my kids are still in the pre-school phase. My manners went out the window a while ago and most meals involve me trying to shovel some food in my mouth before my cheeky darling tries to pull me by the hand or climb onto my knee.

Here are some of my other non-negotiables:
- Not letting a child over the age of 2 sit on my knee while I eat.
- Not letting a child with a pooey nappy sit on my knee.
- Toileting and showering in peace. These are two things that I like to do alone.
- When I'm cooking dinner the children need to entertain themselves and do something that does not require my supervision.
- When dining, the children are either at the table or away playing quietly — not distracting the other diners.

Helpful parenting phrases

I've adopted some great parenting phrases lately that have helped to get my message across. One of my favourite sayings these days is adding 'end of story!' to the end of a sentence when I'm trying to emphasise that I won't be swayed and that's my final word. My other mantras these days are:

- 'You get what you get'. This can send a clear message and also avoids that whole 'I want a pink cup', 'I want a green cup' thing.
- 'Once is enough'. My mother-in-law uses this with our daughter, which is much nicer than my usual response of 'I heard you the first time!'
- 'Kitchen closed'. This is a great one for after snack or meal to curb the constant catering that comes with being a parent.

Things we thought we'd never do

There are many things we witness our friends who are parents doing that we swear we will never do ourselves when we become parents. Letting our children watch TV, letting our children go out of the house with no shoes and snotty noses, having masses of toys all over the house. Everyone believes their own child will be the best behaved, most well-turned out child of all. They will be able to entertain themselves, sit quietly in the corner, share nicely, play nicely and have beautiful manners. We never dream our own children will turn out just like all those other snotty-nosed children out there. Likewise we believe that we will be the perfect mum to our children. We believe that we will read and play with our children and never shout. We'll make monkey-faced pizzas for dinner and our children will love our cooking and eat dinner all up. Reality is that you just do what you have to do to get through each day and you just need to let some things go.

There is nothing more annoying than trying to speak to a friend on the phone who is only half-listening to your conversation because she is talking to her children half the time.

 Before I had children, I would regularly phone one of my best friends at home in the UK who had three young children. Half our conversation was her talking to the kids, telling them off and, even worse, leaving me hanging for 10 minutes while she changed a child's nappy. I swore I would never do the same when I had children. The other day my sister phoned me to wish me a happy birthday. When I accepted the Skype call, her baby was sitting in front of the computer. We then had a very frustrating half-conversation as she waltzed around her kitchen preparing dinner while I was trying to talk to her. At the end of the call, I hung up the phone, annoyed and frustrated and explained my frustration to my mum who was visiting, asking, 'Do I do that?'

My mum nodded, advising me that I did that often — put Skype on with the kids eating breakfast in front of it and go off to make myself a cup of tea, leaving Mum and Dad to talk to non-responsive children who were trying to eat. How frustrating! I have now made a pact to myself to lock myself away to have a quiet conversation in future with anyone calling me. My children can fend for themselves for 10 minutes!

On the other side of the coin, Nat tells how it's hard when her mum calls her for a conversation and she really cannot talk as she has three kids to get fed and organised. Her mother wants to have a five-minute conversation with her but might be calling in at the most inopportune moment, when she's trying to get the kids out the door or they're in the middle of mealtime. It is hard in those situations to give yourself to the person on the other end of the phone and to concentrate on what they're saying.

Is there ever an opportune time to have a quiet phone conversation with a friend or relative once you have children? Maybe the best thing to do is to let regular callers know when the best times to reach you are and the don't-even-waste-your-time times. When they do call, and provided it is a good time for you, then take yourself away from the children and concentrate on the friend calling you for the next 10 minutes and, if it's not a good time, just let them know.

The happiest mother in the world

 I had a series of one-on-one chats with mother and father friends about the wonderful topic of marriage and parenting. First on my list was a couple who I see once a year at most but who are the first to come to mind when I think of wonderful marriage and wonderful parents, probably because I just love the way they treat each other. The clincher for me, however, was when Heather updated her Facebook status as 'The happiest mother in the world'. Wow, I thought, how many mothers would describe themselves with such confidence and joy? They've been through the baby years and here are some of her pearls of wisdom:

⊚ If something is going on with us he reminds me that we need to keep working at us. We need to stay strong together as a unit and not let ourselves drift apart.

⊚ Communicate. Never go to bed angry. Never go to bed back to back.

- Say I love you every day with simple gestures of affection such as a hand on the shoulder or a hug in the kitchen. It's easy to get caught up in the chaos and forget to do that stuff.
- Take time out for what you love. Let each other have a day every now and then. Once a month I give Lain a 'man pass' — a certificate to do fun things, i.e. go skiing or for a long mountain bike ride.
- Create 'us time'. The kids have four grandparents so having the kids for sleepovers allows for 'us time'.
- Continue to do things we've always done, e.g. tramping.
- Stay passionate.
- Get out every weekend and do something as a family.

IOTTM tips to help mums thrive

- Ensure you build in 'you time' on a regular basis. Whether it be going out for a walk at the beginning or the end of the day, swapping babysitting with a girlfriend while you get a haircut or playing 'tag out' with your hubby.
- Do something you love! It's too easy to 'lose yourself' in parenthood. Make sure you take time to have a hobby and do something for you! For some it's mountain biking, for others it may be reading a book on the couch in the sun. Whatever it is — something you used to do pre-kids or something totally new — make the time to do it! If you feel fulfilled and inspired, your relationship will be better off too.
- Tell your husband that you're taking some time to yourself. Let them know a day or so ahead and generally how long you'll be gone for. Don't faff around making meals and laying out clothes. Not only will this make them feel incompetent but it will magnify your role as the primary carer.
- Keep in touch with your girlfriends. You could have girlfriends over for 'Stitch 'n' bitch night or clothes-swap or a book club.
- Daily chats (and sometimes rants) with girlfriends.
- If you are feeling overloaded and under-rested, try to get some sleep and some help around the house until you feel on track.
- If you feel that you are completely losing track of reality, if you have stopped being able to make rational sensible decisions, if you cannot get through a day without wishing it were over, if you have stopped living in a normal, safe way or if your moods or behaviour frighten you, then you need to get some help from your local GP.

⊚ Make time for exercise. It could be a walk with the pram or putting your baby in a crèche and going for a swim or even investing in a couple of weights and a Swiss ball and doing a mini workout in front of the TV with your children playing around you.

CHAPTER EIGHT

The more the merrier?

You want another one?

So you've done it. You've made it through the first year of your first child! You clink glasses with your husband, parents, in-laws and anyone else you invite over to toast your child's first birthday. While you are inwardly patting yourself on the back, watching your delightful child try to pull herself up on the furniture, there is a tap on your shoulder. 'So,' they whisper, 'are you going to give her a little brother to play with?'

Actually, if you even make it as far as the first birthday before being bombarded with questions, hints and suggestions from other people, then you are doing pretty well. I obviously looked permanently exhausted for the first year of my child because nobody dared mention it to me, but I have heard of other mums who have returned from the hospital to nosy questions about producing more offspring.

You and your husband may already have considered it. Or you may well have had a dreadful time of it and pushed it far into the depths of your mind. If you are thinking about baby number two, you may spend ages trying to work out the best age-gap. There isn't one, and your fertility may not always co-operate anyway. Whether there is 13 months between them or four years, that first year with a baby is tough yet magical. Baby number one is hard because you don't know what you're doing and you're learning on the job. It's also a precious time because you can fully focus and immerse yourself in that baby. Baby number two is hard because you are now managing a toddler, while having to get up through the night to feed the new baby. Twins are a whole different story altogether!

Jacqui's story: 19-month age gap

 If you have a small age gap between your children, then, in effect, you have two babies. Sometimes you may have two of them in nappies, two of them needing daytime sleeps, two of them needing to be carried everywhere. It's tough! Jack, my eldest, started walking at 15 months so he was a very new and wobbly walker when my second child came along. As a result I gave myself a very sore back, lugging the new baby in the capsule with Jack balanced on my other hip, not to mention managing heavy double buggies. Very bad for the posture. What with changing two lots of nappies and managing naps for both children, I rarely left the house.

However, on a positive note, having siblings close together is great as they grow older. The older child tends to be a great source of fascination to the younger one and they do play together and keep each other busy — until it all turns to custard, of course, which it always does in the end.

On the other hand you hear stories of shattered mothers with young babies, trying to juggle breastfeeding with 4-year-old's playdates and kindy runs. It can be tough entertaining an older child who is not happy to stay home all the time while you tend to baby's needs. On the plus side, there is only one lot of nappies to change and often a 4-year-old can be quite adept at entertaining themselves and can even help Mum by fetching things and entertaining the baby.

When you are pregnant, people with one child tell you how tough it is and to enjoy being pregnant while you can. I grew increasingly frustrated at the tales of woe I would hear from Mummy Friends about 'you won't be able to run a race again without needing to stop for a pee halfway through.'

If you listened to all those so-called 'advice givers' your legs would be firmly crossed for the rest of your life. Yes, it is going to be tough having one, two, three or even four kids but, with some good systems in place and some great patience and love, it's going to be lots of fun too.

The only advice I am going to give is for those times when you are breastfeeding your baby and you have a toddler vying for your attention too. Have a 'special' box full of toys, books and stickers that your child only gets to play with while you are feeding. It can be books that are easy for you to turn the pages of and read with one hand, or special stickers for them to play with and stick, or a special DVD or toy. Anything to make them feel you are still looking out for them while you are feeding so that you are not feeling pressured and guilty about ignoring your older child.

Nat's story: 20-month and 2½-year age gap

 Our age gaps were 20 months between baby number one and number two and 2½ years between number two and number three. I'm a big believer that 'there's never the perfect time' so if you think you're 'ready-ish' then start bonking! Once Ruby turned 1 it was 'game on'. Baby number three was a tougher decision, about whether we really wanted another baby. After 8 months of deciding, we decided that we did!

It's definitely a bit easier if baby number one is 'up and running' before number two comes along, but there are pros and cons for everything. A friend just had baby number two after five years of trying! Now she has a 6-year-old and a newborn. That's easier in some ways but harder in others. I like to think that no situation is 'perfect' and you just make the most of what you're dealt!

The more the merrier (child number three and four?)

Some people say having a third (or fourth) isn't a major shift. 'You just tuck them under your arm and get on with it.' I asked strangers and friends alike what it was like having three kids when we were in the 'deciding stages' before number three. One dad assured me 'number three is sweet, easy as.' (I wondered what his wife would have said.) Another mother warned me, 'Three is not three times the work! It's *four* times the work!'

One particular conversation with husband and wife (independently) intrigued me as their responses were so different. The mother who had three said she was 'all done' having kids, said three kids were great and a lot of fun. The husband (who according to the wife would be happy to have another) said, 'She's always grumpy.'

It's hard to know how to react when people look at me with my baby in a stroller, and other kids walking or on scooters and make comments like 'Ooh, you've got your hands full.' I know they're acknowledging that three is lots of work but part of me can't help but wonder if it's a polite way of saying 'your kids look out of control' or 'you look like you could use a hand'.

Just the one

It must be annoying when people say 'Oh, just one?' To get some insight, I spoke with some friends and some IOTTM Facebook followers who have just the one child.

'I personally don't believe there are any disadvantages at all to having one child only, and that there are many advantages. From a parenting viewpoint, what is important is ensuring they are exposed to and experience strong relationships of all kinds.'

MC, Auckland, girl 6 years

'There are lots of advantages "for me" to having one child. The hardest thing personally is that you are the playmate. They are not off in another room playing with their sibling . The biggest thing I've had to overcome is feeling guilty that she doesn't have a sibling. I am over the guilt now but I still feel a bit sad that she doesn't have a sibling. It may be easier when she's at school and there are more "only children" around.'

Ngaire, Auckland, one daughter aged 4 years

'Making sure he's well rounded and doesn't turn into a self-centred "the world revolves around me" kid cos I've taught plenty of those. I am also a teacher so have made some interesting observations about family dynamics over the years.'

Laura, Auckland, one son aged 3 years

Why one?

'We've been trying so it's not really a "choice". Everybody assumes that he will have a sibling. People say "you don't want too big a gap". Initially I just smiled and cried inside. Now I say we tried and we can't and we're lucky that we have him. Have we given up? No, but I have health problems which make it tricky and I like being able to give him all of my attention. It's about counting your blessings instead of thinking "if only". Relatives of ours can't get pregnant at all. When people close to you can't even have one I feel lucky to have one!'

Laura, Auckland, one son aged 3 years

'My husband and I are only having our wee daughter Libby. She is coming up for 6 months now and we get so many comments that we are selfish. But my husband has two adult children and I had such a hard journey to have a successful pregnancy that the thought of going down that road again is too hard. I just want to enjoy my girl and watch her grow.'

Natasha, one daughter aged 6 months

'I love having one child, it was a mutual choice with Mark and me. Sometimes I regret not having more but when I see others with more kids I'm indifferent. Different strokes for different folks. We get to focus on one child's needs, go to every rugby game or cricket match, there's no refereeing between the kids, don't have to listen to fighting all day.'

Tanya, one son aged 5 years

What annoying things do people say?

'The assumption that I can't possibly only have one is annoying. Acquaintances and strangers in the shops asking "have you only got the one?" especially if they're having one of their moments. I have quite firm boundaries with him (probably because I'm a teacher) so it really irritates me when people respond in this way. You can see they're thinking only-child syndrome.'

Laura, Auckland, one son aged 3 years

'There is a bit of public perception that "it's easy" having one child. And a few people have said "how can you do that to her?" For us, having a sibling isn't a good enough reason to have another child. We try to provide those relationships in other ways, for example with cousins.'

Ngaire, one daughter aged 4 years

'I don't find it annoying when people ask me if I'm having any more but it is annoying when people give their expert opinion on how Thomas will end up spoilt, rude, arrogant, unable to share or a serial killer! People always assume he is missing out on something but in fact he gets all of our attention, better holidays, more toys, clothes and our time, to name a few. There is also the assumption that I'm not as busy as other mothers therefore my house should be cleaner or I should be baking.'

Tanya, one son aged 5 years

What was it like being an only child?

'The main thing I dealt with as an only child was loneliness. I so wanted a sister to play with at every age. I felt like my friends with siblings were part of a club and I didn't belong. I did get to travel and go to a private school for 13 years, things I may not have been able to do if I had siblings, but I really wanted someone to go through everything with and to take some of the scrutiny off me!'

Jodi, only child and mother of two

Twins

I once babysat for friends with 7-year-old identical twin boys — I've never really spent much time around twins and there's just something so fascinating about them! I spent the first five minutes just looking at them, my head going back and forth like I was watching a tennis match. When the parents returned home, I asked them what was the most common question people asked about the boys. Interestingly, 'Who was born first?' topped the list.

I was so intrigued that I asked the parents Tim and Michelle to come into the studio to share their stories and tips for 'parenting twins'. While Tim suggests booking friends who offer help in to a specific time and date to get through the 'dark ages', Michelle recommends writing a 'letter to yourself' at the end of your pregnancy to look back on.

 Parenting Twins: ifonlytheytoldme.com/41

We've also had some insightful comments from followers on our IOTTM Facebook page:

> 'Make sure you don't have people singling one out as being "the cutest" or "prettiest" or "smartest". It's a really natural thing for people to do with twins, but it could be so damaging when they're old enough to understand.'
>
> **Kathy, New Zealand**

> 'Having twins is awesome. The first four months is seriously hard work and you wonder "How are we ever going to do this? Raise two babies who need the same thing at the same time?" But once you are rocking a routine and find your groove it all just falls into place and you marvel every day at what an amazing bond they have and feel ripped off that you aren't a twin!'
>
> **Sian, New Zealand**

Many parents also recommended joining a multiple birth club. For example, the Auckland Central Multiple Birth Club strives to 'address the special and unique needs of families experiencing a multiple birth, by providing and sharing information, advice and support to those involved with the care and raising and well-being of multiples.'

Top tips and words of wisdom for parenting twins

- ☉ Be prepared for sheer hell on wheels for the first six months, then when you've got them sussed, sit back and marvel at them and yourself!
- ☉ Keep a feeding journal/timesheet with name of child and which side or how much bottle they got. Things are such a blur that you forget.
- ☉ Join a 'parents of multiples' group for advice, support and baby gear.
- ☉ Twins are harder in a lot of ways at the beginning but once they turn 2, the joy and laughs more than double.
- ☉ Hire a baby whisperer, au pair or friend to help.
- ☉ When friends offer help, book them in and give them a specific date and time. And text to remind them!
- ☉ It gets even more interesting and fun when they are teens and then adults.

> *'My girls always have a willing buddy to play with, stick up for each other, make each other laugh, and of course gang up on their parents when they're not listening/being naughty!'*
>
> Ingrid, Canada

Twins plus one

As a proud mother of three (a three that includes a set of two) it's hard for me to admit but my emotions were mixed when I found out that the second baby we were expecting was actually our second and third. Why then wasn't I doubly happy to find out we were going to have two babies?

My initial reaction was one of worry about our first son, Matthew. He would just be turning 3 when the twins arrived and I was achingly concerned about how he would feel. My husband and I planned to do everything we could to make Matthew feel as loved as always and we were committed to making sure he had one-on-one time with both of us, but the truth is, I also knew that these babies were going to occupy a lot of our time and attention.

The other thing that surprised me is that I felt like I was grieving the beautiful first year of bonding I had already pictured having with our new baby. While I knew things would be different this time round because an older brother would be a big part of our daily routine, I had still imagined a calmness to the infancy of our second similar to what I had known when Matthew was a baby. I was used to being able to respond instantly to the every need of a newborn. Matthew's infancy had been blissful. When we weren't playing together, he was breastfeeding or napping on me, or he was happily nestled in our carrier as we went for a walk or as I got some things done around the house. How could I create that same bond with two babies? I couldn't 'wear' them both at the same time. I couldn't bounce and lullaby my way around the house with both of them cradled in my arms if they were both crying and upset. There were no guarantees I could even breastfeed them both.

As our due date approached we did everything we could to make Matthew feel excited about having a brother and a sister on the way. He seemed to be a typical toddler, thinking that more is always better (except when it comes to certain vegetables) and we played this up telling him he was so lucky that he would have two babies instead of one.

I was very fortunate to have an exceptionally easy twin pregnancy. I was able to be very active so Matthew didn't notice a difference in how I played with him. The twins, Will and Pippa, were born at 36 weeks and were healthy and strong enough to come home with us after 48 hours, so Matthew, who was home with two sets of adoring grandparents eating pizza and ice cream, barely had time to notice that we were gone.

In our first week together as a family of five, we figured a lot of things out. First and foremost Matthew seemed to take to his role as big brother very naturally. Some of the things we did to help this along included keeping him enrolled in his pre-school programme full time. While I would have loved to have him home with me, dropping him off to spend the day with his little friends and enthusiastic teachers gave me time to focus on the babies. When we all went to pick Matthew up, he was excited to see them (instead of resenting having to wait around while I breastfed and changed them all day). It also meant that I felt OK giving Matthew some extra attention after school, as the babies had had me to themselves all day long. Once my husband got home from work we each strapped a baby in a carrier and tried to keep things as normal as possible for Matthew. I remember several dinners where my husband and I stood bouncing and eating, each with a baby strapped to our chest, while Matthew happily chatted away (sometimes almost shouting to be heard over a crying baby or two) about his day at school or about what he hoped we could do on the weekend.

The other key thing that helped soothe my worries about Matthew's adjustment was that my truly amazing husband agreed to take our just breastfed but seemingly insatiable babies every evening and juggle both of them (solo) as they sometimes wailed for 20–30 minutes (it happened to coincide with the peak of their 'witching hour') while I tucked Matthew in, in the same relaxed way I always had. I didn't want Matthew to feel rushed while we read stories or talked about his day. This was the greatest gift my husband could have ever given me as a mother and I am sure it helped Matthew adapt to his changing world. Of course my husband and Matthew had their own chance to say goodnight undisturbed but it wasn't nearly so trying for me since I had what the babies wanted and what my husband couldn't provide — breasts.

As for how I would ever form the same close bond with two babies at once — of course it happened. I had to remind myself often that Will and Pippa didn't know any different. We also decided early on that we weren't going to stress over getting them on synchronised routines. With an older sibling we didn't want to be tied to a rigid at-home napping schedule that would divide our family on weekends with one parent staying home with the babies while the other was out with Matthew. Will and Pippa learned to nap and feed on the go. I was happy that they weren't always asleep at the same time. Sometimes their naps overlapped for a bit but more often one was awake while the other slept which gave me the time I craved alone with each baby. Of course it meant that daytime naps for me didn't happen and it likely hindered our attempts to create a predictable night-time schedule, but that's what we did because that's what we felt most comfortable with.

So now they are 6, 3 and 3 and I've learned that I have more than one lap for reading stories. (Will and Pippa define each knee as a separate lap and Matthew seems content to sort of drape himself around my neck by lying on the back pillows of the couch behind my head.) It's perfect. Our three kids are wonderful friends — helped by the fact that there is only three years difference from oldest to youngest. Life is great with one plus twins.'

Sarah, Canada, twins plus one

The toddler years

Will things suddenly get easier once we're out of the nappy stage? Will we be consistently getting a full night's sleep and will our libido go through the roof? Is that a resounding *no*? Life will still be busy. Laundry will still be laundry. Coffee group catch-ups and music class will be replaced with doing the kindy and school run. The kids will grow taller and we will all grow older. Our love will also grow. We will continue to face parenthood challenges of self-doubt and the joys of brimming with pride and love. We will admire our spouse and get aggravated by them as well.

Mealtime mayhem

 One of the most frustrating things about raising children is their inability to enjoy the food you spend ages preparing. They call it the 'fussy eater' stage but as far as I can tell, it is far from a stage.

When a baby first starts solids (mush), they are fascinated by the new textures and tastes filling their mouths. They seem to take to it really well and you congratulate yourself that you haven't got a fussy eater, until a few months later and the novelty of the textures and taste has gone out the window and they think it is more fun to throw their food than to eat it.

Later, as they get older, they may no longer throw their food at you but there will be battles for many years to come.

There are many techniques to tricking your child into eating their food. Feeding your child as a choo-choo train (only works the first time), distracting them ('look over there' while you shove a spoonful in their mouth), pretending to eat it yourself, clapping every time they eat a mouthful, music, TV. While these methods may be successful the first time, in my experience they fail consister after that.

Mealtimes, for many mums, are a pain in the neck. Even when your child is at the preschooler or early school age, they can be fussy and painful, refusing to try new things, clamping their mouths shut, saying 'yuck' and 'I don't like it' and turning up their noses at dinners you may have spent ages preparing.

I tried everything, from making faces with food to disguising disliked food items in other items and pretending that disliked foods were other things.

In the end, after getting severely stressed about the fact that I was sure my toddler was fading away to nothing, I went on a 'fussy eater' course. It was the best thing I ever did. Not only did I realise that my own child was not a fussy eater by other people's standards (there was one child on the course who was 5 years old and ate nothing but one certain brand of yoghurt, often 10 of them a day), but Diane Levy, a New Zealand child psychologist who took the course taught us such gems like 'toddlers can survive on fresh air for five days' and 'you are a parent, not a smorgasbord'.

Diane taught us that if your child doesn't eat what you put in front of him then not to lose your cool but simply remove it and say sweetly, 'That's fine, you may leave the table now.' The key is not to lose your temper and not to serve an alternative. When they realise that they will not be getting anything else then they may sulk initially but, after three days of you being firm, they will accept that if they are hungry, they have to eat what you put in front of them as the restaurant is now closed and nothing else will be served.

It changed my life as the mum of a toddler. I no longer get upset when the children don't eat anything — but likewise they know that if they don't eat their dinner then they won't be offered anything else so it is either eat up or be hungry.

When visitors with children come to the house I continue to hang firm, refusing to give in to whining children who don't eat my lasagne. I refuse to have one rule for my children and another for visiting children. My house, my rules. I have upset many a child (and a parent) as a consequence of my firm eating discipline.

Once when some friends came over for an early barbecue, I served up dinner only to have their two children point blank refuse to eat it, making faces and yucky comments. 'That's fine,' I said sweetly. 'You may leave the table.'

One of them whispered something to their mum and she in turn looked up at me and asked, 'Can Ashley have a sandwich instead?' 'No, sorry,' I replied calmly, 'it's sausages and salad or nothing tonight.'

'I can make it,' she insisted, 'just a Marmite sandwich or something easy.'

'No,' I replied again, 'I am not a smorgasbord.' (I love that line.) 'The rule in this house is that they eat what is put in front of them. If they don't want it, then that is fine but there is nothing else.'

My children watched me keenly to see if I was going to fold. I wasn't. The other mother started insisting that Ashley only sometimes eats sausages and if she wasn't in the mood then she tended to make her something else.

I started to lose patience. No wonder her children were so fussy, I thought.

'I am not a smorgasbord,' I repeated. (I *really* love that line!) 'If she doesn't want it, that is fine but there is nothing else.'

Sullenly, Ashley watched me. 'Well, can I have ice cream now?' she asked.

'No,' I replied, starting to enjoy myself. 'Only clean plates get dessert.'

Of course by this time my children had finished their plates and were waiting patiently for their dessert. I put out ice cream for the three children who had finished their dinners and none for Ashley.

She started crying and went to complain to her mother. Her mother looked at me pleadingly.

'Diane Levy's course for fussy eaters,' I said. 'Best thing I ever did.'

Funnily enough the next time that family came for a barbecue, Ashley quickly ate her entire plate. It just takes sticking to your guns and being consistent to make something like that work.

I asked Diane to share her tips for a stress-free mealtime:

- Our job as a parent is to offer food to our child when they are hungry. It is up to them what they do with it.
- If you know you have a fussy eater then do not overspend time and energy on making dinner as you will be fraught and tense before you even serve food.
- The end of the day is always the time when they are most exhausted so try to make this mealtime as easy for everyone as possible, e.g. carbs could just be a sandwich or pasta if that is easier than peeling a potato.
- Breakfast — your child may not be hungry as soon as they wake up in the morning — they could be a 9 a.m. eater, for example. If it means a honey sandwich in the back of the car to get them to kindy in time then that's fine too.
- Children's tastes change. They may love broccoli on Tuesday but hate it on Thursday. Just take a deep breath and know it will change again by Saturday.
- You can never win a feeding battle — it will end in tears — so don't battle and don't get uptight about how much your child eats.
- If your child doesn't want to eat their dinner and says they're not hungry then say 'that's fine' and let them get down and put their plate to one side. If they come back 10 minutes later and say they're hungry, say 'That's fine, darling.

I saved your dinner for you' and offer their dinner again. If they say they are not hungry for dinner but they are hungry for ice cream then let them know pleasantly it is not going to happen!

- If they genuinely don't like something then don't keep putting it in front of them. By constantly offering it you are not taking into account their feelings and likes and dislikes.
- Change mealtimes around. Make it a picnic dinner or dinner in the garden.
- Sit down with them and have your meal at the same time, as children always eat better when you are eating with them.
- Children can be extremely stubborn and battles over mealtimes can be constant and depressing. Take the mileage out of the food and let it be appetite driven. Serve what you know the child reasonably likes and take the hassle out of mealtimes.
- Don't make a big deal out of a meal.
- If your child refuses to eat a meal, don't then go and make another meal for them. You are not a smorgasbord and your kitchen is not a restaurant!

 Diane Levy: ifonlytheytoldme.com/36

A helping hand

> 'As is common with other mothers, of course we want to appear that we can do it all ourselves. It is silly — I am always quick to help others, but have difficulty accepting help. I am working on this'.
>
> Daria, Toronto, three sons aged 4, 7 and 9 years

 Offers of help are bountiful with the first baby, fade out after the first initial months, and are even more scarce when additional babies come along. When many of our friends had their second baby I made a point of offering help and doing random acts of kindness (such as arriving with dessert, taking their toddler to music class so they can sleep at home while the baby sleeps) because I knew that these were rare and treasured gifts when dealing with a newborn.

I'm a generous person but I'm also good at asking for help. A cup of sugar from the neighbour, babysitting from friends. I think some people fall into the 'I don't want to bother them' trap, while others would rather be seen as 'competent' and 'handling it'. I'm a firm believer that most people enjoy being asked for help. I also believe in 'what goes around comes around'.

A new mother friend recently cancelled a playdate as she'd had a terrible night and was exhausted. I immediately offered to take her toddler to the park with my kids while her baby (and she) had a nap. She jumped at the offer! Another friend with a 3-year-old and a 1-year-old (past the 'baby stage') was appreciative but slightly offended when her neighbour brought round a dinner.

Are there unwritten rules about offering help or is it based on your relationship, personality or ages and stages? When a friend had her first baby, I made her a placard which read: 'Never be too proud to ask for help'. She treasures it.

Accepting help from others is key to keeping on top of things at home. People will and should offer. Rather than be a martyr and pretending that is everything is 'fine', accept the help that is offered. If someone phones and asks you if they can do anything to help, say, 'Yes, please, I don't have time to cook so a meal for the freezer would be greatly appreciated.' When a friend calls to ask if they can come and visit, agree and ask if they could go via the supermarket for you and pick you up fresh milk and bread that you otherwise won't have time to stock up on yourself. When a visitor pops in, tell them you need someone to hang out the washing, put a wash on, do the dishes for you, mind baby while you take a shower. There is *nothing* wrong with accepting and asking for help.

How to help a friend and how friends can help

Before I had children, a good friend of mine who was pregnant with her second told me: 'The best thing you can get a new mother is not a set of bibs, or a pretty outfit for the baby, but dinner for that night.' I took the hint and when I went to visit her with her new baby I took lasagne and made her day!

Likewise, coming from the UK, I was blown away by the generosity of neighbours, friends and colleagues when I had my first child. Meals were left in baskets on the doorstep with notes. People turned up to visit and brought their own (and my) morning tea, not expecting me to do any entertaining, and our freezer was packed full of goodies from generous friends. I have never forgotten and make sure I do the same for friends who have children now. In fact, often your friend is exhausted and — no offence — really hasn't the energy to see you. Don't even ring the doorbell — just leave the meal in a container on the doorstep with a note and text to say it's there after you leave. Then they don't feel the pressure to entertain you and you feel like you are doing something beneficial.

For friends with other children, when baby two, three or four come along, the best gift you can give apart from a meal is to take older siblings off their hands for a couple of hours. It helps Mum by giving her a break, and it keeps the older sibling entertained.

Are you good at asking for help to make your life easier? We asked some mothers this question and here's what they said:

'Sometimes, but in reality it's a no. I feel like a failure as a parent if I have to ask for help.'

Anna, Dunedin, two sons aged 1 and 3 years

'I find it incredibly hard to ask for help. I am not sure if it is because of my "Britishness", but the thought that I cannot do it by myself is overwhelming. However, when I did have a tough time with breastfeeding, I got to the point that I knew that I just had to ask for help. The hardest thing I ever did was to pick up the telephone and call a helpline. But once I had opened that door, the help flooded in and Plunket got me through it. Without them I would have been in serious danger of spiralling into post-natal depression. The best thing I ever did was admit I need help and ask for it, and I have absolutely no regrets.'

Jacqui

Eleanor Black, author of *Confessions of a Coffee Group Dropout,* said: '... my first few months at home were the hardest of my life and, honestly, I was afraid to ask for help for fear of looking like a bad mother. Besides, whenever someone did try to help me, I was incredibly sensitive to any perceived criticism and drove them away with my frantic attempts to appear competent and in control. It was ridiculous, but also it's an all-too-common reaction to motherhood, I now understand.'

Tips for visiting a mum with a new baby

It is tough being the visitor and the person being visited (the visitee). Here are some tips to make it easier:

Tips for the visitor

- Call/text the day you are visiting to make sure it is still convenient — things change constantly with babies.
- Take morning tea or snacks with you — chances are the new mum will be breastfeeding and ravenous but won't have had time to do the shopping.
- Check with the new mum if she needs any other bits and bobs or groceries picked up before you come over (milk, tea, bread etc.).
- Take dinner for the family that evening. They will love you for it.
- Knock quietly in case baby is sleeping.
- While you are there, you look after mum. Make the tea, do the dishes, wipe the kitchen bench and put some order back into their lives.
- Check if there is anything else you can do for them before you leave, e.g. hang out a wash, put a load in the washing machine, stack or unload dishwasher etc.

Tips for the person being visited

- Don't be afraid of putting off the visitor if it is no longer convenient or you have had a bad night with the baby.
- Don't feel you have to bake or put on anything special for morning tea. A packet of gingernuts or just a plain cup of tea is fine.
- Check you have milk, teabags, coffee — that's all you need. If you are running low on milk, ask your visitor to pick up some on their way over.
- If they ask if they can get you anything then tell them not to worry about a gift for baby but dinner would be nice.
- Stick a note on the door if baby is sleeping and tell them to go around to the back door.
- Sit back and be looked after.
- Don't be afraid to ask if there is anything else you need them to do before they leave — especially if they offer!

Power hour or 'tick the list'

Here's a great thing to do for a friend regardless of the age of their child. You don't need to have a 'baby' to be in need of and appreciate a helping hand. I love the idea of going to a friend's house and gifting them a 'power hour' to help them achieve, tidy, sort whatever is bugging them. Examples include the Tupperware drawer, putting photos in albums or overhauling their wardrobe. It's always more fun to help and share the occasion with a friend.

Meals on wheels

 One Thursday I arrived home very late from work to discover a meal in the fridge from my fellow writer and friend, Nat. There was a note with it which said simply: Bolognese Pasta, made with love, Nat.

Nat had recognised my current struggle of 101 things to do and had helped out in a practical way by supplying my family with dinner. The New Zealand tradition of helping each other out with meals is just incredible. When I first arrived in New Zealand eight years ago, we had bought our first home. Moving-in day it was total chaos. Everything (and I mean everything) was packed in boxes and the realisation, when we arrived in our new home, that we didn't know which of the boxes contained the kettle and mugs was a disaster.

Then our fairy godmother arrived in the form of our dear friend, Annette, with a basket in hand, filled with freshly baked muffins, a large flask of hot coffee and several mugs, a Tupperware container of milk and a big pot of home-made soup and fresh bread. It completely blew me away. I had never encountered such thoughtfulness and generosity. Hubby, however, was quite nonchalant. 'Yep,' he agreed, 'that's just what you do here.'

And he was right. I have now witnessed the constant generosity of New Zealanders many times over.

When I had children, I really realised how important receiving and giving that help was. I remember going to a friend's baby shower and sitting there with lots of other non-baby friends, proudly showing off our completely inappropriate gifts of baby jumpsuits with domes up the back, when one guest arrived with a large lasagne instead of a beautifully wrapped gift.

She looked at the rest of us, raised one eyebrow and announced knowingly: 'The best gift you can give any new mum is a meal. Nothing else. Just a meal.'

It stayed with me for a long time and, funnily enough, years later when I had my own children, the mother whose baby shower I had attended all those years ago was the one who turned up to visit, armed with frozen lasagne, fresh bread and a pint of milk. I almost kissed her that day. I had a 4-week-old baby and hadn't yet managed to leave the house. We were down to the emergency evaporated milk in the cupboard and had resorted to crackers and Vegemite for breakfast in the morning in the absence of bread. She understood.

When my non-baby friends went on to have their first children, I offered the same service and the system continues, an understanding between mums that they will help you, and that you will help the next person out in the same way.

I love it. It is an amazing and brilliant New Zealand support system that I believe should become a worldwide institution. If I could nominate it as a worldwide law then I would, and thus I am writing about it today in the hope that all you readers overseas can forward this on in the hope that it takes off in your own countries too. Such a simple and cost-effective way of supporting families is a must.

Subsequently, I have joined (and managed to persuade many other mothers, Nat included, to join) a New Zealand charity called The Guardian Angels. The charity has been set up by New Zealand mums to support the families of children in long-term or intensive care in hospital. These families are so caught up with spending every waking hour with their child in hospital and with being there for their child, the last thing they want to think about is what they are going to eat that night. The Guardian Angels is a group of mums who twice a year cook up a storm for those families who need that help. We cook and bulk freeze lots of meals that are then collected and supplied to the local hospital. The meals are given out to those families who really have no time or thought to cooking for themselves as they are too busy being with their children in hospital.

It is an incredible and really easy way to help other families and, again, it would be amazing if this charity system could be adopted worldwide.

Where is the village?

We are led to believe that 'it takes a village to raise a child' but many women don't have a real village. We have e-communities like Facebook and blogs but often no real other person to give us a break on a regular basis.

'I live the "American dream". I live in the suburbs, we have money and a car, and yet, no one is ever around. We have no community ties anywhere.

'My advice would be to find a tribe and live close to it. By tribe, I mean people who parent like you do. Take breaks, have some "me time", nourish your body and soul and make sure your spouse is on board.

'The reason why I am unsatisfied with my own parenting is because I want to have one day where I don't have to ask something three or four times or have to threaten a time out before it gets done. My children really like to push boundaries and it gets to be frustrating. I try to be calm, cool and collected, but more often than not, I get mad, have a temper tantrum myself and put everyone on time out.

'I don't like being that type of mother. I hope it will get better as they get older. My husband works out of town a lot so I am on my own most of the time with little to no real support.'

Alisha, Calgary, three sons aged 1, 3 and 6 years

Grandparents

'I never think of myself as a grandparent. It's a process.'

Cecile, Adelaide, grandmother of four

'It is a huge thrill when a grandchild is born. The same huge relief baby is healthy that the parents feel. Grandparents feel personally involved. Hold the baby, gaze at the baby, enjoy the helplessness and innocence of the baby. Acknowledge the parents' achievement. If at all possible visit often to form a bond with baby and marvel at your own child now in the mother/father role.'

Lynley, 10 grandchildren
(Nat's mum)

Out-of-town grandparents

 Staying with my parents I tend to actually relax. To sit down for more than three minutes at a time and to let other people cook and do the dishes. It's bliss! The get-caught-doing-something-good feeling knows no age limits. At the age of 35 there I was wanting my dad to see me wiping the table just so he knew that I wasn't totally freeloading!

Another time, we were camping at a friend's place for New Year's and we began discussing the topic of 'well-meaning' grandparents and the gifts they give. Both the sets of grandparents in question were overseas and only got a chance to see the grandchildren in person once or sometimes twice per year. One dad expressed a bit of frustration about his American in-laws: 'Why don't they send books or ask us what we want? We don't need more crap!' The other mother (with her parents in Italy) said that she sent a detailed list of exactly what to send: some nostalgic patriotic gifts from 'home' and other practical gifts for the kids.

It's tricky being a grandparent. Wanting to be involved but still have your own life. Wanting to express your love and lend a hand but not wanting to overstep your place. Parents wanting help (to varying degrees) and everyone dancing around each other trying not to offend.

Living in Canada and away from the rest of the relatives, I only grew up with grandmothers who visited once a year. I feel so fortunate that our kids have both sets of grandparents and one set of great-grandparents! I have some friends whose parents passed away before they had kids so they never got to share that experience. I really feel for them, especially on Mother's Day and Father's Day.

Both my parents and my in-laws live out of town so our relationship is one of 'live-in visits' a few times a year. Most of our holidays are spent with us visiting them or them visiting us. It's a fine balance. Length of time is key, as is a 'date night' or night away as a couple if you can swing it and a bit of personal space now and then.

My relationship with my in-laws is great, and has been enriched since having kids. But for some, the 'in-laws' can feel more like 'outlaws' if your relationship is strained. Keeping it civil and even feigned friendship is good for the kids but sorting it out if possible is even better.

 Grandparents and In-Laws: ifonlytheytoldme.com/11

I wish, I wish, I wish my parents were nearby. Not at the other end of the world. Being from the UK and having married a Kiwi and bringing up a family in New Zealand, I miss my parents so very, very much.

Not only do I miss them myself but I ache to have them involved in my children's lives. They miss all the milestones. The births, the birthdays, the first days at kindy and at school. They miss the first crawl, the first steps, the first words and often it eats me up that they can't be there for those important times.

That's not to say they don't make a great effort. They do try very hard. They flew out after the birth of both children. We flew back to the UK for my son's first birthday and Mum flew out for my daughter's first birthday. They Skype often and we send photos and pictures over regularly. Skype is wonderful as they get to see each other, however Mum has confessed how hard she finds it when she just wants to hold and hug them and they are not even interested in holding a conversation with her.

My parents try to come out as often as they can and likewise we try to return often too, although as we are no longer DINKS (double income, no kids) we don't have the disposable income to pay for four flights back to the UK any more. Mum and Dad are now retired which means they are time-rich and income-poor.

This year they visited New Zealand as part of their gap-year-grandparent project and it was the most time we had all spent together in ages. It was wonderful, not only for me but for my children to really get to know their grandparents and to learn to get used to them and feel comfortable with them. Mum and Dad spent as much time as possible with them, although they found it exhausting at the same time. We cannot wait for them to visit again.

> 'Just enjoy it and soak up all the cuddles and open love and trust that your grandchildren can give you. Priceless!'
>
> Magda, England, grandmother of four
> (Jacqui's mum)

I am lucky to have wonderful in-laws here in Auckland, New Zealand. They are divorced but they come together for important family occasions and are a great source of help and support to my husband and me. Anything from babysitting duty to dropping in meals, taking the children for haircuts and just 'popping in' for a quick cuppa and to catch up with the kids. It's wonderful.

I have the two extremes. In-laws here in New Zealand who adore the children and help out often and my own parents who are as far away from New Zealand as you can get and only have Skype to connect them.

'Being a grandparent is wonderful! You see the next generation of the family and recognise some of the traits from your own children. It brings back so many memories. The good points are that you are able to enjoy them and give them back at the end of the day for Mum and Dad to continue with all the hard work and tiredness that comes with being a parent. The bad points are that if I disagree with something, then I have to keep these opinions to myself! Not always easy.'

Magda, England, grandmother of four
(Jacqui's mum)

Local grandparents

I sometimes wonder what it would be like to have 'innies' — grandparents who live in the same city, who can pop in at a moment's notice or pick the kids up from school and kindy, who can babysit and occasionally do the washing. I know there are also drawbacks but it would be pretty handy, right? My friend Tanya's dad drops her son at kindy every day and her mum makes them family dinner every night! Oh, what I would give to have that evening meal cooked for me!

While some grandparents are 'actively involved', others have a more 'only when it suits' approach. In the research for our book, I interviewed someone whose own mother had an 'only when it suits' attitude. She thought it was because she (the grandmother) had raised her own family without grandparent assistance so surely her own daughter could do the same.

Remember, grandparents have already raised their own kids — you. They've done the hard stuff, just like you're doing now. There is nothing wrong with asking for help but let them have fun too. Grandmas love to spoil their grandchildren. Let them. Let it be an unsaid thing that they get special treats with Gran and introduce rituals such as regular special outings that only happen with the grandparent.

For instance, in our house it is known that Nana is in charge of hair cuts. Once a term, each of our children takes it in turns to have a Nana Day. Nana Day involves being picked up in the morning by Nana (usually the child who is going is so excited that they are sitting waiting by the front door for when she arrives). They are then taken directly to Nana's hairdresser — I have tried suggesting that they are preschoolers and only need a $10 cut from the shopping mall but Nana likes to take them to her own posh hair salon, so who am I to complain? It's her thing and even though it costs her four times the price, it's what she wants to do. After their haircut they are taken for a fluffy and cupcakes at the garden centre café then either to the park for a walk or visiting Nana's friends. Then it's home for a special lunch, stories, jigsaws and games and a special — often new — DVD before it's time for home.

The kids love it. They put on their best clothes, brush their teeth and comb their hair faster than any other morning when they know it is a Nana Day. And, Nana loves it too. Not only because it is her own special time with an individual child, but because she controls the day and it unfolds how she wants it to, without me looking over her shoulder making comments like: 'They need to eat all their greens before they're allowed ice cream' or 'They're allowed no more than twenty minutes television.' On Nana Day anything goes, rules are broken. She can give them biscuits for lunch and I couldn't do anything about it. Nor would I want to as it's her special time.

 Having grandparents living in the same city is, it seems, a mixed blessing. The level of benefit to detriment depends on the overall relationship. I've seen this with my sisters and parents as well as with various friends and neighbours. A friend has both sets of grandparents in town. One she describes as more proactive than the other in terms of helping and spending time with the kids. Another friend who lost both of her parents (one before and one soon after the birth of her first child) has a similar situation. Her in-laws are helpful with the kids when asked but do not readily offer. Whether they are busy, unconfident, wary of imposing or not wanting to be too pushy, she doesn't know. Throw into the mix differences in parenting styles and ethics that come with generation changes and unique personalities and it is always going to be tricky to get right.

Create the situation where the grandparents can spend quality time with the kids, without you hovering around.

> 'I am more relaxed with grandchildren than with my own children. I can help in practical ways and offering any support I can. Just listening and being there. I think it is also good to help give the parents a break by having the children overnight sometimes (where practical). The children and grandparents get to enjoy one another without the interference of Mum and Dad.'
>
> **Magda, England, grandmother of four**

> 'You really feel the love grow when you're the sole provider. It happens three times as quickly as when the parents are there. You care so much about the little children when you're a grandparent. When you're the only one there it's magnified and you rise to the occasion.'
>
> **Lynley, Wellington, ten grandchildren**

It is up to you (the parent) to manage things with the grandparents how you want them to play out. If you want the grandparents to be actively involved with the kids then don't just use them as a babysitter or nanny service but invite them for the fun stuff too.

Top tips for a thriving relationship with the grandparents

- ☉ Acknowledge the experience that they have.
- ☉ Try to interpret offers of advice and assistance positively instead of as a negative reflection on your parenting.
- ☉ Let them spend quality time with the kids, without you hovering around.
- ☉ Get both sets of grandparents together once a year with the children, if possible.

- Arrange to spend quality time with them without the kids. It's amazing what an uninterrupted conversation can do!
- Say thank you in words, flowers or returning favours.
- Let them know what you value/appreciate them doing with the kids. Positive reinforcement will show them that you noticed and encourage them to do more of it! For example, 'Thanks, it really helps me when you back me up and insist that the kids use good manners.'
- Ask them questions about what it was like for them as a young parent. It's amazing what you'll find out. Ideally record the conversation as a memento.
- Cherish the memories that you have of them as parents and the moments they spend with your own children.
- Let grandma spoil them.

Hosting guests and staying sane

It's hard having guests at the best of times. With children involved things get even trickier.

Being a guest in someone else's house you are super-conscious. You don't want your child to wake everyone up so you sleep with one ear open all night. If they so much as whimper you're up like a shot, shushing them. While they might wake at 5 a.m. on a regular basis at home, you can control it by slipping into bed with them, bringing them into your own bed or persuading them to go back to sleep. If they wake at 5 a.m. at someone else's house then you're up too, trying every technique in the book to ensure that the rest of the house remains sleeping.

A recent trip back to the UK meant that jet-lag disrupted our entire family's sleep patterns. We were staying with my sister and her husband and new baby in London. They were up through the night, feeding baby, so when our own daughter woke brightly at 3 a.m. believing it was a brand-new morning we were forced to rise too. By 5.30 a.m. our entire family was showered, dressed, had had breakfast and was pounding the pavements of London waiting for a café to open for much-required coffee.

It was understandable for the first morning but then it became a kind of norm for the week we stayed in London. The nights were unsettled with our new nephew waking constantly and then, as we were sharing a room with our youngest, we were woken (if we had actually fallen asleep at all) by her at 3.30 a.m. Conscious of not wanting to upset anyone in the house, we became London zombies and were well known and very nicely treated by the local café owners who would sometimes arrive to open up and find us sitting on their front step. Sleep (or rather a lack of it) killed us and by the end of our stay we were extremely grumpy guests.

From my sister's point of view, I know that delighted as she was that we were staying, she also found it a struggle having a toddler (which she was unused to) in her house along with her new baby. A nervous first-time mum, she watched my daughter, who was a typical 3-year-old, like a hawk, concerned that she was too rough with her baby. Furthermore, my sister, with a non-crawling baby, had never had a need to put special things out of reach and so she was alarmed by the inquisitiveness and delight with which Sasha touched everything.

Then there was the difference in routines. With a 5-year-old and a 3-year-old in tow we often needed to get out of the house first thing in the morning, to run off the children's energy. We would be out in the morning, returning for lunch and a nap in the middle of the day. Then revived, we would be keen to do stuff in the afternoon. My sister, however, had a new baby and was still on a three-sleep-a-day routine, confined by sleep and feed times. The fact that she was also up through the night with her baby meant that she would often go back to sleep during the day. Everyone was tired, everyone was grumpy and I think that everyone was relieved when it was time for us to move on.

House rules

To ensure a successful stay by guests, it helps if the guests and the hosts are upfront at the beginning. You need to share what your routines are with your guests or your hosts. Let each other know what works for your family so there are no surprises. Also, ensure that it doesn't just fall to Mum to cook dinner and run around after everyone. Take it in turns for each couple to be in charge of dinner for the night. They can do what they want: barbecue, take-outs, roast dinner, organise a babysitting for the adults to go out. It takes the pressure off the hosts being expected to organise everything.

If both guests and hosts have children then it might be an idea for each couple to take it in turns to babysit so that everyone gets a night off.

Putting things into perspective

I remember one time visiting my hubby's in-laws. I'd been up all night with a breast infection and rock-hard lumpy boobs. Having slept three hours in total all night, I was woken by our toddler at six-ish and hubby, instead of taking her down the other end of the house, put her in bed with his parents (the room next to ours) and proceeded to work on the computer. Later after a 'debrief' it turned out while I was lying there fuming and thinking 'What is he thinking? Doesn't he know I can't sleep when I can hear her?' he was listening to his parents chatting and playing with Ruby and thinking 'Isn't it adorable how much they love each other?'

It was a timely reminder to look at things from others' perspectives instead of focusing on the impact on me.

It's easy to become quite insular in the baby years when you're so focused on doing laundry, making and cleaning up from meals, snacks and more snacks.

I remember being frazzled by my day with the kids then Matt coming home and telling me about his stresses at work. It did make me glad that it wasn't me at work.

It's a fine balance between acknowledging the stresses that accompany the joys of parenting as well as putting things into perspective and recognising how fortunate your individual situation really is.

At 18 months Jonah had a raging fever as a result of an ear infection. He was dehydrated and we took him to the after-hours clinic for two hours of observation, antibiotics etc. It wasn't serious compared to many situations but the doctor said things like 'I don't want you to worry but he's only 18 months and he's not out of the woods yet. We want to make sure that his infection hasn't moved to his lungs.' By the time Matt arrived and Jonah was lying on the patient table in nothing but a nappy I couldn't even talk or make eye contact. I was on the verge of breaking into tears. It's moments like this that put it all into perspective. The frustrations I sometimes feel when he wakes at 5 a.m. or when Ruby won't give me two minutes' peace — bring it on!

IOTTM tips for managing toddlers

⊙ There is no 'right' time to have a second or more child. Whenever it's right for you and your partner is the time to try.

⊙ When managing breastfeeding a baby with a toddler vying for attention, have a 'special' box full of toys, books and stickers that your child only gets to play with while you are feeding.

⊙ Mealtimes are stressful. Make it as easy for yourself as possible.

⊙ If your child refuses to eat a meal, don't then go and make another meal for them. You are not a smorgasbord and your kitchen is not a restaurant!

⊙ The end of the day is always the time when they are most exhausted so try to make this mealtime as easy for everyone as possible.

- If you know you have a fussy eater then do not overspend time and energy on making dinner as you will be fraught and tense before you even serve food.
- With grandparents, cherish the moments. Let them spend quality time with the kids, without you hovering around.
- Arrange to spend quality time with them without the kids.
- Say thank you and let them know what you value/appreciate them doing with the kids.
- When friends come to visit and ask if they can help, say yes please and tell them how. Ask for help if you need it. Keep a list of visible 'tasks for visitors' on your fridge.
- Appreciate the moments you do have with your children, your husband and your own parents and remember to keep things in perspective. Is it really that much of a big deal that Jamie won't eat his broccoli?

CHAPTER NINE

Whatever works

Returning to work

Returning to work brings with it a tonne of questions and self-doubt, judgement from others (or a self-belief that you are being judged by them), inner turmoil, loss of confidence, trepidation and also excitement.

It could be that you are dying to get back into the swing of things at work, to be the person you were before you had your child. To wear the pretty dresses again, to reclaim your status as an 'important person', to linger over coffee discussing project deadlines, or simply to be out of the house.

Or it could be that you *have* to return to work; that if you had the choice you would much prefer to stay at home but the company needs you, you need the money, you have made promises that you now must keep, or you could be doing a maternity/paternity swap with your partner.

Alternatively, you may have made the decision not to go back, whether it's because being a mum has fulfilled you in ways you never imagined or that you simply are not paid enough to justify the cost of childcare.

Whatever your decision, be prepared that it may differ from the decision you had made prior to having your child. It may be a tough decision to make. It's not only about whether you will go back to work but also about why, where and how?

Working mum

Before and during my pregnancy I had absolutely no intention whatsoever of being a full-time mum. The thought couldn't have been further from my mind. In fact, I was determined to work right up to the point when I gave birth. I just loved my job, you see. Obsessively. And I was determined 'not to change', like other women did when they had their children.

Luckily a smart colleague and friend who had been there before me persuaded me of the importance of having some time to myself before baby came along and so I reluctantly agreed to take four weeks off prior to its birth.

When my son, Jack, arrived I wasn't particularly taken with motherhood. In fact, I missed my working life to the point that I would take him in for weekly visits, catching up with the news of work and putting my two pennies' worth in whenever I could. I did, however, realise that my intended maternity leave of four months may not be quite enough, so I doubled it to eight.

I was, however, happy enough to get back to work and into the swing of things again. Working full time for a young ad agency and managing a child in full-time daycare wasn't so easy. Jack was sick constantly and my husband and I would often compare whose day was busier/more important to determine who would stay home to look after him.

I was struggling with managing my pre-baby persona at work. I could no longer go to the dinners or nights out like I used to and I felt estranged from my fellow colleagues who had no concept of my rush out the door at 5 p.m. each day, my journey home with a screaming tired baby, the fact that I then had to spoon-feed him dinner, bath him and get him to bed and then think about our own dinner before logging back on to the computer to do another two hours' work.

Within a month of going back to work I fell pregnant again and I only had eight months of work before once again I left for maternity leave. This time I was much wiser. I took the full four weeks off happily before baby number two came along — not only to put my feet up but also to be able to spend some quality time with Jack before having to share myself around.

I took the full 12 months of maternity leave I was entitled to and I stayed away from work and let those who were still there just get on with it.

Life was much harder managing two children so close together and the year flew by. I realised how hard it would be to go back to full-time employment and manage two children in daycare. I resigned from work and this time I was quite happy to be a full-time mum, throwing myself into fundraisers, kindergarten committees and whatever else came along.

When my children were aged 4 and 5, I went back to full-time employment after four years of being at home and loving it. Being a working mum is hard work, there is no doubt about it. But being a full-time at-home mum is hard too. Your children know just how to wind you up when they feel like it and the lack of adult conversation can be a killer.

In the movie *I Don't Know How She Does It* starring Sarah Jessica Parker, her character juggles motherhood and working life constantly. Determined not to be different to the other mums, she takes her children to school and kindergarten, thereby arriving late at work; passes off store-bought cakes for the bake sale; misses her child's first haircut; catches lice off her children, all the while trying to protect her professional image of an investment adviser.

Being a working mum I often feel the main challenge I face on a daily basis is never really being able to do everything 100 per cent.

If something goes right at work, inevitably it goes wrong at home. If all is good at home, then chances are I will have dropped the ball at work. It feels impossible to be in top form in both camps. If I am taking my children to kindergarten and school, then I am running late for work. If I am working late to try to meet a deadline, I won't get to kiss my children goodnight. It's a never-ending of juggling act of keeping a million balls in the air.

This week my son turned 6 years old. I haven't even managed to get out and get him a present. How bad is that? For once, a self-confessed cupcake queen has had to *buy* a cake!

My in-tray is overflowing. My 'to file' tray is a mess, and that's just at home. Dinners are turning into fast-food frenzies. Three people last week told me I looked 'so tired'. (Please don't say that to a working mum.)

The house is a mess, the car needs to be fumigated, the cupboards are bare — and my husband even went out and bought me a facial.

And what happens when children are sick? Well, basically if both parents are working then they just cannot get sick — there isn't time. And if they do, it becomes a juggle of work, friends who can help out, mother-in-law and nanny.

So, with that in mind, here are my pros and cons of being a working mum vs a stay-at-home mum:

Working mum pros	Working mum cons
You get to dress up and wear nice clothes.	Your drycleaning bill is astronomical because of the amount of food, snot, vomit spilled on your best jackets and skirts.
You get to wear heels.	You cannot walk in heels while carrying a baby or toddler.
You get to feel important.	You miss being the most important person in the world to your children. Nanny is instead.
You actually get to hold a decent conversation.	You miss the endearing little things your children say and do.

Working mum pros	Working mum cons
You *love* what you do.	You miss doing fun things with the children.
You build adult relationships.	You don't know any of the other class mums, which is a problem when it is a teacher-only day at school and you have no one to call on to help you out.
You have your own salary.	You never have time to spend it.

Stay-at-home mum

 It can be a bit of a shock going from independent, working woman to mother. Even if having a baby was something you've planned and longed for, it can still be a massive adjustment waking up each morning to feed, love and care for a baby and embracing your new role as mother.

Whether you're at home with the kids, working full time or somewhere in between, it's good to ask yourself 'Who am I doing it for?' and 'At what cost?' Jacqui talks about the juggling act that comes with trying to work, spend time with the kids and run a household. I have been observing some of my 'working mother' friends lately and I have to say, they look so stretched. I am kind of dreading that stage. I recently read the book *I Don't Know How She Does It* and I frankly think it should be called *I Don't Know WHY She Does It*.

While it's not healthy to judge others, it is natural to see what others are doing and question or reaffirm your own situation. Many mothers (and fathers) find what they expect to do regarding maternity leave and returning to work is quite different to what they want to do when the time comes.

My first child was in daycare three days a week at the age of 1 while I worked. Now I look at my third child (18 months) and it baffles me! I can't imagine putting him in childcare more than two mornings a week at this stage — and I haven't even done that yet!

It seems you can't really anticipate how you will feel until you're actually in the situation. One friend tried for three years to get pregnant and eventually did through IVF. Then, when the baby was born, she was 'bored' after two weeks at home with baby. Some people just need to work. Another friend who was 'never having kids' changed her mind as she approached 40 and went from career woman to fully embracing motherhood. She was swooning with love for this baby and her new-found role as mother which was so unexpected but wonderful to see! You can anticipate how you will feel when baby arrives and how you'll react to motherhood but the truth is it's a journey that's constantly changing.

> *'I used to think that I couldn't imagine not going back to work. With baby number one I felt bored after about nine months and I wanted normality. With number two I was never bored. I love it! I want to stop the world and treasure it!'*
>
> **Jude, Christchurch, two daughters aged 22 months and 4 years**

Being at home with children is wonderful yet exhausting. I'm loving the relaxed 'what playground should we go to today?' stage but the domestic grind of keeping a tidy home is relentless and it's a constant juggle between playing with the kids or getting things done, not to mention the huge responsibility looking after the kids' health and well-being while keeping them safe from accidents and other scary moments 24/7.

One of our Facebook followers asked us to write about 'losing one's identity and struggling to get back into work in a new field when you're looking after two kids and pushing 40'. So many mothers we know are at that stage where they want to do 'a bit of work' but not necessarily in the capacity or the same field that they worked in pre-kids.

Blue sky

Write a list or mind map brainstorming what your 'ideal' life would look like right now. Consider what you're good at and what you love to do. For me it would be take photos, write, and help people. For someone else it might be fashion, music or fitness. Consider also what's important to you such as flexible hours, proximity to work or recognition. Be honest and open-minded. It's amazing what you'll discover when you start thinking about yourself, something you may not have done for a while . . .

Whatever works

The 2011 US census discovered that more mums are returning to work before their child's first birthday than ever before. Reasons vary from women having achieved a higher educational status, having children later in life (and therefore getting further up their chosen career path pre-children), and/or a greater financial need.

Returning to work can sometimes be the only option for some mothers. Others want to go back to the career they have spent years carving out.

However the juggle between mum and career woman can sometimes be tough. Often you feel you are racing from meeting to soccer game, trying to please everybody and as a mum, you are the one who suffers. Fitting in exercise, breakfast, making packed lunches, showering, feeding babies, getting everyone dressed and making yourself presentable, all before 7.30 a.m., is hard work. Dashing between daycares, school and the office is no fun either. You're often running late and seem to be in a state of constant catch-up. Washing piles up, breakfast dishes don't get done until night, friendships filter out and you are constantly frazzled.

Perhaps people should tailor their lives to best suit their situation and needs. If you have grandparents or siblings in town that can (and are willing to) help you out then integrate them into your weekly lives. If both of you are working, you need some solid systems and routines so that everyone knows what they are doing all of the time. It needs to work like a well-oiled machine. Try having systems for drop-offs and pick-ups, e.g. Dad does morning drop-off, Mum does evening pick-up. Give everyone (who is old enough) jobs, such as clearing breakfast things away, washing up, making packed lunches so that it doesn't all fall to Mum in the morning.

Sometimes instead of 'rolling along', it helps to ask yourselves 'is that really the best or only option for our family?' At one stage I was doing 12 pick-ups and drop-offs a week while the kids were at Montessori at opposite times of the day. After a few months of this, I was getting a bit resentful and wasn't 'at peace' with the situation so hubby and I brainstormed some options. He tweaked his work schedule to do a late night once a week so that he could do the drop-off one morning a week.

> 'We had our children in a foreign country with no close relatives. My wife and I both worked in companies where having children was rare so there was little social interaction with other parents from work. Moving recently to Montreal has helped with that and we have been out, had people over, and had more "us" and "me" time in the last two months than the last four years combined.'
>
> **Colin, Montreal, two sons aged 2 and 3 years.**

If just one partner is working then there may not be the stress/rush factor in the morning; however, the one left home can sometimes feel resentful. When Dad is working nine to five (or longer), that means Mum is responsible for the kids for 10 hours (give or take) a day. By the time Dad comes home, Mum is exhausted and wants Dad to take the kids off her hands, whereas Dad wants to walk in the door from a hard day at work and relax. It is important to communicate and have systems in place that give everyone a break. For instance, a weekend is everyone's weekend. Yes, it's Dad's time to kick off his shoes and recover from a week at work. But it is also Mum's weekend too and parenthood should be shared on the weekend so that everyone is happy.

> *'With him working so hard and especially working at home most nights, I often feel invisible, like I'm interrupting him to have a conversation or like a secretary wanting to put something in his calendar.'*
>
> **Anon, New Zealand**

> *'The work and home life balance is difficult. After a tough day at work it can be hard to dedicate yourself to your children when you get home and you're tired and burnt out. This can leave me feeling like I'm letting my kids down.'*
>
> **Elton, Oamaru, two daughters aged 2 and 7 years**

> *'Before we had our baby I felt that my husband and I were more equal. I never really thought about the division of roles between male and female. Now that I am at home I really noticed the division between the roles of the breadwinner and homemaker and feel it has had a bit of a negative effect on our relationship. My husband's job has suddenly taken on a whole new level of importance. He worked before we had a baby and managed to do lots around the house and he would still be working if we didn't have a baby. I always expected to take on more around the house but I am working from home and I don't always feel like spending all my time doing housework. The housework situation is a bit better now but for a while there he basically stopped doing anything. From speaking to my friends this seems to be quite common.'*
>
> **Lauren, Wellington, one daughter aged 6 months**

WHATEVER WORKS

'We constantly fight. He believes he shouldn't have to help with our daughter just because he works and I stay home with the baby.'

Anon, Calgary

'We have taken on very traditional roles (housewife and breadwinner) which we didn't have before. It creates pressure for him to stay in a well-paid job even if it's not very fulfilling. I am mostly glad to be at home but feel lost in terms of career.'

Rebecca, Christchurch, one daughter aged 4 years

'I feel less resentment than I did after our first child. Having each worked part time and shared parenting we both have more of an appreciation of what the other has to do. I still feel a bit of resentment about night parenting, but my husband deals with our older child if he wakes and then has to go to work in the morning. There's not much resentment these days. The first was harder as neither of us knew what to do or how long it would all last.'

Anna, Dunedin, two daughters aged 1 and 3 years

Mothers are their harshest critics. There are so many ways you can approach motherhood: stay-at-home mum, part-time work, full-time work. The options are endless but often so too are the expectations.

My friend Rachel lamented that her neighbour said, 'I could never have my toddler in daycare five days a week!' In my homeland of Canada it is quite common for mothers to have a full year's paid maternity leave and then to return to work full time while their children are in care.

Various parenting books will advise on different philosophies and techniques for raising babies. We went routine for our first and demand for our second. My advice to those expecting or in the midst of the first year with baby is to do 'whatever works', particularly in baby's first three months. If Mum is getting frazzled and Dad finds it easier to stay at work than come home it may be a good time to look at your situation and see what you can change to make it less frustrating.

Sometimes when mothers are venting to their girlfriends they discover what it is that is truly bothering them and what would ease the problem. My cousin (formerly a lawyer and now an at-home mother) was saying how it was difficult getting used to not earning any money herself and therefore being overly cautious with the spending. 'But all I want is a cleaner!' she suddenly said. Problem solved.

Work-life balance and earning a crust

'Work-life balance has always been very important to me. I very rarely work weekends, and have never brought work home. I always try to be with the kids for the first and last hours of their days, and my wife is very understanding in allowing me to have some evenings out.'

Tim, Christchurch, two daughters aged 1½ and 3½ years

While some dads feel tremendous pressure as the primary breadwinner, others admit that sometimes work is more fun. At work he's on to it and in charge. People respect and appreciate him. At home he's in trouble. Home too late, not doing enough or doing it right with the kids. It's the classic case of the husband having more fun at work than at home. Make home fun too, mums!

 More than sleepless nights and 2-year-old tantrums, the hardest thing I've found about the baby years is reconciling my role as mother and worker. The work-life balance and ongoing self-inquisition over how many hours and how to fit it all in. Daycare versus no daycare, when to work, how much to work...

Personally, I went back to work full time when Jack was just 8 months old. I had actually planned to go earlier but, like most new parents, had completely underestimated how much being a parent would change me. When I did have to go back to work, it surprised me that I was rather half-hearted about going, especially as I had always loved my job pre-children.

It took me a while to get back into things and I found that I was no longer the frivolous time-waster I had been before. Without realising it, before children I had frittered away lots of time: chatting by desks, making copious cups of tea, spending time thinking and planning. Suddenly I didn't have the luxury of time. I would race in after everyone else arrived (after dropping my child at daycare) and be the first to race out in the afternoon. Work time became focus time and I was more efficient than I had ever been in my life.

Meetings ran to schedule and to agenda — very unusual in advertising! Projects ran to timelines. Creative reviews were prompt and honest — I no longer had time to 'cushion' bad feedback. Whips were cracked and accounts ran smoothly.

I soon realised that to have a happy, healthy family life and a good solid work life, other things had to give. I cut back on friends, and weekends and evenings were precious. If I had missed my son all day, why would I then go out in the evening and miss his bathtime and bedtime too?

Of course, things at work had to give as well. Advertising is a social environment and there are often leaving drinks, welcome drinks, birthday dinners, client entertainment functions and so on, and I could no longer afford the time, nor the energy, to go to those functions. Work became primarily work and not so much part of the social calendar as it had before children. Family time was just that.

'The thing that suffered the most was the "me time". Family time was good. When I went back to work part time when my first was 9½ months I realised that it was too much. I felt good about doing it as it meant that my partner got to be a part-time dad and my baby was not being brought up by a stranger, but the sleep deprivation killed me and was hard on the family. When our baby was 19 months I dropped to 10½ hours a week as my partner went full time at his job. This was hard in a different way. I had to concede to daycare when I didn't want to, but didn't want to give up my job completely either. After the initial four months of my child crying and clinging to me every time he had to go to daycare (he only went two half-days a week and was securely attached to us, so it took a bit of settling in) he was happier and so was I. Keeping house and making good, quality time for family was a bit harder but do-able and we were all happy with the situation after those first few months.'

Anna, Dunedin, one son aged 2 years, baby on the way

'I returned to work with my first baby at 3½ months and full time was too much but it definitely helped me to feel like "me" again. Second time round I will probably do two days a week at 4 months old. I'm totally open-minded this time. My husband would agree that I'm the type of person who needs balance.'

Kelly, Christchurch, one son aged 4 years, baby on the way

Do what works for you

I remember when Ruby was just over 1 and in daycare three days a week while I worked. I remember being amazed that a friend (with two kids) was still not back to work. I just couldn't comprehend being home all the time or not working for two whole years. My sister with her 8-year-old (and three younger kids) hadn't worked for eight years! Now my mindset has done a total shift and I must say that for me, with baby number two the desire to 'work' totally plummeted.

'Going to work makes me realise how happy I am to be at home with the kids.'

Nat

Is it the hardest job I've ever had? I suppose so but I still don't love thinking of it as a 'job'. Sometimes I look back at jobs I've had and things that I've achieved in wonder that I did it, whereas now it would be so daunting or so far from my realm of comfort or interest. I was once lead singer for a band and an outdoor instructor at Outward Bound being responsible for 12 lives at sea for three days. When I went back to work after baby number one my care factor had definitely diminished. I often felt resentful, thinking, 'I gave up my maternity leave for this?'

'It's not the nappy changing, the lack of sleep, the peculiar breasts or the responsibility. It's not missing out on hen weekends, having to wear practical clothing or negotiating a pram around Sainsbury's. Coming to terms with the fact that **you** are now a mother can be very hard and it takes a long time. Learning how to fit this in with all your other roles and personalities is your key to survival in the first year.'

Liz Fraser, *Yummy Mummy Survival Guide*

WHATEVER WORKS

I can totally relate to this. I was guilty in the early stages of parenting of feeling like I had to qualify myself as being a mother, 'but I used to be a project manager'. Project manager ironically is a great title for motherhood too! I was definitely caught in a bit of an identity crisis, trying to please everyone. I would drop my kids off at daycare (the minimum time of one morning and one afternoon a week — see, here I go again) and hope that I wouldn't run into Mike and Joan, a lovely elderly couple on our street who I assumed would think that a mother should be at home, raising her kids. Fortunately I had a job and employer who was very accommodating to my changing needs as a mother. I went back to work three days a week after our first child but only four hours a week (two days a month!) after our second. My motivation to work completely plummeted after having our second baby. My new mindset was I have the rest of my life to work!

Figuring out what's right for you and your family is really tough. Rather than trying to impress everyone (so high school) I think I was trying not to offend anyone or make them feel like I was doing a disservice to my kids.

Mothers' guilt

 Ask any honest mother how they feel on an average day and the answer is often the same: 'Guilty'.

If we work we feel guilty for leaving our child in childcare or with a nanny, even if work is a choice as a career mother, not a necessity. You would be lying if you said you never felt guilty for not staying at home with your child. If your child is with a nanny you feel guilty and jealous that someone else is doing all the things you want to do with them, and getting paid for the pleasure. If your child is in daycare, you hate the fact that they are just one of a number of snotty-nosed children at that establishment. Mothers, feeling guilty for taking too much time off work, will often drop their sick child at daycare even when they know they really should be at home recovering.

So, you feel guilty for leaving your child and going to work but at the same time you feel guilty for not giving your work 100 per cent. You may have been the office star in a previous life but, unless you are a callous cow and not in the least maternal, I defy you to challenge me that you are still giving your office 100 per cent post-children. Let's face it, you are probably one of the last people at work in the morning, prising clinging hands off your smart suit to be able to get into the office. You'll be one of the first to leave in the evening, needing to get back in time for the nanny to go and so that you at least get a quick hour with your child before they are due in bed.

'OK,' you may say, 'but I don't take lunch breaks like I used to.' Maybe not but, boy, do you need them now. Let's face it, it's the only chance you get to do your banking, posting, bill payments, any other maintenance and to eat a meal sitting down. And honestly, you can no longer put in the long hours, work the weekends, and often you need to get home because little Johnny is vomiting or is covered in spots.

So, you feel guilty that you are no longer as good at your job as you once were. If you are anything like me you may pick up your child from daycare after a crazy day at work — feeling even more guilty if your child is the last one to be picked up — no mum wants that for their child — then you bundle them into the back of the car and while they sit looking at you from their car seat you spend the majority of the journey home on the telephone to the office trying to put out the fire that happened at 4 p.m. as you were trying to get everything clear for the day.

You get home and feed them something out of a jar, hurtle them through their dinner and bath time with a quick story at bedtime and then say goodnight, and quickly return the phone calls to the office that have been beeping on your mobile for the last hour while trying to grab a take-out menu from the wall chart to order food in before your hubby gets home.

Hubby gets home and you feel guilty that you haven't had time to cook anything, let alone shop, and that you have spent all the money you have earned this week on take-out to make life easier. You flop down in front of the TV with a glass of wine, exhausted.

Before going to bed you look in on your child sleeping peacefully and looking so angelic that you feel terrible that you haven't spent any time with him today and you wish you had given him three stories instead of rushing through one. Then, feeling pretty stink you fall into bed an hour later making excuses for no nooky because, really, it's the last thing you feel like. As you lie there in bed, you can't sleep anyway because you are so wired and thinking about all the things you need to do tomorrow, and you feel guilty for not giving him any intimacy and wishing that you had.

And then it all starts again the next day...

You no longer catch up as much with friends — you can't do the drinks thing after work because it means you don't get to see your child at all. You really cannot be bothered to go home, go through the night-time routine with him and then get ready to go back out into town for drinks as you are just exhausted by that time. Weekends are so precious as it is the only time you really have to see and spend quality time with your family. So, friendships develop into telephone friendships, vaguely promising to catch up at some point in the future. And you feel guilty for that too.

Now, that kind of guilt is all to be expected of course. But what about the 'stay-at-home guilt'? If you don't know what this is, let me enlighten you.

No woman, no matter how perfect everyone may think she is, can honestly do everything. So, if you are a relaxed mum and put your children first and spend most of your time playing and reading to your children, chances are that your house is a tip and so are you.

If you are an anally retentive kind of mum, then you probably need the house to be spotless, all the dishes done and breakfast things cleared up, under the table to be swept, benches to be wiped down, yourself to be showered and dressed, before you can even face sitting down to read your child a book. I'm talking about the 'I'll play with you after I've just put the washing on' mum.

When a child asks you to play or to read them a story, it is the sweetest thing. And it won't last for ever. It is incredible how quickly they stop asking you.

How disheartened would you feel if a friend you were asking for tea kept on giving you excuse after excuse. How would you feel? You would stop asking. Put yourself in your child's shoes. He isn't mature enough to listen reasonably to your excuses and their plausibility. All he knows is he is being put off, yet again. If you really do finish the dishes then go and play with him then good on you. But if you finish the dishes and then just need to hang out the washing after that then chances are you are disappointing someone who really isn't asking for the earth — just for some time with his mum.

It's hard, I know. I am one of the biggest culprits. I cannot face the day unless I am showered, dressed and ready for the day. I cannot leave the house as a pig-sty. Everything needs to be cleared away first. But I am trying to improve so that if my child wants me to see something, I see it then and there and do the dishes afterwards or that I do the dishes, then play with my child for 20 minutes.

Someone once told me that you should read your child at least three stories a day — not only from an educational standpoint but to share closeness and intimacy with your child while spending good mum time with them. If you can try to read those three stories in the morning then you know you are on the right track.

It's not just about keeping on top of everything you need to do. Cooking, cleaning, shopping and general household maintenance might not sound like much on top of childcare, but when you are home full time, each of those items needs even more care and attention. Otherwise the place is always a mess and there is never anything nutritious to eat. Getting your child to help you complete your tasks is often the best answer. If you need to clean, give them a cloth too. If you need to sweep, give them a small brush. If you need to garden, give them a spade.

Sasha and I have had some hilarious moments cleaning the bathroom together. She just loves being Mummy's little helper. And I have got some great pics of Jack taking down the washing for me in the nude!

While I am racked with guilt every day, Nat is the positive opposite. 'Life is too short to be guilty. Just enjoy the moment,' she quips.

Look out, Super-mum, here comes Wonder-mum

My parental survival saving grace and the secret to my sanity is that I simply don't believe in perfection. I don't do guilt. I understand 'feeling bad' — if you feel bad that you spent too much time tidying up rather than doing puzzles with your 2-year-old. But guilt just seems to have so much weight behind it. If you feel 'guilty', then do something about it. Change your life and lose the guilt. My husband's favourite tagline of late: 'Whose problem is it?'

As for perfection, I strive for greatness and even excellence but I don't believe in things being 'perfect'. I don't believe in Super-mum. When you see a mum who looks like she's got it all together you can react three ways:

1. You can compare yourself and feel like crap.
2. You can look at her and think negative thoughts.
3. You can be inspired. I believe in Wonder-mum! As in, 'I wonder how she keeps her house so clean...'

I strive to do a great job as a mother but I don't beat myself up about it. Mothers are too hard on themselves and we seem to spend too much time lamenting what we could have done better rather than enjoying the moment.

Just the other day I was at the crucial stroller and scooter stage of leaving the house to take my son Jonah to kindy. Despite having had four-plus hours to 'prepare', there I was, in all my flustered glory. Honestly, perfection isn't even in my hemisphere. I'm just trying to get by. I suppose I should mention that while I don't do perfection and guilt, I am good friends with their evil step-sisters frustration and resentment.

Solo mothers are my true Wonder-mums doing all the work and the play, sorting all the logistics, tantrums... and not having a partner there (for whatever reason) to share the load and the joys at the end of the day.

Enough with the Super-mum saga! Instead of striving for perfection we should encourage mothers to just be themselves, be proud of their parenting and to ask for help if needed. So many of us do not have family nearby so we should encourage the 'village/community' feeling by offering and accepting help as part of what we do.

Choosing childcare

It's not only choosing to go back to work that's a minefield but the whole childcare conundrum is a challenge also. Are you lucky enough to have local grandparents who don't mind helping out? Or are you going to have to start looking for alternative options, e.g. a nanny, au pair, childcare centre, home-based childcare (either in your own home or in the home of a 'shared' nanny) or even a friend you pay to help you out?

Whatever you decide will be based on your needs, e.g. whether you are going back part time or full time or even if you are able to work from home some days. Other factors in your decision will be:

- geographic (near to home or near to work)
- financial (often childcare centres are more cost-effective than a private nanny)
- convenient (if you know you are going to have an 8 a.m. meeting every day then it may be easier to get someone to come to your home rather than rely on a childcare centre that doesn't open until 8.30 a.m.)
- emotional (who will look after my wee darling and keep them as safe and happy as I will? Not to mention the fact that nobody wants a complete stranger looking after their precious cargo).

A good friend of ours decided to hire a nanny for her first child when she returned to work (when her child was 6 months old). She resigned five months later, citing the fact that she couldn't stand that 'someone else' was raising her child, doing all the things she wanted to do with him and being the first person to experience all those special moments. She declared that if she had placed her baby in a childcare centre, she believed that she would have remained at work.

No matter what you decide, one key tip is to get on the waiting list. Even if you are unsure whether you want your child to go to a childcare centre, visit a few and put your child's name down, even before they are born. The best ones get snaffled up early on and waiting lists are long. Also, have a plan for childcare and then a back-up plan. You never know what's around the corner.

A mother with something to prove

I put Jack in a childcare centre close to work full time from 8 months old. It was a disaster. He contracted every bug going (my father-in-law named the place The Petri Dish), he would cry and cling to me every day and would have to be prised off me. I would sit in the car outside the office crying and asking myself what I was putting my child through. He was often the first baby to be dropped off at the centre and the last to be picked up due to a demanding job and a stubborn mother (me!) who thought she had something to prove.

I had chosen the daycare centre based on its proximity to my work. I thought that would enable me to stay at work longer and pick Jack up later than I would have had to if I had needed to travel 30 minutes towards home for a daycare. Due to this stupid decision, not only did it mean that I was the only person able to do the pick-up and drop-off (if I have chosen close to home, hubby or my in-laws would have been able to help out more), it also meant that I picked up a very tired little baby at the end of the day. He would cry the entire journey home in the car and then by the time I got home it was close to 6 p.m. and I still needed to feed, bath, and settle him to bed.

With my second child, I did almost the opposite. I had had such a hard time with Jack at daycare that when I did eventually return to work after four years at home, I decided to get a 'Hot Nanny' (more on her later). Ironically, due to their different personalities, Jack would have been better suited to me not returning to work at all, whereas Sasha would have thrived in a daycare situation where, as Nat has said to me, she would have been running the place!

A mother with a diminishing desire to work

During my career as a 'mother' I've employed a nanny, shared a nanny, tried Montessori and daycare. Like Jacqui, I went back to work early for possibly the wrong reasons. As project manager for a new business (there were only four of us), I felt that I should and could handle it. I put Ruby's name on the list at daycare but didn't want her to start there until the age of 1 as she seemed too young. So I knowingly went for the expensive option of a nanny who would come to my home and care for my darling while I worked two days a week from home. It was great but I literally was not making any money. The transition to daycare went smoothly and I upped my hours to three days a week.

With baby number two, I worked even less. I took eight months off and gave work the explicit instruction not to call, email or ask me to do any work. I then worked 12 hours a week while both kids were at daycare. Mathematically speaking the more kids, the less cost effective daycare becomes. Add to that the fact that my passion and interest in 'work' significantly diminished, I soon dropped to 10 hours a week and then to none at all. Only when my third child was 2 did I start working again and this time it as on my on business: Go to Girl Social Media & Networking.

'Hot Nanny'

 I used to swear that I would never hire a hot nanny. How could a woman even contemplate such a thing? It's hard enough having a strange woman come into your home to look after your children, take them out to the park and all the other fun activities they do as well as see them reach their milestones while you're working. If she's good-looking as well, that would just be a killer.

In the movie *Sex and the City 2*, Charlotte's hot, braless nanny jumps up and down with the kids, much to the delight of the men. However, when it came to choosing a nanny and I had a choice between the hot and the not-so-hot, I chose the hot. Why? Well, suddenly when it came to choosing someone to look after my children, whether she was hot or not no longer mattered. All that mattered was that she fitted in with them, got on with them and would truly enjoy and care about them.

A fellow school-mum has also hired an extremely hot nanny, and they are happy with her — and that is all that matters. In fact she came home one day to witness the nanny having a water-fight in the garden with her kids — soaking wet and even hotter — or so the next-door neighbour seemed to think as she noticed his tongue hanging out of his mouth.

Did she care? Did she heck! To the nanny it was just fun with the kids, and that's exactly what my fellow-mum saw too. Squeals of delight and hilarity that they had managed to get her wet with their water pistols. Genuine fun.

Who cares whether my nanny is hot? As long as she is good and kind and caring to the kids and they are happy with her, that's all that matters.

Getting out the door

 Getting out the door with children can be a mission at the best of times. Throw in trying to get to work too and it's nearly Mission Impossible.

Our house is chaos in the mornings. Hubby and I dance around each other trying to each get ready for work, while getting children ready at the same time, as well as trying to sort out breakfast, make beds, clean teeth, iron shirts, organise packed lunches, missing school books . . .

I am trying to get myself into a routine, but no matter how organised I think I am, at 8.15 a.m. on a weekday morning it always turns to custard. Usually I am racing around half-dressed, eye pencil in hand, yelling at children to clean teeth, get shoes and socks on and get their school bags ready.

At 8.20 a.m. I am still yelling, while simultaneously making two packed lunches and throwing in whatever is in the fridge together for me.

At 8.25 a.m. I haven't stopped yelling. 'Jack, I've asked you three times to clean your teeth!' 'Sasha, why have you taken your shoes off? Put them back on now.' 'Guys, stop arguing!' 'Jack, where's your school bag?' 'Sasha — put your coat on!' 'Sasha, I said *put your shoes back on now!*'

All the while I am writing my list for Hot Nanny to know what needs doing after school and what the children will have for dinner. At 8.30 a.m. I decide to help out by getting down the noodles from their high perch at the top of the pantry. As I balance tentatively on the top of the stepladder, I feel rather than see that I have knocked against a large glass jar full of rice on the top shelf. In slow motion it wobbles then tips and, my hands full of noodles, I watch aghast as it crashes onto the new kitchen bench, taking out a large chunk of pristine white marble, then bangs onto the floor, shattering glass everywhere and sending rice into every tiny crack and under every single element in the kitchen.

'No!' I cry, not believing that this could really happen to me at what is now 8.35 a.m. I stop the children crunching over broken glass in the kitchen as they come to investigate the crash. I know there is no way I could possibly leave this for the nanny to clear up so out comes the broom, vacuum cleaner and everything else to attempt to clean up as much as possible.

By the time that is done I have lost all composure. It is 8.50 a.m. as I run — in heels — to school, with one child dragging on one hand and the other one balanced on my hip. Hurriedly I kiss him goodbye. 'Don't go,' he pleads, not liking not being 'settled' as he normally is. I brush the top of his hair. 'I'll see you tonight, buddy,' I reply in a rush.

Next I scamper out to the kindergarten a few streets away. My daughter is not, however, going to let me get away that easily. 'No! Don't go, Mummy! Don't go!' she screams. She is sobbing her little heart out. The teachers help prise her off me and tell me just to go. I know they say not to look back but I can't help it. My memory is of this little sobbing face pressed against the gate. I am brushing back tears as I get into the car at 9.10 a.m. that morning. At times like that, being a working mum is hard.

I feel like a bad mother. I feel awful. What a failure. My mobile rings. It is a client telling me that they are waiting for me — I am late for a meeting I completely forgot about. Now I feel even worse. Not only am I a failure as a mother, but as a worker too. And that's just the start of the day.

Couplehood and work

The whole maternity leave/work thing can put a bit of pressure on the relationship. Money stress, time stress, the new division of the domestic duties, identity shifts and of course the tiredness. It all adds up! It can be tricky if you and hubby are not on the same page. For example, if you are keen to get back to work and he would prefer you to be home with the baby (or vice versa), there may be conflict ahead. Try to keep communication open as both of you may find your views evolve over time, and with each additional child. Go back to the 'blue sky' activity and try to create or 'design' the lifestyle that best suits you both.

Depending on your and hubby's job, try not to go back to work too early. Enjoy your maternity leave and the first six months or year (depending on how long you have) with baby. You can 'work' for the rest of your life. If your husband or partner is lucky enough to work for a company that is willing to offer paternity leave then take it up! Not only will it take childcare pressure off both of you when you go back to work but, importantly, it enables your partner to really appreciate what it is to be a stay-at-home parent and to spend quality time with the baby.

IOTTM tips for a work-life balance

- ☉ Be open to changing expectations. What you thought you might want pre-children may well change.
- ☉ Do what works for your family: Stay at home, part time, full time, flex time. Try a bit of 'lifestyle design' and create the work–life balance that actually works for you as a family. You'll be much happier as a couple too!
- ☉ Weigh up the pros and cons of you returning to work. You may find that the financial and emotional cost outweighs the benefits of you returning to the workforce.
- ☉ Consider your child's personality as much as possible when choosing childcare options. If your child is an outgoing go-getter then chances are he'll

love the busyness of daycare. If he's more sensitive then consider a nanny or even not going back to work at all.

- Get on the waiting list of your chosen childcare centre early on.
- Have a plan for childcare and then a back-up plan. Murphy's Law and all that…
- Ask yourself 'who you are doing it for?' and 'at what cost?'

 Work-Life Balance: ifonlytheytoldme.com/66

CHAPTER TEN

Keeping kids safe

Being sick while pregnant

 When my eldest child was 3 we visited the dentist for the first time. He was fine. My youngest wasn't even 2 at the time and the dental nurse, playing around and wanting to amuse her, told her to climb up onto the chair and open her mouth wide for a bit of fun. Imagine my astonishment when she turned around and in all seriousness told me to bring her back the moment she turned 3 years of age.

You see, Sasha had suffered from the injustice of her mother being sick while pregnant. Poor Sasha's teeth happened to be forming while I was being ill in the corner and pregnant with her. Not a major, is it? I didn't think so. However, the dental nurse thought differently. You see, the fact that I happened to have a virus while those teeth were forming meant that the enamel hadn't formed on her teeth. Not only that but some of the teeth hadn't formed properly either.

When I told a friend she said, 'But it's only the baby teeth', but it turns out that what happens to your child's baby teeth really affects the adult teeth too. So, everything she was eating and drinking was literally protected by nothing. Which means that it's going through to the gums, affecting the cavities and therefore the future teeth.

So, for the last couple of years, until my child came of age, she has been treated religiously every three months with a dental coating to protect her teeth until she was old enough to go into dental surgery.

Finally, she was old enough to go in and have her teeth done. So, anyone who has been through surgery with a child and a general anaesthetic knows how hard it is to prevent your child from eating for the 12 hours leading up to surgery. You hide water bottles, you tell them they cannot eat and somehow you muddle through.

Tuesday 7.30 a.m., there we were. Bright eyed and eager . . . to get it over with.

Fast forward one hour and a nurse advises me that surgery went well and 12 teeth have been successfully capped and saved and that they will be coming to get me when my daughter comes around from the anaesthetic in the next 30 minutes. I am forewarned that often they are distressed, clingy and weepy.

I heard Sasha come out of the anaesthetic before a nurse even had a chance to get out of her seat. Screaming at the top of her lungs for her mummy, I was packing my bags before they even popped their heads in to look for me. By the time I got to her, two nurses were holding her down and another looking on in horror. The sight of me calmed her for five minutes or so but she got distressed again, to the point that they actually removed us from the recovery ward to a little side room to ensure that we didn't upset the other children.

I have never seen my child so angry. And do you blame her? All she remembered was that people in blue uniforms wearing hats and masks who seemed nice have in some way tricked her, and she has woken up with a sore mouth, a sore head and very unsure of what was going on. And yet the 'nice people' with the masks were still everywhere. They had told me I would have to stay around for another few hours to ensure she recovered from the general anaesthetic but I literally begged them to let me out. To be honest, I think they were quite relieved to get rid of us.

And, once we got home, she was my daughter again. She wanted hugs, kisses, stories and snuggles. And slowly she lost her anxiousness, although her mouth still hurt.

One mother once told me that it didn't matter what her child ate while a baby and toddler because the baby teeth would fall out anyway. Believe me, after going through the last couple of years, I can tell you all right now that whatever your child eats now affects their future teeth, so look after those baby teeth. The health of the baby teeth ensures the health of the adult teeth and nobody wants to affect those, right?

My 4-year-old now has a silver mouth. I have told her that it is because silver is her favourite colour and the dentist was trying to make her teeth as pretty as possible. She has proudly showed off her silver teeth to her friends this week and I just keep smiling and telling her how beautiful she is.

Here are some top tips to look after your child's teeth:

- ☉ Avoid orange juice and other juices and sugary drinks when your child is young. Avoid letting your child fall asleep with a bottle in their mouth, especially if the bottle is full of juice. Water is fine. Even toddlers are best to avoid sugary drinks and stick with water. If you must give your under fives juice then give them half juice, half water.

- ⚇ Make brushing teeth fun. Look for ways to engage your children in brushing. Make it seem as if brushing is a fun thing to do rather than a chore. Get your child a fun and colourful toothbrush to start.
- ⚇ Allow your children to brush your teeth. Have fun with that, then allow them to brush their own teeth. Finish by brushing your child's teeth.
- ⚇ Have your child brush their favourite doll's teeth before you brush theirs. Remember to routinely give them the opportunity to brush their own teeth and then follow up by brushing their teeth correctly.
- ⚇ Use only a pea-size amount of toothpaste on your child's toothbrush. Larger amounts tend to be difficult for kids to handle by creating too much foam and overwhelming your child's mouth with toothpaste!
- ⚇ Use a toothpaste that's made for kids. Others can taste too strong and put children off brushing with them.
- ⚇ Avoid raisins and dry fruit whenever possible as they get stuck in between the teeth.
- ⚇ Don't forget to praise, praise, praise your kids for their awesome brushing.

Accidents happen

Children are a massive responsibility. Keeping them happy, healthy and safe day in day out, year after year is a real accomplishment. Despite our constant vigilance, accidents sometimes do happen or we are lucky and get away with 'near misses'. Everyone has a 'close call' story. They almost dropped the baby in the shower, they grabbed their child as a car backed out of the driveway... It's amazing how many stories come out once you get the conversation started. It's half confession time and half a wake-up call to up our game and definitely to expect the unexpected.

When Jonah was 2½ years old I left the room for one minute. In that time he got up from playing in the lounge, dragged a dining room chair into the kitchen and climbed up to where I was cooking pasta. I walked in and grabbed him off the stool completely grateful for what could have happened but didn't. It was totally my fault — everyone knows you shouldn't leave the room when cooking. A close call.

I had another scare a year later when visiting my auntie and getting the kids ready to swim. Jonah (now 3½ years old) lifted the cover off the hot tub while I was one metre away with my back turned. I heard it bang shut, turned around, scanned the area and yelled his name then heard a muffled yell. I lifted the lid and jumped in the tub to grab him!

 We've had a few close shaves with Sasha too. The first when she was just 4 months old. With only 19 months between my children I needed to keep Sasha out of her elder sibling's jealous reach. I found I couldn't leave Sasha on her play mat on the floor unless I was in the room with them both. Not that Jack purposely wanted to hurt his little sister but he certainly had no concept of what it was to be gentle. Once when I needed to do the washing, I put Sasha in a bouncinette chair on the kitchen bench, believing her safe from big brother's reach. I disappeared off to the laundry and as I came back into the kitchen I saw that little Sasha had bounced herself almost off the entire bench. The bouncinette was teetering over the edge of the bench — another couple of bounces and she would be off and I grabbed it just in time.

A friend of ours has a similar story. Unfortunately they didn't manage to catch their child and a hospital visit followed. She was racked with guilt afterwards.

Then there was the time when Sasha, now a toddler, climbed up to the window seat in the lounge and pulled herself up onto the window. We hadn't realised the catch was broken and as the window swung open Sasha, only 18 months, stood teetering on the edge. We caught her in time but were very shaken. A trip to the hardware store followed shortly after to ensure windows were firmly fixed.

Everyone's got a story and I'm a big believer in sharing stories to keep us on our toes. Anticipate crazy random things to happen and hopefully you can be one step ahead.

Missing child

 It's your worst fear. You're in a shopping mall. It's busy. There are people everywhere. Your child is by your feet. Isn't she? You look down and she's gone. You look around frantically and she's nowhere to be seen. You scour faces, backs of heads trying to find her and then luckily you spot her. Face glued against the sweetie shop window, licking her lips and completely oblivious to the fact that she is 'lost'.

My mother tells me that when I was 4 years old, she lost me. I do remember it, partly. She tells me that we were in a supermarket. She realised she had forgotten something from an aisle and she told me to 'wait there', to 'not move a muscle' while she disappeared up an aisle to find her pasta, or whatever it was. I did 'wait there' for what seemed like an eternity and was probably only a few minutes. And then I saw her, or I thought I did. It was her legs, to be precise. I spotted her legs and she wasn't coming back to me, and so I followed her. I followed those legs all the way out of the supermarket and along the road to the post office. It was only when I actually got to the post office that I realised the legs didn't belong to my mum but to a complete stranger, wearing similar tights. By that time I was a little confused . . . and, being 4, I couldn't find my way back to the supermarket. So, I just stood there in the middle of the pavement, confused and a little disoriented, waiting to be 'found'.

I was found 35 minutes later, by which point I was crying and distressed. My mother, when she found me, was crying more though, although I didn't recognise it at the time. She had scoured every inch of the supermarket before venturing onto the street outside.

I, of course, was oblivious to how much drama I had caused, until today when it all came flooding back. So, picture this. I am at work. Busy and a little stressed. Work dramas are unfolding around me as there are issues about a client's advertising placement. I'm in the middle of dealing with it when the phone rings. It's hubby. 'Hi, honey!' I say, pleased to hear from him. He doesn't waste time. He says the three words no parent wants to hear: 'Sasha's gone missing.'

'What?' I respond, relatively calmly. 'What do you mean, "missing"?'

Hubby is not prone to exaggeration or extravagance of words, so when he says the words, 'She's been missing for thirty-five minutes. Hot Nanny has just phoned. Everyone's out looking for her', I know to be a little concerned. Actually more than a little, but I'm trying to remain calm. Suddenly my client's duplicity of advertising is no longer the biggest thing in my mind. 'OK,' I reply, 'I'll leave now.'

'Hot Nanny was about to phone the police,' he reports, 'but I've said to give it five more minutes. If she doesn't turn up by then, Hot Nanny will call and we'll phone the police and head home.'

'Right,' I reply, biting my lip in concern. 'Five minutes.'

The next five minutes are the slowest five minutes known to man. Every minute seems to drag by. I am trying to get my head around my client's issues but, to be honest, they feel insignificant now.

When my colleague calls to discuss them, I am only half listening to her. She blabs on and I nod and agree distractedly, looking at the clock the whole time. Seriously, has it actually only been two minutes? Suddenly, halfway through the call, my mobile rings. Hubby's name is displayed. I snatch it up, cutting off my colleague at the same time.

He says the words I really don't want to hear: 'I'm grabbing a taxi, heading home now. They still haven't found her. The builders are helping look too.' I pale when I realise the implication of his words. We are in the midst of a renovation and there are holes and dangers everywhere around our house. Oh no. 'I'm on my way' is all I manage.

Five minutes later, I'm screeching uphill in my car when my mobile rings again: 'They've found her. She was hiding behind the curtains curled up in a tiny ball in her bedroom the entire time.' Relief rings through in his voice. I realise that I am actually a little rattled. I have to pull over and regain my composure before returning back to the office. Half of me wants to race back home. To shake her and hug her and make her realise the worry she has caused everyone. Not just us but Hot Nanny, the neighbours, the builders and half the people in the street, all of whom have been scouring cracks and gardens. One family even walked to the nearest school for us in case she had gone to visit her brother.

To her, it was just a game. She thought it was hide and seek and it was great fun that everyone was looking for her. She had no concept of how distressed everyone else was. Our builders were even driving around the neighbourhood looking for her, for goodness' sake!

So, yes, although I did tick off my minx of a child for putting everyone through a huge amount of worry, I was also more than a little relieved that it was, to a small child, just a game of hide and seek and that our daughter ended the day tucked up in bed, safe and sound and still oblivious to the dangers of the world.

Stranger danger

There's a balance between giving kids freedom and space and keeping them safe. The message is not really 'don't talk to strangers' because we role model being friendly and saying hello to strangers all the time. It's about teaching them to say no. To not to get into cars or to go anywhere with strangers. If you get lost, stay where you are and ask a mummy for help. We don't want to unintentionally scare our kids but we do need to give them the skills to stay safe.

 I'm just entering that stage where you can take your eyes off the kids for more than a few minutes at a time. I'm so used to hovering over them when we're out and about, but now when we're at a playground I am more relaxed (with my 5-year-old) than I used to be.

I was reminded of this the other day while watching my two older kids from a picnic table at a very crowded playground. I noticed that a group of international tourists were admiring the scene and when I next looked over, one of the men was having his photo taken while holding my daughter! It seemed to be an innocent photo but just felt strange. My husband rushed over and calmly diffused the situation but it was a reminder for us to once again 'expect the unexpected' and to have another 'stranger' talk with the kids about what's OK and what's not OK.

I imagine that most parents have their own 'when I was a kid we used to...' story. For me we used to play Wonder Woman in the ravine down by the train tracks and play out in the street playing kick-the-can until it was dark. Somehow I can't imagine letting my kids do that these days. As kids get older and become more responsible, we want to give them increased freedom but without compromising our sanity and their safety. A recent American documentary talked about the impact of 'helicopter parenting' and having GPS tracking devices on kids. Yes, they're safe, but where's the trust?

We spent two nights at a public campground this summer and it was the first time I'd ever really let Ruby out of my sight in a public place. She was with her friend and they would meet up with other children and we would check in on them now and then. All was well and we had a good holiday but I wouldn't say that I really 'relaxed' (do we ever?). My kids are not 'runners' so while I don't need to worry about them wandering off, I suppose it's more 'other people' that I worry about.

Five top tips for keeping kids safe around water

1. **Supervision and proximity**
   Depends on age and skill but at Glen Innes pool children under the age of 10 need to be supervised by an adult. The closer you are, the faster you can respond.
2. **Awareness and knowledge**
   Proper fencing around pools, being aware of dangers at different types of water (the beach, the pools).
3. **Water-safety skills**
   Teach children water-safety skills through formal lessons or parent, such as safe entry in water, U-turn, floating on back, 'wait' until an adult is supervising them.
4. **Practise and enforce water safety**
   Do progressions and work towards kids practising falling into a pool or out of their kayak. This will have them better prepared for if it does happen.
5. **Know your child's ability**
   Know what they can and can't do. Remember, swimming in a pool is different from falling in.

A friend recently told me they bought life jackets for the kids to wear while playing in the waves at the beach.

Tips for swimming at the beach
- ⊙ Swim between the flags
- ⊙ Swim with adult supervision
- ⊙ An adult should stand between child and open sea
- ⊙ Life jackets and flotation aids do not mean the child is safe. Supervision is always needed.

Tips for swimming in a river
- ⊙ Be aware of current direction and power
- ⊙ Use safe entry when unsure of depth
- ⊙ If in doubt, stay out
- ⊙ Know your limits and the environment

Tips for swimming in a lake
- ⊙ Swimming in open water is harder than a pool
- ⊙ Be cautious of depth and drop-offs
- ⊙ Wear a life jacket if on a boat

Family emergency kit

 You never know what's going to happen so it's best to be prepared! Here are some items and ideas I recommend from my experience in the Christchurch earthquakes.

Shoes

Stash old shoes in your emergency kit in case you have to suddenly run from the house due to fire, earthquake or robbery. Bare feet and broken glass are not a good combo. Have a pair of old shoes (that fit) for every member of your family in your emergency kit, just in case!

Have a family 'plan'

You never know what life is going to throw at you. It pays to have a plan so that your family knows what to do in the case of fire, robbery or natural disaster. Ironically my hubby and I made our 'plan' two days before the Christchurch earthquake so when it hit in the middle of the night we both went into 'auto pilot'. He grabbed Ruby, I grabbed Jonah and we rushed outside to the neighbour's house.

Have an emergency kit

Have an emergency kit ready to 'grab and go', including food, water and shelter as well as: heavy duty backpack, torch and radio with extra batteries, first-aid kit, candles and matches, duct tape, dust mask, multi-tool, whistle, plastic bags, wet wipes, toilet paper and more. Make the time to create an emergency kit that is portable and complete.

Be prepared, not paranoid

In addition to 'child proofing' there are some things you can do around the house to keep everyone safe in case you need to suddenly act in the night. Keep a torch by your bedside (in case of a power cut), keep hallways clear for a quick safe exit and keep your wallet, keys and phone together for a 'grab and go'.

Have a first-aid kit that is full, accessible and portable

You will have a first-aid kit in the house (and possibly car and stroller) but it's also good to have a first-aid kit that is full, accessible and portable. Accidents do happen so it's best to be prepared!

Wonderful water

Water is crucial for hydration, cooking and cleaning. Make sure you have 5–10 litres. Write the date on it and replace every six months.

Nat's earthquake story

 Here's a story that really puts things into perspective. It happened to me and to my family during the Christchurch earthquake.

As a parent you want to keep your family safe and do what's best for them. That's what we tried to do in the face of a natural disaster. I've had lots of people ask me about my 'earthquake story' so here it is.

You could say we've been through a lot of upheaval in the past few years. On 22 February 2011 we had a second huge earthquake (6.8) in Christchurch. Lives were lost, homes were destroyed but we were lucky, we only lost a job. The next day our third (and final) baby was born safe and sound. Again we felt fortunate.

When the earthquake hit, we were all outside and together. I couldn't have asked for a better scenario given the circumstances. Ruby (then 4½ years) was standing by the gate with her bike and helmet. Jonah (then 2½ years) was in the garage getting his tricycle out. As I ran to him I was thrown to the ground then crawled to him (with my pregnant belly) as best I could. As a parent, you know how scary it is when your kids are in danger. Possibly as a tribute to my Outward Bound training, I went into 'practical risk management mode' and was efficient and calm.

Liquefaction started bursting from the lawn and concrete so with the help of our lovely neighbour, we put the kids in the car and I did a mad dash into the house to get keys, wallet and cellphone. We drove around the corner to 'higher ground' and waited for my husband Matt to return from work. The phone lines were crammed so I couldn't contact him for a while. Luckily Matt cycles to work so despite the gridlocked traffic we didn't have long to wait until he arrived and we were all together and safe. We went home to start the process of checking on neighbours, cleaning up, boiling water and cooking on the barbecue. That night I went into labour and our darling 'earthquake baby' Xavier was born.

Our house was damaged but liveable, but with no power, water or sewerage it was not the place for a newborn. My sister bought us all one-way tickets to Wellington where we spent the next three weeks being pampered by her and my parents. Matt's parents flew over from Australia to be with us and to meet their new grandson. With the aftermath of the earthquake, we had decided to 'cast the net' very wide with Matt's job search and took a 'the world's your oyster' approach. He ended up applying for and getting his 'dream job' with the NZ Green Building Council and so a new chapter has begun for us in Auckland. We have relatives in Auckland and my other sister only lives a few hours' drive away.

So now our life has gone from earthquake, job loss, new baby to new city, new house, new friends, new life. People have been amazed by our positive 'glass is half full' attitude. I think that's something that comes from the girl I was back in my Branksome days in Toronto. I remember getting the 'enthusiasm' award in grade 7! Sometimes life gets turned upside down but you have to make the best of it. That's just what we did. The *New Zealand Herald* interviewed us after we moved in a story titled Mum's Secret Labour Pains. Sure we have a good attitude but we also had great luck! We could have lost so much more than a job.

We miss our wonderful friends and our 'old life' but with countless aftershocks in Christchurch we are pleased to have moved on. The Geotech report classified our house as in the 'red zone', meaning the land is not safe to live on. The next time I visit Christchurch it will be gone. Matt loves his job, we have met fabulous new friends and all is well. But we still have our emergency bin packed and ready, just in case...

IOTTM tips about keeping kids safe

- There's not an awful lot you can do to avoid being sick while pregnant. Obviously taking good care of yourself, getting plenty of rest and eating a healthy balanced diet, drinking plenty of water and keeping your feet up as much as you can will help. However, if you do get sick, visit your local GP as quickly as you can.

- Take good care of your child's teeth. Teach them the importance of brushing early on.

- Avoid lots of sugary snacks and drinks for children under 5 years old.

- Keep a close eye on children around water. Never let them out of your sight. It only takes a minute for something awful to happen.

- Don't put children in rockers or bouncinette chairs up high. Children can bounce themselves over the edge.

- Anticipate the worst and expect the unexpected. Children have fingers everywhere and see everything from much lower down than you. Wires hanging out, a TV perched on a table rather than fixed to a wall, a hot iron or kettle on the edge of a surface. All of these are big dangers for young, inquisitive children.

- If you have to leave your child unattended while you are in the shower, in the laundry etc., try to eliminate as many risks from the room as possible.

- Talk with your children on the risks of strangers without upsetting them too much. Have a secret family 'code' for people who are picking your child up from school.

- Be vigilant around water and know your child's capabilities. Make sure you and your children swim between the flags at all times and never be far away so you can run in and grab them, fully clothed if necessary.

- You may think a family emergency kit is unnecessary but just reading about Nat's earthquake experience will make you think otherwise!

 Prepared for Emergency: ifonlytheytoldme.com/72

CHAPTER ELEVEN

Family times

Mind your manners

'I wanna ice cream, I wanna ice cream... I WANNA ICE CREAMMMMMM!'

'Say please!' you insist.

We try so hard to instil good manners in our children. After all, 'good manners will get you far', as my father-in-law always says.

I recently held a party for my 4-year-old's birthday. There was one little girl who stood out from all the rest with her beautiful manners. She would come up to me with her deep brown eyes, tap me quietly on the leg and say 'Thank you for a lovely afternoon tea/cake/game/party.' and I would melt, glaring at my own ill-mannered children who romped around expecting cake and presents and everything else to land on their laps.

'Say please!' I would chant at them. 'Say it! Say please!'

Manners need to be taught as early as the first words. One of the first words to teach your child shouldn't be 'mummy' or 'daddy' or 'yes' or 'no', but instead 'please' and 'thank you'. It will get them so much further in life and it is amazing how we all, especially our own parents, appreciate good manners so much.

There are times, however, when you will want the ground to open up and swallow you as your child, loudly and innocently, delivers some corkers. Here are a few:

- ☺ My 3-year-old daughter, Sasha, at the swimming pools one day, points to a very hairy, rather large-nosed woman and shouts: 'Look, Mum, it's Nanny McPhee!'
- ☺ My same 3-year-old daughter at the supermarket being cooed over by the rather large checkout lady until she says loudly, 'Have you got a baby in your tummy?'
- ☺ Four-year-old Thomas, after having the word 'punished' explained to him

when he had to go to bed early, then said the next day (at daycare in front of teachers, kids and parents) that he would be a good boy today so he wouldn't be 'punched'!

- ☉ The same 4-year-old Thomas on his scooter shouting, 'Mum, I'll be careful not to crash into that big fat man.'
- ☉ Two-year-old Joe, whose mum always tells him his bottom is so delicious she wants to eat it, one day, when having his nappy changed he says, 'Please don't eat my diddle, Mummy.'
- ☉ Five-year-old Victoria, while having her hair brushed by Mum, is struggling and squirming. 'Be still,' Mum says, 'don't you want to be beautiful?' 'No, Mum,' she replies sweetly, 'I just want to be like you.'
- ☉ Four-year-old Jack pointing at a man in a wheelchair asking why he is still in a pram.

We all want our children to be good and kind and caring to others. None of us want to be the mum with the kid who kicks and bites and hits others. But sometimes, despite our best efforts, this may happen.

Lead by example

 If you're a stay-at-home mum, it is impossible not to be driven crazy by your child at one point or another. Toddlers in particular are babies with big shoes. They don't know any better and are often just finding their voice. That doesn't make it any easier to handle when they draw all over your walls with permanent marker or chew your book because it was lying within easy reach, or they cover themselves and your carpet with your best Yves Saint Laurent bright red lipstick.

Try not to shout. Shouting can destroy your child's confidence and make them feel insecure about themselves. It's awful to see your child mimicking you by shouting at their siblings or their friends. You recognise yourself in their actions and only then do you realise how badly you handled the situation. If you are someone who would shout easily then the best thing to do in a situation is to stop before saying anything. Walk away. Go into another room if necessary and just pause for a minute. That minute of pausing is all you may need to diffuse your anger and to formulate a different way of dealing with a situation.

Picture this. It is 4.30 p.m. Your husband has just called to tell you he won't be home for dinner as he is catching up with the boys. The place is a pigsty and you cannot for the life of you find your mobile which keeps bleeping to let you know it is dying. You're wearing your husband's boxers because you have run out of clean knickers. You haven't even had time for lunch and the kids are scratchy and hungry. Then your toddler knocks down the milk you have poured for him and you erupt.

You know it is wrong. You know it is not really his fault that you are tired and bad-tempered but you shout at him anyway. You mop it up, feeling terrible, hug him and say sorry and the moment is gone.

Then three days later you see your toddler shouting at your younger child for playing with his pens, and you see yourself in miniature.

'Be nice,' you tell him, wondering where he has picked up his temper from.

We all do it. We swear we will be perfect parents and never shout or snap at our children but we will. Even the calmest of mothers will, on occasion, lose it.

I am too embarrassed to share my 'lose it' moments because I am ashamed of them. No child is perfect by any means and they will all push our buttons on occasion. But we must remember that they learn their habits from us. So, when we do lose it on occasion, it is important to admit you made a mistake and apologise.

I am forever preaching to my children to be 'good and kind', but I am far from perfect too and I need to remember that little people watch and learn and pick up even when we think they are far from earshot.

It is easy to say hurtful things in anger and even though you may not mean them, they can seriously damage your child. The best check of how you are handling a situation is to think to yourself whether you would handle the situation differently in front of a friend or stranger. Would you shout at your child in front of an outsider? Would you say hurtful things? If you know the answer is no then you need to stop and diffuse the situation quickly.

Other tactics work much better. For instance, I recently visited a friend's house who has two small children the same age as mine. While the children played, my friend and I chatted over a cup of tea. Once our tea was finished, we decided to check up on the children. Three of them were playing really nicely in

one of the bedrooms but the fourth — my youngest — had disappeared. We looked everywhere for her, calling out her name, then finally found her behind the sofa, with my handbag and my favourite red lipstick which she had managed to smear not only all over her entire face eyes and clothes but also over my friend's sofa and carpet.

After getting over the shock of seeing her like that (and realising that not only did I have to replace an expensive lipstick but also possibly a sofa and carpet as well) I paused, and went to get the camera. My friend and I bit our lips as we calmly told Sasha that she must not go into Mummy's handbag again, and took lots of photos at the same time!

Another time I had gone shopping with my two children. It had been a particularly big shop and they had done extremely well for the first half hour before degenerating into misbehaviour, picking things off the shelves and throwing tantrum after tantrum when I wouldn't buy them things. To make things less painful for them, I promised them I would buy them each some new stickers if they were well behaved for the rest of the shop. They seemed happy with that and we escaped from the shop relatively unscathed. They clutched at their stickers in the back of the car for the journey home and as soon as they were home I opened each packet and let them go off and play with them while I unpacked the car and the shopping.

Once I had finished my tasks, I went to track them down, pleased with how successful my 'sticker strategy' had been. As I walked into my son Jack's room, I soon discovered the reason why I hadn't heard boo from them since we arrived home. Every single one of the hundreds of stickers in the huge packet I had given them had been stuck lovingly onto every inch of wallpaper and carpet in Jack's room, and he was just starting on the bed.

My immediate reaction was one of horror, fearing how much wallpaper might be stripped off by the removal of each sticker. Then I looked at Jack's face. The pride in his face was incredible. He wasn't being naughty, just creative. He honestly had no idea that he was doing anything wrong. He was like a cat bringing in a mouse for his family, proud of the art he had created and sure that I would love it as much as him.

I hesitated while I thought how to deal with it. I was on unfamiliar ground. Then I smiled. 'Wow,' I said, as sincerely as I could. 'That's amazing, Jack. Let me get my camera so I can take a picture of it before we have to take it all down.'

I got my camera and Jack posed beside his wallpaper as I snapped away, promising that we would show Daddy when he got home. 'We had better take it all down now and put it back in your sticker book.' I said calmly.

'Why?' asked Jack.

'Because, my darling,' I responded, thinking quickly, 'stickers are for books and paintings, not for walls. It looks really pretty but if we keep them up there then we can't use them again and you want to be able to use them and stick them on other things, don't you?' I kept my tone light and my smile fixed but firm.

He thought seriously for a moment then nodded.

'Come on then,' I said brightly, 'let's put them all in your sticker album so you've got them to play with again later.'

He helped me take every one of them down and put them in his sticker album. None of the wallpaper was damaged and, what's more, he has never put them on his wall again.

I know if I had reacted as I so often do in those situations, with anger and losing my temper and shouting, then things would most probably not have gone as smoothly. There would have been a fight about taking down the stickers, he would have dug his heels in, I would have ended up doing all of the work myself and lunch would have been a long drawn-out process full of arguments and refusals to eat. But by handling it positively, this episode at least can be marked down as a success. We as parents know that if we do what we encourage our kids to do (stop, think, act) we will handle things much better. It's just having the energy and the patience to do that.

Lessons from our little ones

> 'It's good to remember that we can all learn from our kids. In fact they can even be great role models for you, slipping into new environments (kindy, nursery, friend's house, daycare), with new people (caregivers, babysitters, friends, neighbours) without so much as batting an eyelid, taking it all in their tiny stride, while we would be all ends up if put in the same situation.'
>
> **Vaughan, three children aged 2, 4 and 6 years**

 While our kids learn from us we can also pick up bad habits from our kids. For example, I was trying to empty the trash on the computer and Matt was trying to explain to me how to do it. I tried but to no avail. I turned to Matt in a big grump and said 'I'm not doing it.' 'Do you mean "Can you please help me do it"?' he asked. I replied sulkily in a childish tone, 'I guess so.' Just the way kids are sometimes 'angels' with everyone but their mother, sometimes it's easy to be nice to everyone but grumpy with your partner.

Kids can be great role models for us all. I'm not saying we should throw our-selves on the floor in full tantrum mode but being open with our feelings is (most of the time) better than hoping our spouse will guess how we're feeling.

Catch them being good

An effective parenting technique is to 'catch your kids being good'. The same technique can be applied to marriage. This positive reinforcement technique involves praising or acknowledging your kids for good/desirable behaviour. This may be anything from treating their sibling well to staying in bed to drinking or eating at the table instead of walking around with it.

Instead of looking for and pointing out our spouse's flaws, we too should look for the good and acknowledge it out loud. It's a classic case of when someone notices our effort/good behaviour we are more likely to repeat it. And let's be honest, we all like to be caught doing something good or acknowledged for it. If hubby comes home and says with happiness 'Oh, the house looks tidy' after I've vacuumed, it's more likely to result in a repeat performance. Similarly my saying 'Thanks for coming home early' when he makes an effort to come home before 5:30 p.m. shows him that I notice and appreciate and will more than likely mean he will make the effort on a more regular basis.

Perhaps the key is to treat our spouses more like we treat our children. Complete admiration, (mostly) detailed and animated explanation and enquiry, heaps of long cuddles and snuggles.

I tell my kids I love them and how smart and amazing they are multiple times per day but probably only say this to my husband a few times a month.

It's amazing (and sad) how we go to great lengths for our kids but barely look our spouse in the eye let alone give them a passionate smooch when they walk in the door.

Family traditions

 We've started a family tradition of doing something physical on every birthday. Partly to commemorate the physical exertion of 'birth' but also to get those endorphins buzzing! For our son's first birthday Matt and I cycled to the beach playground where I'd arranged to meet 10 friends and their kids for some playtime and shared morning tea. Admittedly both sets of grandparents were visiting and there wasn't room in our car but this was the source of the great idea that was to become tradition!

Special outings

I'm a huge believer in the value of special outings, making time for one child (or baby) to bond with one parent. When you have your first baby it's so important for the mother to step back (I know it's hard) and the father to step up (I know, it's a bit scary) and create some time for Daddy and baby. As baby grows towards toddlerhood, special outings once a month or so continue to be valued occasions. These can be low key such as a picnic in the park, or perhaps once a year it may be a big event like a Wiggles concert. When baby number two arrives, quite often Daddy and toddler will have heaps of time together so the focus of special outings may shift to Daddy and baby and a separate special outing and quality time for Mummy and toddler. I vividly remember a special outing with Ruby while Jonah was at home napping.

I took Ruby to a cafe and it was just the two of us. No rush. She didn't eat much but she loved her fluffy (foamed milk) and having grown-up conversation. Her favourite question at the time was 'So how was your day?'

Now, with three children, Matt and I make a point of taking each child out for a 'special outing' with both Mummy and Daddy once a year.

Slow down and smell the coffee

For some reason, when we become mums our attitude to the most mundane things is severely compromised. Things that never bothered us before suddenly start to really grate us. We may have been the most laid-back of people before but suddenly the colour of our child's backpack really matters!

A conversation with a group of mummies uncovered unpredictable behaviour in the mummy world.

'If anyone had told me before I had children that I would get caught up in a debate about what paint to use to paint a stall at the children's school fair, I would have laughed,' declared one mum.

Why is it that we get so caught up in what lunchbox to buy our children, what to put in the lunchbox, whose child is invited over to play and where every other child is having swimming lessons?

Why is it so important to us whether our daughter does ballet or gymnastics? Seriously, why are we so concerned? It's like we're the ones in the school playground sometimes, not our children.

If only they'd told me I would get so upset about this stuff then I may have been more prepared.

One thing I was unprepared for was the critique of my parenting style and of my children. It is something so personal to have your child criticised in any way, shape or form and you will blame each of your child's social discrepancies on your own parenting, so you certainly don't need anyone else's opinion too. Telling people to 'get stuffed' in a nice way is quite hard to do. But then you have to think, if they are rude enough to put you and your child down, then they deserve to be told to where to get off too.

Unfortunately our own parents can be the biggest culprits. They are comfortable enough and close enough to feel it is their duty to share their opinions with us and, like it or not, we will find ourselves caught up in a battle.

Of course when our parents were parents, things were different. It was normal for women to have children younger, to be the one at home and to be expected to keep house and generally run around after the family. Nowadays, with most of us becoming mums later in life we are used to doing something else, rather than marrying and starting a family straight away. We've had careers where we've been in control and we struggle to balance our own worth with running a family too. Not to mention the fact that communities are no longer what they were when our own parents were parents. Families live further apart and we tend to do much more with the children nowadays: coffee groups, baby gymnastics, water confidence, indoor playgrounds. Life is generally busier.

Of course from our own parents' viewpoint, we are own worst enemies by creating this busyness in our lives. As Magda, grandma of four, puts it: 'I think that parents feel they have to keep the children occupied with activities much more than when we were young. I see parents taking their children out to restaurants and grown-up places much more. They expect the children to behave as mini adults when really the children would be happier running around and playing.'

She may have a point. Often we create the stresses in our own lives. Maybe we just need to slow down and smell the coffee. Enjoy being mums at home, reading, doing jigsaws with our children, playing hide and seek. Those simple pleasures are often the more appreciated, rather than rushing our children between soccer and judo after school. If we're tired from our busy lives, what must our little people be feeling too?

I am one of the biggest culprits in this and a dear friend once told me: 'Children need time to just be children. To learn how to play by themselves, to spend time by themselves. To be bored and to cope with it. To just *be*.' She was right of course and I try desperately now not to cram the day with playdates and other things but to let the children amuse themselves. It is a huge part of learning, after all.

Live in the moment

We live in a time of busyness. At the grocery checkout they ask you 'Having a busy day?' Walking down the street with a double stroller or kid on bike and one in a front pack and people pleasantly say, 'Ooh, you're busy.'

A turning point for me was when we had been doing house renovations for the previous five months and my 'finishing' to do list was at a standstill. I heard myself say to the guy installing our solar hot-water heater, 'I could get so much done if I only had the baby — he sleeps all the time!' He turned to me and said, 'Enjoy it while it lasts. They will be at school before you know it.' I am slowly letting go of my 'must get things done' mentality and trying to be present and enjoy the moments with my sweethearts! Once I had that breakthrough and accepted that when I'm with the kids I'm just not going to get stuff done, I just try to enjoy them.

So many people tell you, 'they'll be grown up before you know it' and 'enjoy the moment'. We may not like hearing it but they are right. It certainly is incredible how quickly they really do grow up. When they are babies and toddlers we feel we are going to be stuck in the moment for ever and we cannot see any way out. However, the reality is soon enough they are gone to school or full-day kindy and suddenly we are missing those middle-of-the-day trips to the library or at the stage where we are no longer pushing a pram around a beautiful park or waterfront on a gorgeous day.

You may feel like you are stuck in a time warp but soon enough that time will change and you will miss it.

Birthday parties and special occasions

Children's birthday parties can be a minefield of etiquette and rules. My daughter Sasha recently turned 4. For the first time I decided to hold her a birthday party — I reckon you can get away with not having one until they enter kindergarten and start making friends.

A few days before, I went to Nat's house for a Stitch 'n' Bitch session. While everyone else who attends our fortnightly Stitch 'n' Bitch get-togethers sew, I don't. Not even buttons on shirts. So, not wanting to be the only one sitting there guzzling wine while the others created cushions, skirts and cuddlies for their littlies, I took along my 'pass the parcel' to wrap up for Sasha's party.

I proudly announced to the other mums that I was going to do pass the parcel the old-fashioned way, just how I had it when I was a kid. Layers and layers of newspaper and no candy in between each layer. The mums applauded me, saying how they totally agreed that there should only be one winner in a game and how PC everything had become around birthday parties and making sure everyone at the party won something.

I was feeling rather smug until one of the mums lamented: 'And as for goodie bags, I think they should be totally banned at all parties.' All the other mums agreed wholeheartedly. Ahem. I had just spent a small fortune on pink bags for the girls filled with lolly necklaces, sparkly wands and love hearts, and green bags for the boys to take home with gold coins and sheriff stars.

Quite honestly I agreed with the mums. I had spent almost $100 on, frankly, a load of crap. Of course when it came to the day of the party, I did give out the bags — just to get rid of them really. Imagine my embarrassment when one dad collecting his son refused to take it. 'We don't do goodie bags in our house,' he said. 'Please take it,' I asked, embarrassed. 'No,' he stated and with boy in tow, strutted off up the driveway, leaving me hanging my head in shame and swearing that it was truly the last time I would ever do goodie bags at one of my children's parties.

Do you feed the parents at a children's birthday party? Nat and I have similar views on this: if it's a 'drop off' party (age 5 and older) I wouldn't feed the parents but at a party age 1–3 where parents generally stay and even age 4 when some drop off, yes, I would provide some healthy nibbles and drink for the parents. You don't have to go all-out gourmet but a platter of veges and dip and a juice or water would be nice.

And then there is the invitation list. If you have to invite most people in your class then invite the lot, or just the boys or just the girls. Leaving just a couple out is just mean.

Then there's the cake. The birthday cake can be a source of great despair, wonderful pride, parental envy and many more emotions.

I recently had dinner with a friend who had earlier that day accompanied his daughter to a 3-year-old's birthday party. He was blown away by the drama of the birthday cake. He confessed that, out of interest, when the cake made its appearance, rather than watch the birthday girl blow out her candles, he instead studied the faces of the other mums at the party.

'You should have seen their faces when this huge pink palace cake came out,' he said. 'It was like every other mum in that room threw up their arms and said 'How am I ever going to compete with that?'

My friend was completely bemused by the theatre of the cake and the other mums' worry. In his opinion there was nothing whatsoever wrong with a bought sponge covered in icing and lollies.

It seems that most of the dads I spoke to were of the same opinion. Another dad who popped in for a coffee one afternoon confessed that he had had to escape the house because his wife was on her third cake — for their child's fourth birthday. 'I keep trying to tell her that the children won't even eat the cake,' he said, exasperated, 'but she just won't listen.'

I am not sure exactly why it is that we put such pressure on ourselves as mums with the cake. Prior to having children I had never baked, not even scones. Then suddenly I had children and was at home and I almost expected that I should be able to bake. I used to get myself into such a tizz over cakes and parties until my mother-in-law bought me my very own copy of the *Australian's Women's Weekly Children's Birthday Cake Book*. An amazing book which encourages you to buy ready-mix cake and spend the time decorating the cake instead of spending the time baking it. Nowadays I just love the adventure of trying out a new cake for my children and feel I have become a bit of a dab hand at it. However, I never care how it actually tastes — in our house only the icing is ever eaten!

Another friend of mine went to a child's sixth birthday party recently. The theme was a Mad Hatter's Tea Party.

When she turned up at the party, she admired the table settings and in particular the big beautiful yellow teapot which was the centrepiece of the table. When she asked her friend where she had bought that beautiful teapot the friend looked at her strangely. It was only when it was time for the birthday cake to come out that my friend actually realised that it was a cake and not a teapot at all. Not only had her friend baked a stunningly beautiful teapot cake, but she had also spent ages decorating it with beautiful iced roses, and had even made two beautiful teacups out of sugar and colouring. For a sixth birthday party!

It does raise the question about who we are actually doing the food for at a party? Surely it should be the children, rather than to show off to other parents? Although often we do get pulled into the game of competition, sometimes without even realising it. My same friend has decided to abstain from the whole cake drama herself and instead pay someone else to do it. She just feels she would rather spend her time elsewhere rather than competing with the other mums over who has done the best cake.

Personally I love making the cake myself. I will spend hours lovingly putting it together. For someone who couldn't cook for toffee before children came along, my new-found skill is something to be proud off and, quite honestly, I will happily show off my birthday cakes to anyone who cares to look.

The rest of the spread is pretty basic though. Cheerios, marshmallows, popcorn — nothing that is going to take up too much of my time. And sausage rolls for the adults, of course!

Hosting a fab birthday party

Invitations: who and how?

The size of your guest list will depend according to the age of your child and your budget. In the early years it tends to be family and your own friends that you invite along to celebrate your baby or toddler's auspicious occasion. When they're turning 2 or 3 it's still a 'parents stay' party so you could be looking at some large numbers, especially if siblings are included. At age 4 they start to choose their own friends a bit more. Some parents will 'drop off' and some will stay.

Paper invitations, email and electronic invitations are the usual ways to invite the guests. My daughter received the most original birthday party invite I've seen. It was a 'rock star' theme party and the invite was a 'backstage pass' laminated card on a lanyard that they all wore to the party. They hired two rock chicks who ran games, pumped the music and kept the 20 kids (boys and girls) entertained for two hours. My friend (the host) was thrilled with the party and happy to pay what it cost.

Themes

Carnival, tea party, Scooby Doo mystery, pirates, princesses... There are so many 'theme' ideas depending on the age, stage and interests of your child. Check our Pinterest Party Ideas board for some inspirational images! I love the idea of a kids' cardboard playhouse as an interactive party idea. Pick your theme and let their imaginations go wild!

My son originally wanted a clown for his 4-year-old party but the $200+ charge made me cringe. He was happy with the fabulous face painting and balloon-twisting Fairy Jane who had the children entertained and looking lovely for a well-deserved $100.

Other cool party ideas include a Lego party (the guy arrived with masses of Lego and kept kids entertained with challenges and games) or hiring a bouncy castle.

Ruby just went to a 6-year-old 'beauty salon' where the girls did each other's hair and make-up then the dad got a make-over care of the giggling girls! What a sport with his multi-coloured fingernails, rouge, eye shadow — the works!

Venues

We invited friends to meet us at the local park when our kids turned 1 and 2 — no prezzies, bring a plate, very low key. I love the idea of a free/outdoor venue. As the kids get older you may host parties at home or decide to book in at a venue. Here are some great party venue ideas: roller-skating party, trampoline party, swimming, indoor rock climbing, YMCA, Stardome...

Top tips for a happy birthday

- ◉ Plan and stick to your budget. Birthday parties can be a big expense. Choose your numbers and venue with your budget in mind.
- ◉ Have a Plan B. Your child may have their heart set on a certain theme or venue but availability or cost may pose a problem. Have a back-up plan just in case.
- ◉ Ages and stages. Be aware of the age and stage that your child is at when selecting who will be invited, the time and plan for the party. If they're between 1 and 3 years old they may still nap in the afternoon so a morning party may be a better option. If they're turning 6 then a party at 4.30 or later is fine!
- ◉ Clear instructions. Be clear on your invite about what to wear, whether siblings are invited, directions to house or venue.
- ◉ Relax and enjoy. Try not to get too caught up in the cake and theme details. Remember that this is a monumental occasion as you mark another wonderful year with your child. Take some time to enjoy the occasion and reflect on all the memories of the past years.

Getting your child ready for school

Sending your child off to school for the first time can be daunting, both for the child and the parent. There are certain things that everyone needs to know to make their life easier.

Recently I was lucky enough to meet with Samantha Knowles,

a new entrant teacher at Meadowbank School in Auckland, who armed me with her top tips for getting our children (and us parents) ready for school.

What tips can you give to get your child used to the school they are going to attend?

- Visit the school as often as you can before their start date. Most schools offer official visits where your child will get to sit in what will be their classroom with their new teacher at least twice before their actual start date. Most of the time this is not a full day but more a 'taster' day of a few hours.
- Apart from these official visits, go on your own visits with the family before your child is due to start. Go in the afternoon when the school is coming out and watch all the children coming out of school, and visit on a weekend, walk around the school grounds and explore, play on the playground and try to work out which classroom your child will be in.
- Find out where the toilets are and the water fountain before your child starts. It will make it heaps easier for them on that first day.
- Talk about school with your child and the kind of things they will do there. Some children can be overwhelmed when they start school, not realising that it is different from kindy. One child I met couldn't understand why they weren't allowed to play all day like they were at kindy and kept on asking 'Where are all the toys?'
- Meet with other families who are attending the school your child will attend so that they know at least one friendly face already at the school before they start.
- Choose a preschool or kindergarten that 'feeds' into the school that your child will be attending to make it easier when they go to the school, so they at least have one or more friends at the school before starting.
- Go and buy their uniform together. Make it a big deal and exciting for them so they start to get enthused about wearing it.
- Take them to buy their lunchbox and bag and let them have a say in which one you buy.

Should you teach your child basic reading or writing skills before they start school?

No, it's not at all necessary. In fact, often when children arrive at school having been 'taught' by parents or preschool teachers, school teachers find they have to 'unteach' them.

If you do want to try teaching them before they start school, then make sure you spend time on the lower-case alphabet, not the upper-case.

Children need to be able to recognise their own name when they start school. Do spend time getting them to recognise their name. Write it out for them, put it on their bags and items and on their bedroom door. Some kindies have a system where a child has to find their name among lots of names. Our kindy also encourages children to 'sign in', i.e. to try to form their name with a pen or pencil as they arrive at kindy.

You don't need to teach your child to read before they start school but do spend time reading to them. What you do want is for your child to enjoy and appreciate books and reading so that they are enthusiastic and want to learn when they arrive at school.

What kind of items should you pack for lunch or morning tea for your child?

Ideally don't give them items which need to be unwrapped as children can struggle to unwrap items by themselves and teachers don't have the time at lunchtime to unwrap children's lunches for them.

A tip is to buy a compartmentalised lunchbox where you don't need to use any sort of wrapping. It keeps items fresh and separate and makes things easier for the child.

Pack healthy nutritional things for lunch: apples, bananas, cheese sticks, sandwiches, filled pita breads or left-over pasta, raisins, nuts and seeds, dried apricots, bread sticks, mini sausages, yoghurt or fruit pots are just some ideas.

Avoid calorie-full but nutritional-nil items like chocolate and sweets.

What can you do to make your child's first week easier?

If you've done the visits and you've done the uniform and they know some people at the school before starting, then you are halfway there.

It is nice to make a bit of an effort if you can and try to make sure you as parents are there for their first day. Don't just drop and run but at the same time, try not to stay too long as the longer you stay, the more you can upset them.

Understand that they will be tired and overwhelmed that first week. Maybe drop some of the other activities you normally do with them for the first term at least and just let it be school for a while until they get used to it.

Remember they have probably been used to lots of free playtime and suddenly they are going to have to sit in a classroom and listen, and sit still a lot of the time. That is tiring for children so be aware that they may be overtaxed when they get home and therefore 'wired'. Spend time just 'winding them down' after school. Read stories, do a jigsaw or drawing together, and a warm bath and early bedtime will help them recuperate.

The key thing is to relax and be excited about their first day. If you are relaxed and excited then your child will sense this from you and they will be relaxed and excited too.

What other tips can you give to new parents?

Try to get to know some of the other parents if you can. Apart from the fact it means you can organise play dates which makes things easier for your child, it also means that if ever you are running late, then you at least have one or two people to call to stay with your child until you get there.

Often schools have a class coordinator for each class. Find out who yours is and introduce yourself. Ask for a list of parents in the class and their telephone numbers and organise coffee with those who are keen. We all need to be able to help each other out as parents at one point or another and just knowing the other parents slightly will help you if ever you need it.

If you are regularly late then have a plan in place that your child knows and understands and make sure the teacher is aware of the circumstances, e.g. organise for your child to wait in the classroom or at the playground until you arrive.

Avoid putting your child's name in large letters on the outside of their bags in the case of strangers; this ensures that they cannot call out your child's name to them and 'lure' them into a situation.

Finally, often parents are more worried about the first day than the children. We need to relax and be calm, then our children will feed off us.

Thriving (not just surviving) in the school holidays

I have yet to meet a parent who is as excited about the school holidays as the children. Even if you are excited initially, chances are by week two you'll be counting the hours until kindy and school open their doors again.

For starters, if you're a working mum you have the logistics to organise and worry about. I watch with sympathy as my fellow working mums around me spend the weeks leading up to the holidays trying to palm their offspring on to grandparents, in-laws, siblings and even unsuspecting friends. A colleague has three children she somehow needs to distribute every holidays. She can often be overheard trying to persuade friends to host various playdates with her own children throughout the holidays — the problem is, being a working mum, the playdates need to begin at 8.30 in the morning and won't actually finish until after 5.00 p.m. Not something a lot of people would be willing to take on. When all else fails and grandparents declare they have had enough, she enrols them into school holiday programmes, but even these have their drawbacks with cost and time limitations often attached. We also have to remember that school holidays are designed to give the children, as well as the teachers, a rest!

Personally, I am lucky to have a Hot Nanny on hand, so holidays have yet to become an issue. However, having been there previously, I know how even a Hot Nanny's nerves can be frayed by the end of the school holidays, so here are some tips and ideas designed to get you through those long days.

Cold and wet weather ideas	Fine weather ideas
An indoor treasure hunt — hide little notes around the house. Children love trying to find them.	A treasure hunt — bury some clues in the garden and make sure there is a prize to find at the end.
If you are lucky enough to live near snow then there is no end to the fun you can have: build snowmen, tobogganing. If not, find an indoor ski centre and go tobogganing. Finish off with hot chocolates in the café.	The beach — even if it's not warm enough for a paddle, there is heaps of fun to be had building sandcastles, clambering over rocks and running around the beach.
Ice-skating parks — indoor and outdoor.	Parks — visit new parks in different locations to mix things up and keep the interest there.
The zoo — even if it's wet or cold, wrap up warm and head out to see the animals.	The zoo — the perfect all-weather location.
Museums — most museums put on special school holiday programmes but even if not there is usually lots to keep young people occupied.	Take the bikes and scooters out for a long ride and run off some energy.

Cold and wet weather ideas	Fine weather ideas
Library — not only a great place to occupy the children but it means that you have plenty of books for other wet days too. Often libraries also have puzzles, CDs and DVDs to rent out too.	Pitch a tent in the garden — if you don't have one then make your own up with sheets and chairs and whatever you have lying around. Have a picnic lunch out there.
The movies for a special treat is always popular.	A ride on a ferry/boat if you live near the water.
Swimming — you're wet anyway so you may as well get wetter.	Find an outdoor pool, local padding pools and if you are lucky enough to have an outdoor water park, even better.
A ride on a tram, train or bus — never ceases to excite and amaze little people.	A ride on a tram, train or bus — never ceases to excite and amaze little people.
A visit to the DVD store and home-made popcorn is a great way to occupy long wet days.	Butterfly farms and botanical gardens — lots of interest for little ones.
Music shows — sometimes local orchestras put on special shows for children. Otherwise grab some spoons, pots and whatever else you can find around the house, on some children's music and make your own music.	Climb some trees, run around a field and take a long walk — explore some different locations from normal, go on a nature walk of your own — take a book of insects or birds with you and see how many you can spot.
The theatre — there are often plays put on specifically for children during holidays. These are often far cheaper than adult plays.	Water play — fill bowls and cups with water, mix with food colouring, give children spoons and mixers, or use their own toy tea sets and let them play.
Indoor playgrounds, inflatable centres and other fun places.	Visit a local farm — often they are open for the children to visit and pet the animals.
Indoor climbing centres, from age 3.	

Cold and wet weather ideas	Fine weather ideas
The Golden Arches — a real treat for the holidays. Mix it up — head out for an early breakfast and have a play on the playground.	Pack a packed lunch, a rug and go down to the latest park, take some books with you and make an afternoon of it.
Ten pin bowling, laser shooting, indoor mini-golf.	
Baking or even having a make your own pizza competition.	Picnic tea in the garden.
Make your own playdough. Playdough keeps little ones occupied for ages.	Chalk-drawing on the driveway. Chalk-draw a road and play with toy cars outside.
Visit the $2 shop and stock up on stickers, paper, feathers, colourful sticks and other bits and create your own crafts.	Make a mud pie and paint the side of the house with mud-paint.
Curl up with cushions on the floor and lots of books and puzzles.	Take a ball and practise throwing and catching it — children are never too early to start to learn.
Build a 'town' or 'farm' with Lego or other building blocks and bring it to life with toy animals/dolls.	Find some old wood and get them to decorate it and hammer in some nails so they feel they are 'building'.
Musical statues.	Chase bubbles around the garden.
Visit the art gallery or an observatory.	Pack some bread and head to the nearest duck pond.
Get the children to sort through their toys and books and put together a pile to donate to charity. Let the children come with you to take them to the charity shop and give them each a coin to spend at the same shop — not only will they enjoy the exercise more but they will learn about the concept of giving.	Get the spades out in the garden, do some actual gardening with the children or bury some toy dinosaurs in the garden, give them shovels and let them find them.

Cold and wet weather ideas	Fine weather ideas
Organise an indoor adventure course where children have to crawl under tables, through chairs, balance on items and carry an egg on a spoon.	Organise an 'adventure course' in the garden, using trees, trampolines, items to jump over and whatever else you can find.
Have a story-writing or colouring-in competition.	Chasing games — place a scarf into the elastic at the top of his trousers and chase him while you try to grab the scarf.

My Hot Nanny has a great tip. On the first day of school holidays this time around, she turned up with large colourful sheets of paper, pens, glue, feathers and stickers. Together, with the children, she drew up a 'table of activities' for the children to do during the holidays. Each child got the chance to choose what they wanted to do each day and then the children spent hours filling it in, colouring and decorating it. The tables were stuck onto the fridge and when hubby and I arrived home from work that night, the children were delighted to show us all they planned to do during the holidays. Not only did the activity itself take them all morning to complete, but they feel thrilled that they have been part of the planning of what they are doing this holiday and are excited about each day to come.

IOTTM tips for great family times

⊙ Instil good manners in your children early on. They are never too young to learn 'please' and 'thank you'.

⊙ Instil in your children the need to be good and kind to others from a young age and, of course, lead by your own example. If you demonstrate good manners and nice behaviour, your child will too.

⊙ Try not to shout at your children, no matter how frustrated you are feeling — it strips away their confidence and they learn your bad habits. Take five minutes, bite your lip and walk away. Once you are calmer, return and deal with the situation firmly but calmly.

⊙ Catch your child and/or husband or partner being good. It is easy to be caught up with the grumpiness of life but finding something to praise your child or husband will ensure a repeat performance of the good deed.

⊙ Start your own family traditions — children love getting into them. It could be as simple as a picnic every Easter with an Easter egg hunt or a group of families getting together for a regular pizza night to celebrate a special occasion or just regular TV Fridays.

- Birthday parties for children. Don't let yourself be bullied into 'keeping up with the Joneses'. Organise a party or gathering that suits your budget, time, family and child.
- If your child is about to start school, spend some time visiting the school, playing in the playground and familiarising your child with the school before they start.
- Enjoy the school holidays and make it really fun by all taking it in turns to choose an activity for different days. Then the children also feel like they have had a say in what you are all doing and will take ownership.
- Don't overthink or overplan holidays with children. The simplest holidays are often the most fun for children — sand toys at the beach, movies and popcorn, bikes in the park. Kids love that stuff.

 Birthday Parties: ifonlytheytoldme.com/69

Life after babies: What lies ahead?

When we first started writing this book, Jacqui and I each had a toddler and a baby. Now those 'toddlers' are in Year 2 at school and those 'babies' are 5 years old! Suddenly all those comments that people made about 'it going so quickly' seem to be coming true, but we still vividly remember the amazing moments like baby learning to crawl as well as the challenging ones like endless nights of broken sleep. But what lies ahead? What do the 'middle years' hold for us?

Here's what some of our Facebook fans said:

- That classmates can give them the sex talk if you don't get in early enough. My son was told at 7 so that fast-tracked it for us.
- Grumpy hormones in girls.
- I wish I had known how much I would suddenly miss having them around. In the preschool years you just want a day to yourself, then suddenly they are all at school and you miss those little daytime trips to the library. Appreciate each age and stage.
- I have a 7- and 9-year-old and there is not a doubt in my mind that I'm in the 'sweet spot' between preschool tantrums and preteen hormones. The best advice I was given was to enjoy this time.
- Enjoy this age. The kids are capable, interesting, and like responsibility. They also love spending time with their parents and they still tell us everything. Beautiful.

Here are some final If Only They'd Told Me Tips to enjoy:

- ⊚ Slow down and smell the coffee. We spend so much time rushing through life that it is easy to miss those special moments. Stop and savour them.
- ⊚ Try to spend one-on-one time with each child. They love the intimacy of spending quality time with a parent or other family member and you will love it just as much.
- ⊚ Enjoy the moment. The people who say it are those who have been there. They recognise how quickly time goes and your children grow up. It really is important not to rush through life but to enjoy each moment with your children and family.
- ⊚ Let your children just *be* children — don't fill their day with tonnes of activities and playdates. It is important for them to learn just to be by themselves and it is important for them to learn to be bored and how to find entertainment by themselves.
- ⊚ Take some time to relax with your child and to enjoy reflecting on your memories of the last year.
- ⊚ Remember to cherish your marriage/relationship for it, too, is growing and changing all the time.
- ⊚ Love yourself, you're doing an important and amazing job!

We have loved writing this book and sharing our parenting journey, tips, joys and challenges with you! Thank you to all the parents from around the world who have contributed with interviews, blog and Facebook comments and surveys. Thanks to the 'experts' who we brought in to our studio in person or via Skype to share their knowledge. And a huge thanks to the many people who supported us with our Kickstarter campaign and helped to make this publishing dream a reality.

Thanks to our husbands for helping us to follow this dream. To Nat's husband Matt for all of his technical wizardry with our weekly podcast and for all his technical support and tips for our blog site, and to John for his emotional support of Jacqui while she juggled full-time jobs, writing and being a mum.

Thanks to our children too — Jack, Ruby, Sasha, Jonah and Xavier — for their patience while we took many writing 'retreats' and retired into other rooms trying desperately to find peace while putting this book together.

Thanks to our parents as well. Being a parent ourselves has made us realise just what an important job it is and has given us both a much better appreciation of our own parents and all they have done and are still doing for us. It certainly takes a village.

Cheers, *Jacqui and Nat*

Recommended Reading

Ashworth, T and A Nobile. (2007). *I was a really good mom before I had kids*. San Francisco, Chronicle Books.

Black, Eleanor. (2011). *Confessions of a Coffee Group Dropout*. Sydney, Allen & Unwin.

Brown, Jaquie. (2012). *I'm Not Fat I'm Pregnant*. Auckland, Random House.

Chapman, Gary. (2010). *Five Love Languages Men's Edition*. Chicago, Moody Press.

Cockrell, O'Neill and Stone. (2008). *Babyproofing your Marriage*. New York, HarperCollins Publishers.

Fray, Kathy. (2005). *Oh Baby... Birth, Babies and Motherhood Uncensored*. Auckland, Random House.

Grant, Ian. (2012). *Fathers Who Dare Win*. Auckland, Random House.

Grant, Ian. and Mary Grant. (2009) *Growing Great Marriages*. Auckland, Random House.

Latta, Nigel. (2013). *The Modern Family Survival Guide*. Auckland, Random House.

Levy, Diane. (2007). *Time Out for Tots and Teens and Everyone In Between*. Auckland, Random House.

McGrory Massaro, Megan and Miriam J. Katz. (2012). *The Other Baby Book*. Massachusetts, Full Cup Press.

Photography by Hope Photography

Photography by Fotoman Ltd

Photography by Fotoman Ltd

CONTACT DETAILS:
comments@ifonlytheytoldme.com
www.ifonlytheytoldme.com
Facebook/IOTTM
Pinterest/IOTTM
Twitter/IOTTM

Published by Jacqui Lockington and Natalie Cutler-Welsh
50 Meadowbank Rd, Meadowbank, Auckland 1072
New Zealand
www.ifonlytheydtoldme.com

Copyright © Jacqui Lockington and Natalie Cutler-Welsh, 2014

The moral right of the authors has been asserted.

First published 2014

ISBN 978-0-473-27476-4

Produced by Mary Egan Publishing
www.maryegan.co.nz
Edited by Tracey Wogan

7157650R00149

Printed in Great Britain
by Amazon.co.uk, Ltd.,
Marston Gate.